THE YMCA AT
150

The
YMCA
at 150

A History of the YMCA
of Greater New York
1852-2002

PAMELA BAYLESS

YMCA *of* Greater New York

333 Seventh Avenue
New York, NY 10001
212-630-9600

www.ymcanyc.org

The YMCA at 150: A History of the YMCA of Greater New York, 1852-2002
By Pamela Bayless
Minda Novek, Picture Editor
Includes selected bibliography and index.

1.   Education—19th and 20th centuries.
2.   Education—Adult.
3.   Education—Vocational.
4.   Nonprofit organizations—New York City.
5.   Physical Fitness—19th and 20th centuries.
6.   Social history—New York City and Brooklyn, 19th and 20th centuries.
7.   Social history—Religious Associations—Young Men's Christian Associations.
8.   Social history—War work—United Services Organization (USO).
9.   Youth—New York City.

Published by the YMCA of Greater New York
Manufactured in the United States of America

ISBN: 0-9717857-0-8

*Designed and produced by Pauline Neuwirth,
Neuwirth & Associates, Inc.*

Contents

Foreword

A GREAT DEAL CAN be learned about the history and people of New York State by studying institutions that are an outgrowth of the population's needs and the natural course of human progression. New York's role as the Gateway to Freedom enabled it to figure prominently in the birth of many outstanding institutions that continue to serve New Yorkers today.

The YMCA was started one hundred and fifty years ago by a group of young men who assembled in a neighborhood church in the area known today as "SoHo" to form a local social service organization. Their goal was to assist other men arriving in New York and Brooklyn from farms and villages in the United States, as well as other countries, and YMCA members offered to help them adjust to urban life. Far from their own families and familiar communities, these newcomers sought a home away from home where their needs—in spirit, mind and body—could be met. The members of the New York and Brooklyn Associations, formed respectively in 1852 and 1853, stepped up to the challenge with educational and employment programs, physical fitness activities, religious meetings and referrals to lodging houses.

Ours was a progressive society and the YMCA likewise evolved over time, showing an ability to respond to community needs during various periods in American history. In the nineteenth century, the YMCA created programs to help groups affected by war, population shifts and industrial growth. Not long after the Associations were founded, the United States entered into civil conflict over the issues of slavery and states' rights. While staunchly abolitionist, the New York YMCA formed a commission to administer medical relief to soldiers in camps, in hospitals

and on battlefields. In the decades following the Civil War, the face of New York City and State changed and the YMCA expanded too, adding new units that included African Americans and immigrant groups. As industries such as the railroads became more important, the YMCA offered special programs for their workers. In a changing society, it was recognized that younger boys needed special attention, and so the YMCA's camping programs were created. Around the turn of the century, YMCAs were a well-established part of life in all five boroughs of New York City.

In the early twentieth century, the YMCA expanded its scope to create opportunities for more New Yorkers and helped women in their efforts to gain greater rights in society. As women assumed a more active role in American life, the YMCA allowed them to become members and eventually would include girls in all Y programs.

Major events such as two World Wars offered the YMCA unprecedented opportunity for service to the country's military forces and, during the Great Depression, the YMCA was looked to for its vocational programs such as skills training and job placement. Social progress in the form of racial integration was attained nationally in the YMCA in the 1940s, and achieved earlier in New York City Branches. In the later twentieth century, the YMCA addressed new problems affecting children and families.

When New York City began witnessing urban problems in the 1950s and unrest in the 1960s, the YMCA responded with programs to address poverty, youth unemployment, delinquency and drug abuse. The Association made its programs more accessible to neighborhoods most in need of support. Throughout a municipal fiscal crisis and national recession, the YMCA maintained a firm commitment to the city and its people. As women entered the workforce, the YMCA created child care programs and expanded its other programs for individuals and families. In the 1960s, an increased interest in physical fitness drew many to the YMCA, where they could swim and benefit from other sports programs year-round, including basketball and volleyball.

For 150 years, the YMCA of Greater New York has been a model of public/private partnerships, maintaining a solid relationship with the city's business and civic community. Early lay leaders such as William E. Dodge Jr., J. Pierpont Morgan and Cornelius Vanderbilt II were among the most prominent businessmen and philanthropists of their time. Former elected officials, such as Governor Thomas Dewey and Mayor John Lindsay, served on the YMCA Board as well. This commitment remains strong in the present-day YMCA, where many city leaders and elected officials support the Association's initiatives for New York City youth, its community centers and its programs.

At the start of the twenty-first century, the name "YMCA" has grown far beyond its original intent and scope of service, and today reflects the rich diversity of New York City. Its members and participants range from the very young to the very old, from women and girls to men and boys, and people of all faiths. Yet, the name YMCA is venerable and has come to symbolize a caring community where everyone is welcome. The variety of programs that define the contemporary YMCA, both within its Branch buildings and outside its walls, follows the Association's traditional triangle of spirit (values), mind (education) and body (health).

In the past decade, the YMCA has become a presence in approximately 200 public schools in every school district in the city through the *Virtual Y* and *Teen Action NYC* after-school academic support programs, as well as through a full range of other leadership activities. These initiatives draw upon the YMCA's many decades of experience in education and interest in our youth and school programs.

Adults continue to find courses at the YMCA, from English to computers, preparing them to find jobs. Others come purely for enjoyment, as participants in Active Older Adult programs, a writing or ceramics class, or for the satisfaction of volunteering through tutoring, coaching or mentoring a child or teen in need of a supportive, caring adult role model.

In its entirety, the YMCA in New York City is the product of fifteen decades of identifying community needs and devising programs to meet them. In doing so, it leaves no one out and is as diverse as the city itself. The YMCA of Greater New York, the largest YMCA in North America, strives to address community needs in bold ways. The history you are about to read captures the evolution, activities and essence of the YMCA of Greater New York, an organization that has evolved in ways its founders could not have foreseen.

But as much as it has changed and adapted to the times, the YMCA retains certain elements that are basic to its longevity and success. Its values continue to espouse respect, responsibility, honesty and caring. The YMCA's advocacy for children and families enables the YMCA to help many.

On its 150th anniversary, this YMCA has proven to be as resilient as the city it serves, adapting to changing times and communities, surviving wars and financial downturns. This is most recently in evidence through the Association's response to the events of September 11, 2001, and their aftermath, when it rose to the challenge by making its 20 neighborhood-based Branches available to meet a variety of community needs. In the decade ahead, the YMCA will become an ever more valued community resource as it serves one in ten New York City youth, building their competence and confidence in programs emphasizing values, education and health. The Association will lead the city as a community-building organization for youth, families and adults, reaching out especially to new Americans.

While it is many things to many people, the YMCA is fundamentally an organization that builds strong kids, strong families and strong communities—by people helping people. Large and complex, comprising thousands of members, staff, volunteers and program participants, the YMCA of Greater New York presents many faces to the city and the world. In this history of the Association, you will discover the strength of the YMCA in New York City based on belief in the power of the spirit, mind and body.

The Honorable George E. Pataki
Governor
The State of New York
July 2002

1

✦

1852–1880

An Idea from London Takes Root in New York

HOW GRAND THE Crystal Palace must have seemed to a young New Yorker traveling in the mid-nineteenth century to the Great Exhibition in England. This first world's fair was situated in London's Hyde Park and housed in a mammoth iron structure sparkling with more than a million feet of glass. Encompassing more than 13,000 exhibits, the Crystal Palace made a magnificent showcase for the art, architecture, and products of the burgeoning Industrial Revolution and specimens of the natural world. Concerts on the world's largest

organ and daring feats by the tightrope walker Blondin in the Palace's arched center transept thrilled more than 6 million visitors in a single year.

Like many who journeyed to the Great Exposition, George H. Petrie, a 24-year-old merchant representing his family's New York–based import business, was also captivated by a flyer handed to him at the fair. Members of a fledgling organization in London, the Young Men's Christian Association (YMCA), were passing out hundreds of thousands of invitations to individuals at the Exposition, encouraging them to inspect the Association's rented rooms and discover its work. They were hoping to recruit members for their Association and also to encourage visitors to start similar associations where they lived.

A curious Petrie made his way to the stucco house at 7 Gresham Street, and was enchanted by his discovery. "During a residence of some twelve months in London, in the years 1850 and 1851," he later recalled, "I was brought into contact with a number of leading Christian brethren who were heartily engaged in the work of the Young Men's Christian Association in that city, and through the secretary, Mr. T. H. Tarleton, I was afforded the opportunity of learning all the main features relating to the aim and working of the association."

The YMCA quarters presented quite a contrast to the dazzling Crystal Palace. There, Petrie encountered several rooms comfortably furnished with tables and sofas that offered young men a welcoming home away

The first YMCA occupied rooms at 7 Gresham Street in London, including a library, reading and social rooms.

from home. He admired a small library stocked with well-chosen books, current newspapers, and journals; a room for refreshments; and classrooms where English literature and several languages were taught. But he was most taken with the Association's overarching aim, achieved in those rooms, to provide a fellowship where young men could congregate to pray, study the Bible and strengthen their Christian faith in like-minded company. Even as the wonders of England's Industrial Revolution drew visitors to the Crystal Palace, the earnest members of the YMCA were trying to counter the dislocations it was causing among countless young men new to its teeming capital.

The YMCA was founded in London in June 1844 by a shop clerk named George Williams, a 23-year-old Protestant from a village in Sussex who had found employment in the world's largest city. He was troubled by what he saw there—limitless snares and temptations awaiting him and other unsophisticated new arrivals

drawn to jobs in shops and factories. Young Williams was quite distressed, too, by their living and working conditions. These young men, he observed, "were treated as though deprived of mind, as though formed only to labor and sleep, and to sleep and labor, so that they could only go from their beds to the counter, and from the counter to their beds, without a moment for mental or spiritual culture, without the disposition or even the strength for the performance of those devotional exercises which are necessary for the maintenance of a spiritual life."

Living above the drapery establishment that employed him, as was the custom, Williams began mobilizing his fellow shop clerks to help them reinforce their faith in Christ and lead a virtuous life in unfamiliar and sometimes hostile surroundings. As evangelical Christians, the young men felt compelled to spread the word and bring others into their circle. The object of their Association, as spelled out in its first constitution, was "the improvement of the spiritual condition of young men engaged in the

George Williams, a young dry-goods clerk new to London, founded the YMCA in 1844.

George Petrie visited the YMCA in London in 1851 and actively campaigned for an association in New York City.

drapery and other trades, by the introduction of religious services among them." Within a year, "mental" would join "spiritual" as a desired improvement. Williams and his fellow employees won financial and moral support from his sympathetic employer, George Hitchcock, whom they had converted to Christianity. Hitchcock thought the YMCA a fine idea and enlisted other prominent businessmen, lawyers, and bankers to the cause.

In the fall of 1851, Petrie returned to New York and his family firm, J. and A. Petrie at 27 William Street, convinced that his city could greatly benefit from such an organization. With New York in the throes of rapid industrialization and growth, multitudes of young men from America's small towns and farms were seeking employment in the city and, in their loneliness, finding many temptations to stray from upright paths. Petrie began trying to convince his friends of the necessity for an association. One November evening he met with three friends and described the London YMCA to them, stating his case for the establishment of an association in New York. But, as he later wrote, "Although these gentlemen's Christian love and impulses were strongly favorable to the movement, I confess a feeling of disappointment came over me that they did not so enthusiastically enter into the idea of our city's need for a Young Men's Christian Association."

But Petrie, a graduate of New York University (NYU), did not give up. He continued to prod a growing group of men, including Howard Crosby, a professor of Greek and later chancellor of NYU, and two prominent Protestant ministers, Dr. James W. Alexander and Dr. Isaac Ferris, who became "considerate and hearty espousers of the subject," Petrie recalled. The men met throughout the winter, and by spring had enough momentum to map out a tentative

organization. They were cheered and emboldened to learn that in the few months since Petrie's return, a YMCA had been formed in Boston, the latter in December 1851. (It was the second North American YMCA, following Montreal's founding that same year.)

The group of men, meeting in Petrie's home on April 21, 1852, resolved to form an association "consisting of members of evangelical churches in this city, to be called the New York Young Men's Christian Association, which shall be conducted on a plan resembling that of similar societies in London and other large cities, and that we invite the co-operation of the Christian young men of this city for the accomplishment of this purpose."

Reverend Ferris offered his Mercer Street Presbyterian Church for a first meeting to explore the formation of a YMCA in New York. On May 28, 1852 some 300 men gathered on Mercer Street, recruited by circulars in their places of business or churches; 173 immediately enrolled as members. Among them was George M. Van Derlip, an NYU student whose report in a religious weekly about the London YMCA had led to its founding in Boston. Meeting again on June 10, the members voted to constitute an association for men under the age of 40 who were evangelical Christians, believers in the gospel of salvation through the atonement of Jesus Christ. The new Association located two rental rooms on the third floor of the Stuyvesant Institute, formerly the Lyceum Theater at 659 Broadway, and formally opened them on September 20.

The momentum and excitement of this new endeavor reverberated across the East River. One year later, on June 9, 1853, 300 men in the independent

The New York Association was formed at the Mercer Street Presbyterian Church.

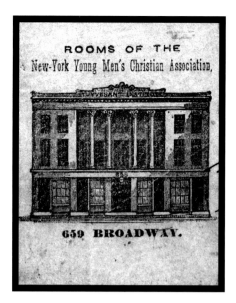

The New York YMCA rented its first rooms in the Stuyvesant Institute, located at 659 Broadway.

George M. Van Derlip

DESCRIBES THE

YMCA

"Young men from the country come up to London, and many are at once led out of temptation. Instead of snares, he finds friends about him, and they are faithful, too. They provide for him a delightful place and a delightful way to spend his leisure. The young stranger can say no longer, 'No man careth for my soul.' This is the best of all."

—Letter published in *Christian Watchman & Reflector,* Boston, October 30, 1851.

metropolis of Brooklyn gathered at the Second Congregational Church on Bridge Street "to organize a Christian Association similar to the one existing in the City of New York." The invitation had pointedly summoned young men to the public meeting who were "connected to the several Evangelical churches of this City," which encompassed Presbyterian, Episcopalian, Methodist, Dutch Reformed, Congregational, and Baptist denominations. (Later, the American YMCA movement would take pains not to specify what it considered evangelical.)

Churches provided the initial meeting places for the Brooklyn YMCA in 1853. The first members enrolled and a constitution was adopted at the Church of the Pilgrims (above). The first public meeting took place at the First Reformed Church (below).

The Brooklyn Association's first rooms were located near City Hall.

Purpose of the YMCA
of the City of New York

"To aid the stranger in finding the proper place of abode; help him in securing employment; furnish him with a place of relaxation under good influences; provide him with some form of entertainment; care for him in sickness; introduce him into city homes; and to lead him into a Christian Life."*

— Dedication of first rooms,
659 Broadway, June 30, 1852.

By December 20, the Brooklyn YMCA had settled into quarters in the Washington Building at Court and Joralemon streets, near the four-year-old City Hall. The municipality was known as the "City of Churches," thanks to its staunch Anglo-Dutch Protestant establishment and widely renowned preachers who were proponents of liberal religious thought. But since the churches focused on their parishioners rather than reaching out to newcomers, Brooklyn was particularly receptive to an organization that was concerned with their welfare. The YMCA's aim of improving "the spiritual, intellectual and social welfare of young men" assured the waterfront city that a diligent and pious partner would watch out for the increasing waves of young men, which had effectively doubled Brooklyn's population from 1840 to 1850.

Charles W. Bleecker became the Brooklyn Association's first chairman and Andrew A. Smith its president. In his initial report Smith, who was of Puritan descent, stated that the Association's objective was "to wage a spiritual warfare against the Prince of Darkness.... It is all important... at the entry of the city... [to have] a conserving and counter-acting agency that shall encircle the inexperienced stranger, with its panoply of protection." Like all of its officers, Smith and Bleecker served the YMCA as volunteers. Paying jobs were few. James P. Root and Pliny Fiske Warner were hired as Association librarians, a key position in the

Charles E. Teale started as an office boy for the Brooklyn YMCA and later became a director.

organization, at $300 per year. An office boy, Charles E. Teale, was hired in 1855 at an annual salary of $50. As an adult, Teale served the Association as a Board member for many years, and was Commissioner of Charities for the Borough of Brooklyn.

The two Associations, formed within a year of each other, would operate separately for more than a century, finally merging in 1957 as the YMCA of Greater New York. As it was for Brooklyn, the New York Association would rapidly become a model for the national YMCA movement and would emerge as visionary by pioneering programs, philosophies and buildings to house them. Through its dynamic leadership, the New York YMCA extended its influence to emerging Associations in North America and throughout the world.

Two Cities at Mid-Century

THE CITY OF NEW YORK had undergone a virtual transformation since the start of the nineteenth century, when its dominance derived from an eminent seaport and its stature as an early capital of the United States. By mid-century the Industrial Revolution was magnifying commercial opportunities there, and both New York and Brooklyn teemed with a populace swollen by new arrivals. Population grew rapidly in the two cities, which were barely more than villages early in the century. From a population of only 60,500 in 1800, Manhattan sheltered more than half a million souls by 1850. Brooklyn, with less than 6,000 inhabitants at the start of the century, counted nearly 280,000 by 1860.

In 1852, pigs and goats still roamed the streets and cattle were driven along them to slaughter. Telegraph poles and elevators were just appearing in the metropolis, but the city was becoming more cosmopolitan by the day. Mushrooming industries had turned Manhattan into a mighty business capital and a powerful magnet for workers from other parts of the country, and the world. This influx, largely composed of young men drawn from America's small towns and farms and European countries

Ferries plied the East River between Brooklyn's waterfront and Manhattan, where city streets teemed with traffic.

such as Germany and Ireland, frequently intermingled on crowded city streets and ferries that transported thousands daily across the East River.

Brooklyn, a beacon of opportunity and progress, offered a picture of contradictions as well. By mid-century, gaslights, horse-drawn street-cars, and locomotive trains had made their appearance, and water was available through a new supply system. But for all their bustling commerce and emerging wealth, Brooklyn and New York were not especially hospitable to new arrivals from smaller, unspoiled locales. Some found the cities quite offensive. The poet Walt Whitman, a country youth who as an adult became a volunteer with the YMCA, wrote in the *Brooklyn Evening Star:* "Our city is literally overrun with swine, outraging all decency, and foraging upon every species of eatables within their reach. . . .

There is not a city in the United States as large as Brooklyn where the cleanliness and decency of its streets is so neglected as here." Nor did Whitman have kind words for New York, calling it "one of the most crime-haunted and dangerous cities in Christendom."

Despite its many ills, urbanization was inexorably taking hold. Brooklyn and Manhattan were ideally situated to become the nation's industrial capitals. Manufacturing, by the 1850s a major commercial sector, was causing capital to accrue rapidly in the metropolitan area. Great banks, corporations, and the country's rapidly expanding railway systems were centered in New York and, on a smaller scale, in Brooklyn. Their prominence as major seaports and transshipment points for goods traveling into and from the United States would only grow. Lured by the promise of

Poet Walt Whitman, who was a YMCA relief worker in the Civil War, found Brooklyn streets offensive in the mid-nineteenth century.

The YMCA offered a more upright social life.

Saloons, theaters, and dance houses presented many temptations to young men.

those opportunities, eager and naïve young men, many of them still boys, were abandoning the comforts of home and family for the promise of opportunities in the new industrial centers. Verranus Morse, M.D., an early and life member of the YMCA, eloquently depicted the predicament of new arrivals to the anonymity of New York in an 1864 speech to fellow members:

> Here, while yet without associates, but yearning for companionship, they will meet with fellow clerks or fellow Boarders, who are beginning to fall into habits of dissipation, but who are frank, generous and social, ready to cheer them with a kind word, an invitation to the drinking saloon, the theater, or the dance house, or to while away their unoccupied time with recitals which will inflame their passions and excite their appetites; and Satan's own suggestion—whispered first in paradise—that a personal knowledge of vice is necessary to enable them to judge wisely and avoid understandingly, will be echoed in their ears; ... that now is a safe time to acquire such knowledge, while they are unknown, and far away from mothers' watchful eyes, fathers' warning voices and neighbors' tell-tale tongues.

Morse, like much of the city's ruling elite, was alarmed that so many strangers were susceptible to what he and others deemed degenerate and immoral activities, with few legal prohibitions to stop them. Citizens of Anglo-Dutch ancestry, among them Astors, Schermerhorns, and Stuyvesants, dominated commerce and social life in New York and had used their Protestant work ethic to fuel the city's astounding growth, forging an enduring bond between Christianity and commerce. Their churches were important bastions of society as well as spiritual sanctuaries, but few felt the need to reach out to the growing cadre of lonely single men.

In Brooklyn, YMCA members expressed concern over "Sabbath breakers" who patronized the city's fifty theaters and more than 600 "groggeries" that remained open on Sundays. Some 30,000 abandoned women also walked the streets, with numerous prostitutes looking to lure young men. But the comfortable classes had little interest in ameliorating the living conditions of newcomers who manned the shops and factories, whose neglected precincts and inadequate living quarters contrasted so sharply with their fine homes on grand avenues, squares, and side streets.

Indeed, the often rowdy behavior and bawdy amusements of these young strangers not only disturbed the gentry's straight-laced morality but inspired fear. A New York YMCA memorandum of 1866 catalogued the prevailing bad influences: billiard saloons whose tables "create a demand for 'drinks,' which are often the stake of the game"; 730 brothels, and theaters "haunted" by prostitutes; gambling halls only too happy to help a young man lose his salary at cards or dice; porter houses and barrooms; and obscene books and papers. "Pretty waiter girl" saloons, of which there were 233 in 1865—nearly equal the number of Protestant churches—welcomed some 30,000 visitors daily, including Sundays.

While nearly half of New York's male population was comprised of men between the ages of 15 and 40 by 1866, a YMCA survey found that the number who attended church services was "less than that of any other class of the populations." It was not difficult to understand why. Established churches had an air of exclusivity and charged more for "sittings" in their churches than these young men could afford. Nor were Sunday Schools or a City Mission targeted to this young population. The survey concluded that "the young men of New York present a wide and most important field for the efforts of the Christian and the Philanthropist." Thus the YMCA took it upon itself to combat the demoralizing influences that beset the naïve and vulnerable new arrivals.

The YMCA reached out to naïve young men who could easily lose their wages at games in gambling houses.

Recruiting Members, Crafting a Program

THE YMCA'S EARLY programs were designed to combat these urban evils. They were primarily religious in nature, taking the form of prayer meetings, Bible study and lectures. In the annual report of 1853 the Reverend Howard Crosby, Association president, observed that "the mental and social improvement of young men are regarded as means to an end, and that end, the single prominent end which we have in view, is the spiritual well-being of the young men of New York—the promotion of evangelical religion among this class of our fellow citizens. This fact must be distinctly marked... This being the case, can there be any fear of the Association becoming too religious in its tendencies? Its whole tendency *must* be religious, if it is to answer its original design."

In 1857, the annual report noted that 50,000 circulars "succinctly stating the character and objects of the Association" were distributed throughout the city, and several thousand copies of a tract entitled *120,000 Young Men* were also circulated to business establishments. Tracts on Sabbath observance were left in shops and saloons. Though the subject of Sabbath desecration came under attack in the New York Association, members quickly decided that working to end it was not their mission: the annual report declared that "it was not regarded as within our province to combat it, except as individuals, or in some other form of organization."

The New York Association formulated two types of membership, which were also adopted by Brooklyn. Only evangelical Christians could be full, voting members; other Protestants could hold associate membership. Given the YMCA's emphasis on evangelical Christianity and its desire to subvert corrupting influences, the initial program was heavily spiritual, albeit in a warm, welcoming social atmosphere where young men could make wholesome friends.

The early New York and Brooklyn programs were also focused on mental improvement. Educational in nature, they centered on a library and reading rooms. In an era that predated public libraries and free reading establishments, the importance of these YMCA initiatives could not be underestimated. "The library of this association is intended to contain everything which can minister to the well-being of man," noted the New York

Rev. Howard Crosby, first president of the New York Association, believed that the spiritual well-being of young men was the YMCA's most important goal.

Association's first annual report. "All true and sound instruction we hope may, in time, be gathered from its treasures." Newspapers and magazines in the New York YMCA library, all donated by publishers, included *Scientific American, Musical World, Merchants'* and *Sailors' Magazines, Photographic Journal, Hall's Journal of Health,* and *American Agriculturist.* Christian and nondenominational newspapers and journals from around the country were also available.

In its founding year, the New York Association established a Committee on Lectures to conduct "an annual course of public lectures or sermons upon subjects adapted to the spiritual and mental improvement of young men." Four years later, at the request of members, the Committee offered classes in languages and gymnastics, although class work would not become routine until 1869. A Literary Society was organized in 1865 "to awaken ... an interest in literature, and induce a desire for mental improvement."

By 1871 a member could choose from courses in vocal music, math, mechanical drawing, natural sciences, bookkeeping, writing, and languages—French, German, and Spanish. A course in "phonography" was introduced in 1877, the very year that Thomas Edison unveiled his latest invention. The Association offered classes at some expense to its coffers, occasionally noting the need for endowments to assure their continuation.

Dues for regular members in both New York and Brooklyn were $2 per year. YMCA men were expected to reach out to other young men, especially strangers, to secure their regular attendance at Sunday church services and to aid them in finding jobs and proper residences.

The Association took concerted action on the new arrivals' pressing need for comfortable, decent living conditions. In 1860 a boardinghouse committee had amassed a register of some 100 suitable lodgings, all of which it had visited and vetted as desirable. Finding such quarters required continuous work. In the mid-1860s, an Association report noted that "the virtuous and vicious are oftentimes herded together in the same boarding house, room and bed. Driven to these places by limited salaries, and unable to afford fires in their rooms, they are consequently led to frequent saloons and like places, where they are exposed to the most contaminating influences." The committee, composed of members in better situations, helped many young men keep up their rent payments by giving them small stipends "to pay board till they can obtain employment, or recover from sickness, to purchase clothes, so that they can take respectable situations," according to the 1863–64 annual report.

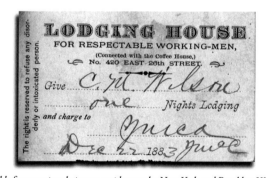

Well before opening their own residences, the New York and Brooklyn YMCAs helped newcomers locate safe, clean and affordable lodgings.

The young Associations quickly spread to new neighborhoods. As they outgrew rented rooms and located larger quarters, the YMCAs established a presence in new communities. In 1855 an Association was formed in Williamsburg, Brooklyn, which was reorganized in 1866 as the Eastern District Association in that heavily German community. In 1864 J. Pierpont Morgan, by then an influential director of the New York Association and soon to be its treasurer, persuaded fellow Board members to leave their shabby and cramped rooms in Bible House at Third Avenue and Ninth Street for larger, nicely furnished quarters at Fifth Avenue and Twenty-Second Street.

Life members of the YMCA, who paid a one-time $20 fee, tended to be well-established citizens. They included prominent ministers in Brooklyn—Henry Ward Beecher, Henry Van Dyke, R. S. Storrs Jr., B. T. Welch, Samuel T. Spear, George W. Bethune and James L. Hodges. In New York they ranged from circus impresario Phineas T. Barnum to William Earl Dodge Jr., a young merchant and civic leader who was elected Association president in 1865.

A WARNING AGAINST Excessive Ambition

 New York Association member Charles Tracy, a lawyer, warned his fellow members in 1853 against worshipping wealth as "the great end of life" in a city that "seems to be altogether given over to the making of money." The YMCA, he believed, could counterbalance the evil of greed: "The Christian Association comes here to the rescue, and calls the young man to higher themes, to ennobling friendships, to improving occupations to the cherishing of the immortal. It occupies the possible leisure with what befits intellect and character, and thus shuts out baneful influences. Something positive must be interposed before the seducing spirit of gain, to pre-occupy the heart; for it is by occupying the soil with good seeds and useful plants, that noxious weeds are the most effectually excluded. The passion for accumulating riches is a fearful and hideous thing, but it may arise as a result of an ill-regulated mind exercised out of proportion in business pursuits."

—Second annual report,
New York Association

Circus entrepreneur Phineas T. Barnum was an early life member of the New York YMCA.

The nascent Associations had little trouble in rallying leading businessmen and citizens as supporters and sustainers. The YMCA was a worthy shepherd for their employees, offering them worthwhile after-hours activities and providing wholesome alternatives to morally bankrupt pursuits. As one member, the lawyer Charles Tracy, observed in the New York YMCA's second year, "The Christian Association comes here to the rescue, and calls the young man to higher themes, to ennobling friendships, to improving occupations, to the cherishing of the immortal. It occupies the possible leisure with what befits intellect and character, and thus shuts out baneful influences."

The YMCA's emphasis on character building had a particular appeal for business leaders. A longstanding apprentice system had once assured city shopkeepers and factory owners of upright and obedient employees. Traditionally a young man would be referred to an enterprise by friends or family, taken under the owner's wing and given sleeping quarters above the store. Under this system, employers inculcated good habits and kept the employee's character and comings and goings under close surveillance. But by mid-century the cities' commercial sectors were growing too rapidly and chaotically to permit this personal approach to continue. More and more manpower was needed, and newly arrived young strangers went looking for work from door to door, asking merchants to hire them on trust.

To address the needs of newcomers in locating adequate work, the two YMCAs quickly established employment bureaus. The New York Association recorded its first job placements in 1865. Word spread, and employers began seeking out the bureaus, knowing that they could find young men there who would pass muster. Businessmen approved of the YMCA's wholesome moral atmosphere as a trustworthy force to mold young strangers into the upright individuals who would be suitable for their establishments.

The YMCA's
Effect on Young Men

The powerful influence of the YMCA is apparent in this letter sent in 1886 by a retired merchant in New England: "To me the Association was a friend in need; the turning of a new and bright page in life, the opening of a door of hospitality and welcome. I was a stranger, just from New England, come to take a clerkship in a dry-goods house. I was boarding at the Cortlandt Street Hotel, and had a small, cold room, on the top floor; I was lonely in the midst of crowds; the hotel and streets were teeming with beggars, and at night from Canal Street down Broadway was a dangerous place; my predecessor (a bookkeeper) had been ruined by gambling, and had appropriated the firm's money; what new and strange temptations were around me and among them the voice of the siren.... The Association did a work which no other organization could do for young men. Certainly my career was influenced by it in a marked manner. The Boarding House Committee afforded me a home more congenial than a hotel; to this I invited a young member of the Association (also a clerk in a wholesale store) the first time we met; the result was, he came and also to the church I attended, was converted and to-day is a Doctor of Divinity."*

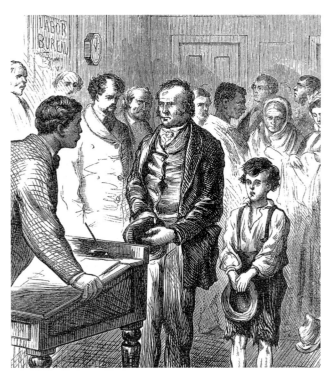

YMCA employment bureaus matched young men seeking work with owners of business establishments.

The YMCA had an even broader appeal to the commercial classes. A number of prominent businessmen and merchants went beyond recruiting their clerks at Association bureaus to a deeper involvement as YMCA volunteers. Like Williams and Petrie, the Associations' founders and officers were uncompensated lay leaders who recruited colleagues and friends such as Dodge and Morgan from the city's leading business establishments. This model took hold successfully in New York and Brooklyn and was replicated across the country. "The New York Association, due in part to its strategic location, gradually became the cradle of the lay leadership of the Young Men's Christian Associations," Terry Donoghue observed in his 1951 history, *An Event on Mercer Street.* "From among its officers and the ranks of its membership were to come many men who were to give new purpose and scope to the Movement, here and abroad."

Within a year of incorporation the New York Association, emboldened by its positive reception, initiated a $50,000 building fund under the auspices of a dozen esteemed citizens. They planned to create an edifice "adorned with every wholesome attraction to win the interest of the young men of the city, and thus lead them to virtue and piety." But due to a gathering storm over slavery and states' rights in the young nation—a storm that would culminate in civil war—the Association was unable to purchase a site and implement this bold plan until 1867.

Battling to Survive in a Time of War

A PATTERN OF energetic, aggressive and at times astonishing growth and leadership came to characterize both the New York and Brooklyn Associations. Day in, day out, YMCA activities were primarily religious in focus. Through what was called "aggressive work," members took to the streets, preaching and passing out tracts, teaching in Sunday Schools, conducting prayer sessions in public institutions, and doing relief work with the poor. Despite the breadth of YMCA work, with its social and educational features, the cities' established churches came to view the young Associations not as allies but poachers on their turf. They eventually caused the YMCA membership to back off somewhat and to issue a statement "that we do not intend that [the YMCA] shall take the highest place in our affections... we hold these organizations as auxiliary to the divinely appointed means to grace, the Church, and the preaching of the Gospel."

Ironically, a financial panic from 1856 to 1858—the worst ever to hit the young nation and deeply felt in

YMCA members often took their evangelistic message to New Yorkers by preaching in the streets.

the two cities—would play a large part in reassuring the churches of the YMCA's good intentions, and in establishing a public profile for the budding organization. After a stock market crash in the summer of 1857, many businesses failed, banks closed, and legions of workers found themselves unemployed and homeless. In response to the crisis that gripped the populace, the Association instigated noontime prayer meetings to alleviate widespread anxieties, drawing businessmen as well as the poor. These daily prayer revivals, which were resolutely nondenominational, soon spread to cities across the country, the New York Association's greatest contribution to the national movement in its first decade.

Its revival activities, however, sparked a split between those that felt the YMCA should be devoted to evangelizing work in local communities, and others who felt it should be targeted just to young men and not the general public. This would become one of the biggest battles in the American YMCA's history, and was finally settled by the Washington, D.C. Association's William C. Langdon, who successfully advocated for the focus on young men at the 1859 national convention in Troy, New York.

Even in its first years, the New York Association gave direction to other fledgling Associations. Langdon approached New York to assume the lead in forming a "fraternity" of YMCAs, remarking in 1854 that the New York City YMCA "is and ever must be, in many respects the most important in the country." Reverend Crosby, as head of the New York Association, refused, stating that a confederation would detract from "local work" in an "essentially local institution." In addition, he pointedly wrote: "We believe [conventions] will tend to produce unpleasant scenes and ruptures on such subjects as *slavery.*" In their stead, Reverend Crosby encouraged "correspondence and chance visits." The young Association wanted to avoid unpleasantries at all costs, a trait that became an ingrained characteristic.

Anti-slavery sentiment predominated in New York and Brooklyn where, in 1827, the state had mandated emancipation and slaves were set free. The Brooklyn YMCA counted the nationally prominent abolitionist, the Reverend Henry Ward Beecher, among its members. (Harriet Beecher Stowe, his sister, fanned the flames of the slavery debate with her 1852 book *Uncle Tom's Cabin.*) Reverend Beecher's pulpit was the Plymouth Church of the Pilgrims in Brooklyn Heights. While he, like other YMCA founders, cherished harmony and resisted being drawn into controversy, Beecher's sentiments against the evils of slavery were clear. In an 1850 article, he had condemned slavery as antithetical to the Christian virtues of

Rev. Henry Ward Beecher railed against slavery from his pulpit at Brooklyn's Plymouth Church.

family and honest labor, and urged helping fugitive slaves to freedom. His church became known as the "Grand Central Depot of the Underground Railroad," with most of its congregation "large stockholders in that line."

Both the New York and Brooklyn YMCAs stood staunchly in favor of abolition. Some Brooklyn YMCA members petitioned the Association in 1854 to oppose the extension of slavery to Nebraska in an act before Congress. But the Association refused to issue a public condemnation. President Andrew A. Smith declared, "As a body, we keep entirely aloof from all those movements which are of a political or partisan character, and sedulously guard against the introduction of topics which only alienate our hearts, divide our counsels, and thence cripple our prosperity and usefulness." After much dissension the slavery theme was dropped from these meetings, setting a precedent of avoiding controversies if they might interfere with Association activities. In ensuing years, the Brooklyn YMCA would refuse to make its rooms available for political lectures.

The hotly contested issues of slavery and abolition roiled the New York Association. The Library Committee voted to ban *Uncle Tom's Cabin* from its reading room in 1853, a move that was upheld by the Board. In 1856 a number of members, led by the young lawyer Cephas Brainerd, took part in a rally for abolitionist Presidential candidate John C. Fremont, only to be lampooned in the *New York Express.* The Library Committee cancelled its subscription to the *Express,* but in this instance the Board moved to expel the Committee. An investigation that followed determined that the Board had acted unfairly, and all directors were asked to resign. More than 150 members also left in support of the Board in 1857, including Corresponding Secretary William E. Dodge Jr., and new members were quickly recruited to take their place.

The official neutrality of the Association on the question of slavery cost the young organization many of its friends. But a policy had been established that, with few exceptions, has characterized the New York YMCA over its 150 years. By not taking stands on controversial public issues the Association has not courted the risk of offending those with divergent opinions, at the expense of a higher public profile through exerting its considerable influence on major issues.

Thirty-seven delegates from nineteen YMCAs convened in Buffalo, New York in 1854 to approve a voluntary confederation of Associations that would support and advance YMCA work in the United States and Canada. The Brooklyn and New York Associations refused to endorse the convention or to send delegates. "Such supposed centralization would militate with the necessarily local character of our field of effort," the Brooklyn YMCA wrote. But by the next year, twenty-two of the twenty-five Associations had approved the constitution for a confederation, including the New York Association, having been assured that the confederation would have no governing authority. The enduring principle of local autonomy was thus established in the YMCA.

By 1857, a rupture emerged in the fragile national conference. As the Brooklyn and New York Associations had feared, the schism centered on slavery and abolition, which were pitting North against South and calling into question the very future of the United States of America. This intense conflict had built to a point where little in national life was left untouched by it, and would soon threaten the existence of the American YMCA movement. Before the Associations could firmly bond with one another, the deep-seated rift grew too large to ignore.

The issue would not, and could not, be resolved within the YMCA. The gulf separating the Associations resounded clearly in this letter to Northern YMCAs from the Richmond, Virginia Association dated May 6, 1861, after the South's secession, and in the response that followed it:

> Brethren: We have determined, by the help of God, to address you in the character of peacemakers. . . As Christians let us discountenance the misrepresentations of each other, which are so frequently made, and

let us labor earnestly in the cause of peace. . . The separation of the South from the North is irrevocable," the letter continued, and the "conquest of either section by the other is impossible. . . . We do not now advocate a war of aggression or conquest," the writers stated, but only wished to govern themselves. "Let us labor earnestly in the cause of peace," concluded the signers, William P. Munford, Joel B. Watkins and William H. Gwathmey. "Let us again unite our prayers and efforts for the restoration of peace and good-will between the Northern and Southern Confederacies."

In response, Noble Heath Jr., the New York Association's Corresponding Secretary, repelled the Southerners' overtures: "Our very existence is imperiled by your hideous 'secession.' No government can stand a year upon such a basis. . . . Indulge me in one word more. Slavery is wrong. You have determined to defend that wrong. You have counted no cost in defending it even before it was assailed, but have been willing even to destroy our Government for fear it might be. May God forgive you; your position is utterly false, and my heart bleeds that men calling themselves Christians can connect themselves with so wicked a cause, even calling it holy, and daring to compare it with that of our God-protected fathers!!

"Your Christians will meet ours in battle. The 7th Regiment of New York numbers many of our members; the 12th and 71st as well; and tomorrow the 9th takes others—active, earnest Christians. . . Upon you and your 'institution' must rest the responsibility of this fratricidal war, and shirk it or dissemble it how you may, God will require an account of every man who abets the treason of the South. I cannot pray for the Southern Confederacy."

When Confederate troops unleashed their fire on Fort Sumter in April 1861, President Abraham Lincoln put out a call for volunteer troops. Legions of men were mustered in the streets of New York, and as they departed for the south a young artist and New York YMCA member, Vincent Colyer, left his studio at 105 Bleecker Street to walk among them, handing them religious tracts. He returned day after day.

Spurred by Colyer's efforts, Noble Heath, Edward Self and the Reverend Stephen Tyng of the Association Board met to discuss the YMCA's role in the Civil War on April 27. They soon formed an Army Committee,

YMCA volunteers ministered to soldiers in hospitals.

mobilizing other Associations to join them in ministering to troops at home and at the front. Soldiers' spiritual needs were a high priority (temporal needs would be addressed by the U.S. Sanitary Commission, which was organized the following month and became the forerunner of the Red Cross). The YMCA published and distributed 70,000 hymnals that fit in a soldier's vest pocket, sending another 30,000 to YMCAs in Brooklyn, Chicago, and Philadelphia, and to the American Sunday School Union. The Committee also furnished troops with religious tracts, Bibles, and prayer books, and requested the Secretary of War to enforce an Army regulation requiring its chaplains to be ordained ministers.

Volunteers from New York and other Associations also wrote letters to ailing soldiers on the battlefront and to their families. The Army Committee visited nearly every regiment that passed through New York, saw that they had the services of a chaplain and furnished books to all who wanted them. A Hospital Committee supplied hundreds of "watchers," or visitors, to local hospitals where sick and wounded soldiers were being treated. The Association convened a Union prayer meeting daily in Fulton Street, and other devotional services were conducted in and around the city on the Sabbath and weekday evenings. Over a six-month period about 150 prayer meetings were organized to sustain soldiers at encampments within a 30-mile radius. The 1861 annual report claims success "in respect to the frequency and regularity with which the prayer meetings are held, and their blessed results in the conversion of souls."

In June, William E. Dodge Sr. presided at a public meeting to raise funds for this enormous effort. The Association's membership and dues were dwindling as young men were called from the city to the battlefields. But the fledgling YMCA managed to raise $2,875 in 1861, spending more than $1,400 alone to print the soldier's hymn book.

In July troops from New York traveled to Bull Run in Virginia to defend the Union, including the 176th Ironsides Regiment. Ironsides, mustered entirely of practicing Christians by Cephas Brainerd, had strict requirements: good moral character and habits, including personal hygiene and abstinence from alcohol and use of profane or coarse language. At Bull Run Northern soldiers met with devastating defeat as troops were soundly pushed back by Confederate forces.

Learning of the disaster, Colyer and fellow Association member Frank W. Ballard left for Washington two days later "to minister to the temporal and spiritual necessities of the wounded and dying men who crowded the hospitals in and near the capital." Colyer remained in Washington, following the men the YMCA had been "watching for" to their encampments and hospitals. He reported back to the Board of "an abundance of work for us to do, work which the physicians and nurses can not do; they have not the time... to talk to [wounded soldiers] on the serious things of the soul." In response supplies poured in, including hymn books, clothing, shoes, cocoa paste, tea, jelly, candles, flour, pork, soap, gum camphor, choice sherry,

Vincent Colyer, a young artist and YMCA member, took it upon himself to minister to soldiers' needs.

Irish whiskey, and cases of wine. Colyer's volunteer efforts were not only directed to white soldiers. Prominent in his work was the establishment of a hospital for black troops and a school for children of former slaves. In 1863, he would raise a regiment of Negro troops and be named its colonel.

Leading this monumental effort quickly put a severe strain on the New York Association. By August Colyer urged fellow Association members to enlist other YMCAs to the cause. In November 1861, fifteen Associations of "loyal states" convened in New York and listened to Colyer's firsthand report from the front. Moved to action, delegates created the twelve-member U.S. Christian Commission. Charged with overseeing ministrations to the sick and wounded, providing them with spiritual and physical comfort, three commissioners were New Yorkers, among them Cephas Brainerd and Reverend Tyng of St. George's Episcopal Church, where J. Pierpont Morgan was a parishioner. The Commission would eventually raise and distribute more than $6 million for its Civil War efforts.

Founding Statement *of the* *U.S. Christian Commission*

"**R**esolved, that it is the duty of the Young Men's Christian Associations to take active measures to promote the spiritual and temporal welfare of the soldiers in the army, and the sailors and marines in the navy, in cooperation with chaplains and others."

The U.S. Christian Commission headquarters in Washington, D.C., was the center of YMCA relief work during the Civil War.

Josiah Dow, a Brooklyn Association Board member, led that WMCA's war activities, including significant fund raising and the distribution of hymnals and religious tracts at nearby camps and the Brooklyn Navy Yard. Under his auspices, the Brooklyn YMCA Army and Navy Committee took shape in December 1861 to focus particularly on needs of soldiers and sailors in Brooklyn. It also called on Vincent Colyer to distribute tents, reading materials and "physical comforts" for them in Washington. The Brooklyn YMCA did not suffer as much during the Civil War as its New York sibling. Although it did not take up new work during this time, monthly meetings continued regularly and it vigorously pursued typical activities such as Sunday Schools, special preaching services and "entertainments" at the Academy of Music. With leadership from John M. Doubleday, the Association managed to raise $5,000 to double the volumes in its library in 1862.

The 1861 New York annual report reveals the pride and patriotism felt by YMCA members: "…in no previous year of its history has our Association given its name and its energies to a work more practical in character or more

YMCA volunteers ministered to the needs of wounded soldiers at the front.

productive of fruit. An institution founded originally for the distinct and specific purpose of 'promoting evangelical religion among young men' and of 'improving their spiritual, mental and social condition' could not but recognize God's beckoning hand in this transfer of its responsibility and opportunity from the streets of New York to the banks of the Potomac."

During this extraordinary time, regular New York Association programs were of necessity set aside in favor of service to troops. Membership was halved and deficits began accumulating. Men who were normally active on committees had departed for camps and fields, and those usually found in prayer meetings were now leading regiments or companies. To keep its missionary work active in New York, the Association decided "to throw open the doors freely to the young men of the city of the Library and Reading room, in the hope that many may be attracted from the haunts of sin, and induced to come with us, that we may do them good," noted the 1862 annual report.

The disruptions of war work were clearly worth the patriotic zeal and missionary fulfillment they stimulated in the Association, according to the 1862 report: "We feel that this [work] gives us an especial claim, not only upon the followers of the Master, but also upon those who prefer a free government to anarchy and ruin. . . The Christian patriot, while he may, and should prefer to expend his time and thoughts upon the things which make for peace, can put in no cowardly claim for immunity from the hazards and horrors of a war in which a nation's life or death must be decided. In the Christian system cowardice can have no place, and indolence no permit."

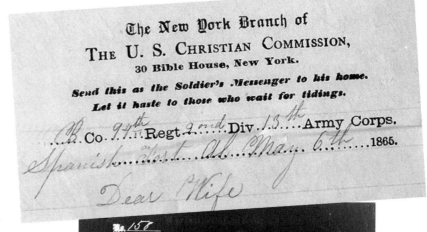

The Christian Commission aided soldiers in sending messages home; volunteers like Walt Whitman personally wrote letters.

"*No* RED TAPE *Here*"

"**A** brave young man, not seriously wounded, came limping up to our tent, and requested some cloths and other articles to dress his wound, himself, as all hands were busy with worse cases. The articles I handed him at once, at the same time giving him a drink of ice-cold lemonade just prepared. 'Ah!' said he, 'there's no red tape process here! You men of the Christian Commission give a fellow what he needs, when he needs it, without a tedious process of waiting for orders, and then waiting for them to be filled. Thank you, gentlemen.' And he turned away with a glad heart."

—United States Christian Commission: Facts, Principles, and Progress, January 1864.

However, grieving members lost in the war, Association leaders were in a state of deep dismay in 1862 and even considered disbanding. Membership rolls were devastated, with only 151 of 1,500 men remaining, and its books showed an alarming $2,400 in debt. Some founders and friends thought seriously about liquidating assets and dissolving the decade-old organization. However, noting the sacrifices members were making in the war, the annual report stated that "Our deepest consciousness repelled the thought" and revealed a determination to reinvigorate the orga..ization: "our minds were thrown back irresistibly upon the claims of one hundred fifty thousand young men at our very door." Thus moved, some forty clergymen met at the Fifth Avenue Hotel and pledged their support. Donations of money streamed in from local churches, allowing the Association to sustain its operations and to erase a daunting debt.

War work was the YMCA's first full-fledged entry into social service, locally and nationally, and it established the organization as one that stepped up to lead in crises. The war effort also represented its first outreach beyond the membership. In all, some 5,000 YMCA volunteers served without pay as surgeons, nurses, and chaplains. Others distributed medical supplies, food, and clothing, and even taught soldiers to read. Walt Whitman, who served as a YMCA relief worker, later reflected on the experience and observed that it gave him "the greatest privilege of satisfaction—and most profound lesson of my life."

The New York Army Committee had spurred a monumental national wartime effort. At a time of grave danger to the nation, the youthful organization's Christian Commission gained approbation nationwide for its efforts, including praise from General Ulysses S. Grant. YMCA "war work," as it came to be known, swiftly elevated the Association's profile with the public, the military and the U.S. government.

Separating the Races

BEFORE THE CIVIL WAR the Canadian YMCAs, part of the Confederation of North American Associations, had challenged U.S. members to live up to their Christian ideals and to speak out in opposition to slavery. Confederation leaders in northern states, however, loathe to alienate white southern YMCAs, had made a conscious effort to avoid the issue. The Canadian Associations were dismayed by the compliance of their U.S. counterparts and separated from the Confederation before the Civil War.

Morris K. Jesup, an early YMCA lay leader, staunchly refused to support businesses that dealt in slavery.

Through their war efforts New York and Brooklyn members had demonstrated sympathy and support for African Americans and their striving for freedom and equal treatment. Among other actions, Vincent Colyer had helped displaced African Americans and aided soldiers based on Rikers Island who had been cheated by bounty brokers. New York Association founder and national YMCA leader Morris Ketcham Jesup, for one, refused to invest in Virginia because of its slave market, and over the years gave $1 million for the education of African-American students.

Brainerd and Colyer were also involved in legal efforts following New York's Draft Riots to help African Americans who were harmed to get financial redress. Colyer prepared the *Report of the Committee of Merchants for the Relief of Colored People, Suffering for the Late Riots in the City of New York* in 1863, and Brainerd served as legal counsel for the suits made.

Despite their fervent support of abolition and color-blind war work, the New York and Brooklyn YMCAs followed the unwritten law of the land: the practice of racial segregation in their memberships. When U.S. YMCAs first formed, most African Americans still lived in bondage although the two cities harbored communities of former slaves. Free black men could and did participate in the early YMCAs, but only in separate Branches or Associations.

After the war, "Colored YMCAs" formed in three cities. Anthony Bowen, a former slave, founded the first in 1857 in Washington, D.C. New York's first YMCA for African Americans was independently organized after the Civil War at 97 Wooster Street, an area with a sizable black population at that time. The New York Association regarded this YMCA, which was essentially a reading room, as a model effort worthy of its support. "An interesting feature of this year's work has been the aid extended in the establishment of the first Christian Association among colored men," noted the 1867 annual report. "While reaching and elevating those of that race in the City, we trust, by correspondence and personal visitation, it will be the means of doing much to induce others throughout the Southern states to unite for the purpose of Christian education and improvement."

In that year the New York YMCA formed a Committee on Colored Association chaired by Abner W. Colgate. Perceiving a need for a religious society "more especially adapted to the growing requirements of the colored young men," the committee set about raising funds to aid the thirty-five members of the Colored Association, who lacked the means to continue their work.

The Colored Young Men's Christian Association became an auxiliary to the "parent" New York Association, submitting a monthly report to the New York Board about its affairs. "Its objects are the same, and...a very large field for doing good is opened," the 1867 annual report stated. "It is a matter of congratulation that this work, at its start, is in the hands of colored men who are well aware of its necessity, and who, it is believed, are thoroughly in earnest. Their wish is to directly influence for good a large class of disreputable young men in their community, whom the excellent religious influences of the colored churches have yet failed to reach."

The parent Association expected those churches to sustain the Wooster Street room with contributions, but in spite of some funds and furniture that came in, more help was needed from the general public. As the 1865 annual report noted, "it is well known that, as a class, the colored men of this city are very poor; and it is hoped and believed that when the existence of this new society shall

E.V.C. Eato was president of the first "Colored YMCA" in New York.

be more generally known to the public, it will not fail to enlist the kindly sympathy, cooperation, and encouragement of those who are so well able to help it along."

In 1867, E.V.C. Eato, president of New York's Colored Branch, became the first black delegate to a national YMCA convention. Eato received a standing ovation and delegates clearly hoped the approbation would encourage formation of similar YMCAs in the South. The following year's Association report noted this Branch's "wide influence among the colored men of the city, and throughout the country. Without any political or sectarian bias, the members aim to instruct their newly liberated brethren in all that will tend to make them useful and happy, and to unite them in efforts for religious education as the true means of elevation. Their room at 97 Wooster Street is the only free reading room and place of social resort of a healthful moral character for colored young men in the city." By 1870, the Branch had grown to more than 100 members and moved to larger quarters above the Freedmen's Bank on Bleecker Street near Macdougal.

The YMCAs would remain separate, with the Colored YMCA regarded by the New York Association as "a distinct and independent organization, our relations to it being that of voluntary intercourse and friendship. Whether this relation should be changed or modified we will not discuss at this time." Unfortunately, this YMCA shut down by 1872, apparently from lack of financial support.

In War's Aftermath, a Leader Emerges

EVEN BEFORE THE war was won and the Union preserved, the New York Association had taken up the business of rebuilding, liquidating debt and rehabilitating its depleted membership. On the national level, the budding confederation of YMCAs had been shattered. The number of American Associations had more than doubled after the financial panic and the Great Revival, but only a

Robert Ross McBurney emigrated to New York from Ulster at age 18.

a member of St. Paul's who was also a member of the Christian Commission, recruited McBurney to the post at Bible House, which the young man took as a stop-gap job for a weekly salary of $5.

Nothing, it seemed, was too small for McBurney's attention and energies. A practical man, he first swept out the neglected rooms and began organizing activities, leading noon prayer meetings and putting the directors to work. The genial McBurney then set about recruiting members, aided by William E. Dodge Jr., who held meetings in his home. He and others who had defected after the Fremont incident were convinced to rejoin. New members included Dodge's cousin James Stokes Jr., 23, and J. P. Morgan, 27, who were also elected to the Board. In a significant departure, the reinvigorated group amended the constitution in 1864 to require that active members only be men of good moral character, under the age of 40, who paid $2 in annual dues. No longer would members have to belong to an evangelical church.

quarter of them remained intact after the Civil War. For the New York Association, this would usher in one of the most dynamic periods in the Association's history. Decisions were made and actions taken that set trends within the movement which endure to this day.

Economically depleted but strengthened in purpose by its wartime efforts, the New York organization turned to a valued young member, Robert Ross McBurney, to lead it in rebuilding. With the national movement lacking cohesiveness, New York under McBurney's leadership would soon come to define the YMCA's focus and purpose nationwide.

Robert McBurney was the prototype of the young man the YMCA was created to serve. An immigrant of Scotch-Irish ancestry from Protestant Ulster, he came to New York at age 18 in a flood of Irish immigrants who were fleeing the potato famine. When he landed in 1854, a former tutor took the young migrant to enroll at the YMCA's rooms at 659 Broadway. McBurney found employment as a clerk in the hat business of a fellow countryman and worked there for six years, while engaging in evangelistic work as a member of St. Paul's Methodist Church. When the business failed and McBurney lost his job, he volunteered for war service but was rejected on physical grounds.

The New York Association, just emerging from its serious consideration of disbanding, needed a young man who could act as librarian, help to rebuild its membership, and raise direly needed funds. Benjamin J. Manierre,

Men carried this membership card.

Young Men's Christian Association
OF THE CITY OF NEW YORK.

No. 7042   FULL TICKET.

Admit *Henry Trumbull Bronson*
To privileges subject to Rules,

RECEIVED   M. TAYLOR PYNE,
Annual Fee, $5.00.   *Treasurer.*
Ass'n Notes,   25   R. R. McBURNEY,
                                     General Secretary.

SUBJECT TO RENEWAL DURING   1192

Turn over.

JOINED — *June /65*

McBurney joined St. Paul's Methodist Church in Wall Street.

During the 1860s, purely evangelistic societies were in decline, and waiving that requirement undoubtedly helped the Association to grow. "Our membership has been increased by many men of sterling worth who join us heartily in the one purpose of most earnest work for the future," the 1864 annual report noted. "By God's blessing we close this year free from debt, and enter upon the new year with cheering prospects of widely-extended usefulness."

McBurney and Board member Cephas Brainerd, whom McBurney promoted as a national confederation leader, strongly urged a wider definition of a ministry for young men and began to exert their influence on other Associations. The New York YMCA set itself a large task—to take care of young men's housing, employment, social, and spiritual needs.

In 1864, the directors showed their appreciation of McBurney, who had solicited the aid of churches with Association programs and finances, by raising his salary to $1,000 annually. But after overseeing the Association's move from Bible House to Twenty-Second Street, McBurney decided to try his hand again at business. He resigned his position with the YMCA to take up employment with a tobacco firm in Philadelphia. Some have speculated that the directors found McBurney deficient in public speaking and desired an Association leader with a clergyman's riveting platform skills. That was not his forte. He preferred, and excelled at, personal contact and the quiet organization of Association affairs.

Within three months, McBurney realized that his departure was a mistake. Still in frequent touch with William Dodge Jr., he communicated his unhappiness with his move. Fortunately the Board had not filled his post, and happily reinstated him. McBurney returned as a director and corresponding secretary, never to leave again. He had found his life's calling.

William E. Dodge Jr., an early lay leader who served as New York president for ten years, was a key figure in the nineteenth-century Association.

At the suggestion of Dodge, an influential Board member, the New York Association added a fourth dimension to YMCA work that continues to be a core YMCA program. In 1866, the constitution was revised to read "The object of this Association shall be the improvement of the spiritual, mental, social and *physical* condition of young men." Through what was called the "four-fold work," YMCA programs were refocused on the "whole man." With leadership from McBurney and Dodge, the four-fold program would be widely emulated in other Associations. Richard Cary Morse, writing nearly a half-century later, observed that "It is difficult to overestimate the value to Association work the world over of what was accomplished within and proceeding from the New York City Association" from 1865 to 1870.

Just as McBurney typified the young man served, William E. Dodge Jr. epitomized the YMCA's lay leaders. In 1865, he was elected President of the New York

The New York Association was represented at the 1865 YMCA convention in Philadelphia by Cephas Brainerd, center; Robert Ross McBurney, seated to his left; and James Phelps Stokes, standing at far left.

Association. His venerable father had risen from humble beginnings, coming from Connecticut at age 13 to work in as a dry-goods clerk in the firm of a family friend, to become a remarkable success in business, earning a fortune in exporting cotton and importing copper and tin. The young Dodge worked first for his father and then formed a partnership with his father-in-law, Anson Greene Phelps. William E. Dodge Jr. set a precedent by introducing business methods in the conduct of Association affairs. He instigated a systematic districting and leafleting of downtown establishments to recruit members, and encouraged formation of an employment bureau that placed 400 men in jobs in 1865. Under his leadership a $250,000 building campaign was launched.

J. Pierpont Morgan was an early treasurer of the New York Association.

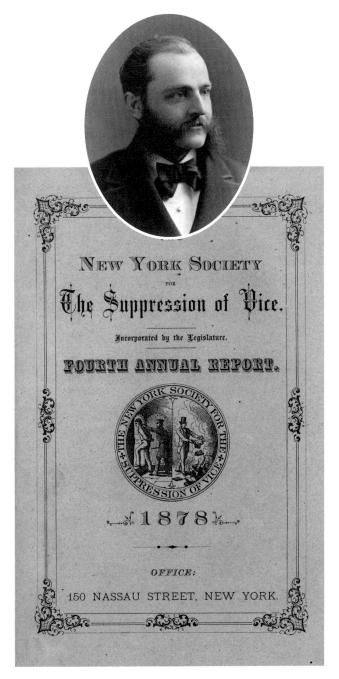

In 1866, McBurney and Brainerd led the Association to survey the social conditions facing young men in the city, and the resources available to them. The survey results were used in fund-raising materials for the proposed new building. A young moral reformer, Anthony Comstock, had been calling the Association's attention to New York's degradations, and the YMCA set about to define them, concluding "that agents for demoralization are fearfully in excess of those of a contrary character." Comstock's primary targets were drinking, gambling, prostitution and pornographic books.

New York YMCA leaders gave Comstock a stipend to support his work, but his growing censorship activities as a special Congressional agent to combat obscenity cast the Association in a bad light. Several YMCA leaders, including the banker Morris Jesup, Pierpont Morgan, Dodge and William C. Beecher, son of the minister, constituted a separate organization, the New York Society for the Suppression of Vice in 1874 and made Comstock its salaried agent for 40 years. Comstock staged seven raids on the Society's behalf. In this way the Association again managed to sidestep direct involvement in a controversial issue.

Anthony Comstock, a controversial moral reformer, enlisted YMCA lay leaders in his cause.

The YMCA's concerns were focused on men between the ages of 15 and 40. "Many are utter strangers from the country and Europe, and pick up friends and acquaintances by accident," the survey noted. "Owing to the change in the mode of conducting business during the past twenty years, the attention of employers has gradually and unnoticed become diverted from the social and moral interests of young men." Even worse, "The proportion of young men who attend services in all these churches is much less than that of any other class of the populations."

The survey report also lamented that their salaries were inadequate to the cost of living and rued an increased exclusiveness in society that made it difficult for newcomers to have "access to that which is beneficial and elevating." The YMCA advocated for agencies that offered young men "facilities for the moral and religious culture. . . without charge or upon terms so liberal as to make them practically a gratuity." Based on their findings, New York leaders fortified their argument to potential supporters that there was great need for YMCA services and the construction of a building to house them.

The YMCA Building Takes Shape

McBURNEY'S HARD WORK, his faith in the mission of the Association, and his skillful persuasion of the lay leadership to keep moving forward convinced the New York YMCA to mount an audacious building campaign just a dozen years after its founding. Early YMCAs were typically in rented rooms that provided a homelike social center; the building was less important than what it housed. But the immigrant leader envisioned a grand edifice that would serve as a beacon to young men and to the larger community. In just five years his dream would become reality when the first purpose-built YMCA opened in the United States. Its importance would extend nationwide as it became the model for Association structures in other American cities.

The 1866 fund-raising appeal described the New York YMCA's services and the economy of its operation. "The rooms we now occupy are totally inadequate for the work we have on hand," it stated. The appeal envisioned a central building with rental portions paying the working expenses of the main organization so that annual charitable gifts could support Branches elsewhere in the city:

The Twenty-Third Street Association building was designed by the prominent church architect James Renwick Jr.

McBurney's building plan, including a central reception area, was replicated in YMCAs nationwide.

"The prominence which such a structure would give to the Association and its work, the assurance of permanence, the character and influence which it would then possess in the eyes of strangers, would add immeasurably to the power of the Association for good, and silently bring young men within the sphere of its influence."

In their plea to philanthropists, the New York directors laid the foundation for a practice still used today. Revenue-generating components, in this instance rental space, would help support the operation so that donated dollars could be directed to programs and services for the needy (the Association had just installed, in poorer districts, a Western Branch on Varick Street and an Eastern YMCA on Grand Street). It also foreshadowed how solid, permanent facilities would give the Association an enduring and distinctive presence in the life of the community.

With $142,000 in hand in 1867, the Board purchased a lot on the busy southwest corner of Twenty-Third Street and Fourth Avenue (now Park Avenue South) and hired renowned church architect James Renwick Jr., who also built Grace Episcopal Church and St. Patrick's Cathedral. Opened in 1869, the imposing Association headquarters incorporated elements that would become standard in other YMCAs. Its novel features would be widely emulated, notably a central lobby with rooms radiating off it so that the secretary could keep watch on all activities. Doors opened on reading and games rooms, social parlors, a basement gymnasium, baths and bowling alleys, and stairways led to educational classrooms, a lecture room, and McBurney's private offices. A large, separate auditorium could be rented for public gatherings. And rent from ground-floor stores and upper-story offices would finance the mortgage debt.

From his desk, McBurney could watch the comings and goings of members.

Everything in this $350,000 structure of dark Belleville sandstone catered to a young man's needs. The Association's defining concept of the four-fold mission greatly influenced the French Renaissance-style building and subsequent YMCA architecture. As new facilities took shape, they too would include gymnasiums.

The opening of the five-story YMCA building was a major event, attended by Vice President of the United States Schuyler Colfax and Governor John T. Hoffman. Reporting on the occasion in 1870, *Harper's Weekly* observed that it was "indeed, fairly entitled to be designated the handsomest club-house in the city." Behind the building's impressive facade were posh trappings—ornate carved woodwork, grand fireplaces, Oriental rugs, and easy chairs. There were limits on what was allowed, however. A billiard table donated by Mrs. J. Pierpont Morgan was hastily relegated to the basement. The game was one of the very temptations that caused the YMCA to be created as an alternative.

The Grand Hall housed major events like the building's dedication ceremony, as well as lectures to promote mental growth in young men.

The basement gymnasium featured equipment for circuit training and body building.

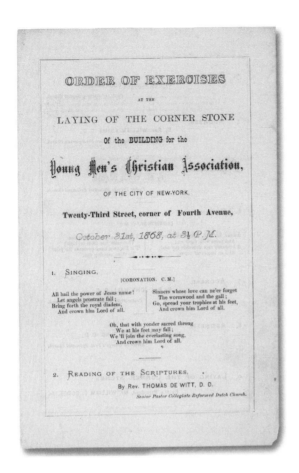

The Association's commodious new quarters allowed it to stretch its programs. In the first year, an evening high school—the first in any YMCA—began offering classes: French, German, bookkeeping, writing, English literature, and vocal music. It was thought that French classes, for example, could aid young men to gain a foothold in exporting, a major commercial activity. Spanish classes were added in 1870. The educational offerings may have appealed more to leaders than their constituents, however. In 1873, the Library Committee reported that "the young men of the Association do not avail themselves of the advantages presented as it was hoped they would—none of the classes, save those in the Gymnasium, are fully attended."

Nevertheless, the Associations did not halt their educational initiatives. They continued to build their libraries; both New York and Brooklyn YMCA shelves were well stocked. The Twenty-Third Street YMCA hosted the American Library Association's first annual meeting in 1877, and the Association agreed to participate in compiling the first Index of Periodical Literature, an epic undertaking. A decade later, when Columbia University opened its library school, representatives visited the

The cornerstone-laying ceremony for the new YMCA building opened with religious exercises.

The library, depicted here in the Twenty-Third Street building, was an important feature of early YMCAs.

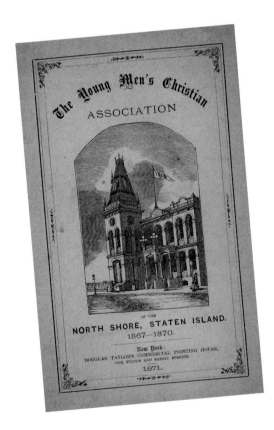

An Association on Staten Island occupied this building at 1590 Richmond Terrace in 1871.

Twenty-Third Street library, taking special note of its catalogue. The library also inspired the largest bequest to date, a gift of $100,000 in 1879 from William Niblo, owner of the popular Niblo's Gardens, an entertainment center in lower Manhattan.

McBurney had his heart set on living in the tower room of the new building. The directors, wary of his workaholic tendencies, were not in favor, believing that he should get away from his duties at day's end. But McBurney eventually prevailed, and lived in the tower until his last day, paying $100 in yearly rent.

The lifelong bachelor, thus ensconced, devoted his life and work to winning young men to Christ. "Boys from the country, in danger of becoming entangled in the snares of the great city, and young men who had lost their way and who might lose their lives for lack of a friend and a chance for manhood, appealed to him," observed L. L. Doggett in *The Life of Robert R. McBurney*. "He was filled with compassion for them, and went to his limit to save them."

During this era a YMCA also opened independently on Staten Island, then a settlement with barely 33,000 inhabitants. This new Association, organized in 1857, rented rooms on Bay Street in Stapleton, which were used for debates and other activities. In 1871, the North Shore YMCA occupied a structure it built in Staten Island's West Brighton section. The two-story brick structure, in grand Italianate style, was topped by a steep tower and featured a paneled library solidly stocked with books and a basement gymnasium. The building, thought to be the oldest Association structure extant, ceased being a YMCA by 1886 and passed to commercial use. Following a fire in the 1980s, only its outer walls remain intact.

McBurney's Influence Extends Far and Wide

MCBURNEY DEVOTED VIRTUALLY all his waking hours to building the Association, locally, nationally and even internationally. He rose in rank through the New York YMCA from his post as librarian to become recording and corresponding secretaries and served continuously on the Board from 1863 to 1882. In 1883 he became its first general secretary, or chief executive, and served until his death in 1898.

At the 1866 convention in Albany, McBurney convinced the national organization to locate its headquarters

Attorney Cephas Brainerd, a founder of the New York YMCA and head of its Army and Navy Committee 1862–65, was a member of the U.S. Christian Commission and chaired the International Committee for twenty-five years. He was known as the "great chief justice" of the YMCA.

one Association, with Branches in local communities. In 1887, when New York's metropolitan organization was established, the Twenty-Third Street building became the parent Branch. McBurney was a key figure in statewide organizing, as a leader of the first two New York state conventions over which he presided in 1869, 1870 and 1875. As the country's most trusted and influential member, he was chosen president at the initial meeting of the American General Secretaries' Conference, in 1871. The following year he attended the triennial meeting of the World's Conference of Associations in Amsterdam.

McBurney had attended the first International Convention of YMCAs in Philadelphia, in 1865, and missed only one, in 1887. He was chosen its president in 1874 but declined to serve because he felt that international work was encroaching on state and local activity. But once the New York Association's work was firmly established, McBurney turned again to international affairs. From 1889 to 1891, he would serve as the first chairman of the International Committee's work in foreign mission lands. Overall, YMCA international work owed much to McBurney, Brainerd and Richard Cary Morse, who spent many an evening in consultation with one another.

in the City of New York. The national executive committee was located there temporarily until 1883, when it was permanently installed in New York. Cephas Brainerd of the New York Board chaired the national YMCA from 1867 to 1892, assuring a long period of New York dominance and earning Brainerd the sobriquet of "great chief justice" of the YMCA.

William E. Dodge Jr. served as an advisor to the national Executive Committee, renamed the International Committee in 1879, for 36 years. In each of those years he was the largest contributor to the Committee's treasury and could be counted on to help in financial emergencies. As president of the New York Association, Dodge provided the national body with quarters in the new Twenty-Third Street building. Other New Yorkers who served on the Executive Committee included McBurney, Benjamin C. Wetmore, Verranus Morse and Morris Jesup. In 1876 it expanded to include distinguished leaders from all of North America. The Canadian Associations eventually formed their own organization and the Committee (incorporated as the International Committee in 1883) was reorganized as the National Council of YMCAs in 1922.

McBurney also developed the metropolitan concept of YMCAs, which prevails today in large American cities—

McBurney's closest collaborators, Cephas Brainerd, Richard Cary Morse and Robert Weidensall, were revered leaders in the national YMCA.

*Richard Cary Morse,
recruited by McBurney,
became general secretary of the
YMCA International Committee.*

Morse, a native New Yorker, came from a distinguished New England family. His father, Jedediah, founded the American Bible Society, and his uncle Samuel F. B. invented the telegraph in 1840. With an educational pedigree including Phillips Academy, Yale, Princeton and Union Theological faculties, the licensed minister started his career as a journalist with the *New York Observer*, a religious publication. He covered a New York Association Convention for the paper, and his report so impressed McBurney that he recruited Morse for volunteer work. Morse's eminent family and religious leanings—he became a Presbyterian convert in the pre-War revivals—made him an ideal lay leader.

The former Yale athlete, described as urbane and winsome, first chaired an Association committee on open-air meetings. These began in the summer and fall of 1868 and attracted non-churchgoers to meetings in Washington Square, near the Eastern Branch at East Broadway and Grand Streets and by the newly established Harlem Branch on Third Avenue. In 1870, the Committee on Open-Air Meetings reported holding other sessions at Chatham Square, the Washington Parade Ground, Tompkins Square, and Jackson Square, each drawing 100 to 500 people. Subsequently, meetings at Houston and First Street of up to 1,000 in attendance were met with harassment, but the net effect was positive. "Some who came at first to oppose, afterward came as attentive and interested listeners," the Committee reported in 1877. "The importance of these meetings cannot be easily overestimated. They reach a class...not reached in other ways."

McBurney subsequently recommended Morse as editor of the national YMCA publication *Association Monthly* and as general agent of the International Committee; in 1869 Morse became its General Secretary. McBurney called hiring him the "best thing I ever did."

Morse shared living quarters for five years on Twenty-Third Street with McBurney, and the two frequently traveled together to conferences at home and abroad. They were described as inseparable by Joel Nystrom, an Association officer in the early twentieth century who spoke of the "lasting intimacy" that developed between the two men. Together they developed many innovative programs and guided the development of the YMCA secretary concept.

Morse, who had "a talent for making young people feel important" according to Nystrom, was deeply committed to the Student YMCA and to Foreign Work, which the International Committee initiated in 1899 under his leadership. In later life, he was described as "a man who had never outgrown his youth." He put other people forward, said Nystrom, and was highly regarded and supported by important New York families such as the Dodges, Vanderbilts, Morgans, Rockefellers, and Colgates. Morse excelled both at creating solid projects, based on thorough study, and raising the funds to bring them to life. His autobiography, *My Life with Young Men*, is thought to be the most significant account of the American YMCA movement.

Religious Fervor
and Secular Outreach

IN THE AFTERMATH of war, Henry Ward Beecher delivered the main address for the Brooklyn YMCA's fourteenth anniversary, on May 21, 1867, from his pulpit in Plymouth Church. The staunch abolitionist and women's suffragist now had other things on his mind. He was concerned that class should not become a criterion for Association membership. "Take a man without regard to his position in society," he admonished his audience, urging that the YMCA embrace "men that have had culture and men that have not." Reverend Beecher articulated a vision that became a guiding principle in the YMCA: "All distinctions except (that) of common manhood, common faith, common hope should be lost sight of. In this way, you will leaven all parts of society."

At the time, membership in both Brooklyn and New York YMCAs tended to be predominantly white-collar,

Dwight L. Moody drew large crowds to revivals in London, where he came to the attention of William E. Dodge Jr.

with many men holding clerk positions in shops and offices. Lay leaders, of course, were a notch above, with business owners, men in finance, doctors, and attorneys heavily represented. Beecher's call would presage an imminent change in the Association's population, as the nation's expanding railroads and coming waves of immigration would swell the ranks of blue-collar workers who would seek out the YMCA.

In the City of Churches, YMCA activities centered on religion and current thought. The Brooklyn Association's reading room, large library and secular and religious lectures by outstanding speakers were major attractions. Courses in French and German were offered, as were monthly receptions and socials. Literary meetings featured readings of essayists such as William M. Thackeray, who spoke on the Four Georges of England, and Lyman Abbott, a lawyer turned minister and one of the YMCA's most active workers. Abbott eventually became editor of *The Outlook,* a national publication, and in 1888 succeeded Beecher as pastor of Plymouth Church, remaining in that pulpit until 1899.

Monthly devotional meetings and Sunday evening sermons by the Reverend Messrs. Beecher, Cuyler, Storrs, and Spear also garnered funds for the struggling Association in years of financial distress after the war. Aggressive evangelistic work, conducting mission Sunday Schools and relief work in times of financial depression would remain the mainstays of the Brooklyn YMCA's program until 1949.

In the New York Association of the early 1870s, religious programming dominated the day as well. On "the Lord's day," typically the YMCA's doors would open at 1 P.M., secular papers and periodicals having been removed. The afternoon could be spent in religious reading or conversation. A five o'clock Bible class was followed by tea and a prayer meeting ending at 7:20 P.M. By 7:30, the Association Hall was nearly filled for a half-hour of singing hymns, preceding the service from 8 to 8:45 P.M. A 15-minute meeting followed in the parlor, and the rooms were closed at 9:30 P.M. But within a few years, Sunday evening meetings were suspended in deference to local churches holding services on that night.

The religious activities proved to be popular. In 1875 the Committee on Lectures reported that the Bible class "has become one of the sights of our metropolis. Such is the anxiety of the members and friends to obtain admission, that the sidewalk before our building is often impassable before the opening of the doors." Attendance at these sessions ranged from 350 to 1,300.

Although urban progress continued apace, with the introduction of steam railroads and electrification of street railways, an economic downturn again gripped New York and Brooklyn in the panic of 1873, the century's worst financial crisis. The stock market's fall caused the New York Stock Exchange to close down for the first time ever, and the ensuing depression lasted until 1877.

The Associations again addressed the financial panic by sponsoring religious revivals throughout the decade, with many of them led by the former head of the Chicago YMCA, Dwight L. Moody. Considered the Billy Graham of his day, Moody was an evangelist who traveled with a singing companion, Ira D. Sankey. Remembered as the greatest religious figure in the American YMCA's first century, Moody traveled to the British Isles with Sankey in 1873 on a three-year evangelistic tour that was considered the greatest revival since that of Methodist leader John Wesley. More than 2.5 million people attended the Moody gatherings in London, including William E. Dodge Jr.

Moody, who attracted thousands to YMCA revival gatherings in New York and Brooklyn, was the greatest religious figure in the nineteenth-century Association.

Revival meetings drew crowds to P.T. Barnum's Hippodrome in Manhattan, and to the Brooklyn Rink. In summer, a special tent was erected near Prospect Park.

From London, Dodge wrote to his good friend, the devout YMCA Board member Morris Jesup, that "Moody is plain, homely and direct; has no views or isms, nor is he at all sensational, it is simply that men are great sinners, and Christ a great Savior waiting and ready to save them. That this is the one great question of life, and should be decided at once."

Moody and Sankey were invited by the YMCAs to hold inspirational meetings in Brooklyn and Manhattan. The Brooklyn Rink and the Gospel Tent at Union Street near Ninth Avenue, near the main entrance to Prospect Park, were the initial venues. The Brooklyn tour concluded in 1875, but Moody stayed connected to the Association in that city. At the time, the Brooklyn YMCA was financially crippled and its future was in doubt. Moody's appeal for funds for the Association proved to be its salvation; he secured sufficient subscriptions to rid it of debt. Two new Brooklyn Branches were subsequently organized, the New Lots and German YMCAs, in 1878. In 1884, Moody returned to help Brooklyn raise an endowment of $150,000, in part through the largest collection ever taken for the Association in a Brooklyn church, where he spoke of the value and necessity of the YMCA and expressed his indebtedness to the organization.

The New York Association also sponsored revivals. William E. Dodge Jr. invited Moody to preach at a YMCA meeting on June 21, 1875 to 200 men, mainly from the clergy. Subsequently, Moody and Sankey appeared at P. T. Barnum's Hippodrome at Twenty-Seventh Street and Madison Avenue from February to April 1876, and typically filled the hall with 6,000 people. They conducted seven services a day every day but Saturday. The revivals and prayer meetings had an enormously beneficial effect for the New York YMCA in that they more than doubled its membership.

Some Board members joined Moody in pressing for construction of a large hall for evangelistic services below Fourteenth Street, but others held out for repayment of the Twenty-Third Street building debt and construction of a new home for the Bowery Branch, which had been performing relief work for three years in one of New York's most derelict districts. The group with the secular interests won, and Moody graciously aided the Board in raising

Ira D. Sankey was Moody's singing companion.

subscriptions of $200,000, with $50,000 destined for the Bowery Branch and the balance to repay the mortgage.

Deemed the "Apostle of YMCAs," Moody had both a spiritual and ecumenical influence. As he traveled from city to city, he brought Protestant leaders together in their first major interdenominational effort. The YMCA's sharing in or sponsoring of these events was a key factor in the growing movement for church unity. Surely influenced by this movement, the Brooklyn Association removed "evangelical" as a requirement for Board membership in 1876.

The *New York Times,* in its 1899 obituary of Moody, noted the great value of his work in promoting the YMCA and of the Association's reach beyond religion. "The beneficence of (YMCAs) is by no means dependent on the religious influence they seek to impart, though it would be both unfair and foolish to ignore the immense force of the religious motive in the workers in this field. But that motive inspires them to a kind of labor that is widely and lastingly beneficent on the whole community. It helps powerfully to form citizens healthy in body and in mind, with sound standards of conduct, and with that habit of right judging and honest dealing which is at once the safeguard and the hope of any people with which it exists."

In one way, Moody held the New York and national Associations back by leading opposition to the four-fold plan of development that required gyms in YMCA buildings. Moody believed that, as in Chicago, those buildings should mainly be halls for evangelistic meetings. Given his powerful influence, the four-fold method was slow to be adopted nationwide, but it finally gained wide acceptance around 1880. Brooklyn, though a pioneer of the concept of physical development, would not open its own building with a gym until 1885.

Promoting Muscular Morality

THE BROOKLYN ASSOCIATION was one of the earliest advocates of physical development. Its rationale was articulated as early as 1856, when Association President Andrew A. Smith stated in that year's report: "It is undeniably true, that the young men of our cities, especially, in order to the possession of that physical development upon which health of body, strength of mind, and even moral stamina are so greatly dependent, require the stimulus and recuperative energy of recreation and manual exercise. The laborious and exhausting requirements of a business life, which most of our young men are pursuing, over-taxes their muscular and nervous systems, and thus it is that in connection with other violations of the laws of health, this strain and pressure on brain and nerves is deteriorating the physical and vital force of the present race of young men. Relaxation, diversion, and animated recreations are a pressing want."

But Smith also recognized obstacles to this course. Public opinion, which had a heavily religious basis at the time, was averse to physical work because it was carried out "under questionable control, or in partnership with evil appliances," in Smith's words. These "healthful and strength-giving amusements," he pointed out, were thought to lead young men to other temptations, so that taking part in them could endanger their reputation and standing in society.

Early YMCA leaders were prescient in believing that a physical program could attract more men to Christianity. Young men could work off steam in good Christian company rather than frequenting inappropriate outlets. So convinced were the leaders that George A. Bell, a Brooklyn delegate to the 1856 International Convention of YMCAs, introduced a resolution advocating gyms in all Associations: "Vital piety and earnest practical godliness are intimately connected with a healthy physical system. . . . The establishment of some such means. . . would doubtless induce many young men whose hearts have not been given to Christ to join the Associations and thus they would be brought under the influence of the members and led perhaps to the prayer meeting and finally to the foot of the cross."

In a nod to the prevailing thought of the times, Bell acknowledged that bowling alleys and billiards could not be part of a physical program. Public sentiment ran high against the former, and even the Brooklyn Association viewed the latter as "detrimental to health and morals."

While they did not persuade other YMCAs early on to address the physical needs of young men, New Yorkers acted on it at home. In 1857, both the Brooklyn and New York Associations offered their first gymnastics classes. A year earlier Brooklyn had formed a committee to consider adding a gymnasium, with influential members such as the 24-year-old Lyman Abbott championing subscriptions to build a well-equipped gym.

But the Civil War had intervened, and physical work necessarily slowed. The issue would not die, however, and was taken up vigorously after the war. Reverend Beecher, in his 1866 address to the Brooklyn Association, urged his fellows to reconsider "amusements for the young," which could keep them from less desirable pursuits and out of harm's way.

Under the leadership of Dodge and McBurney, the YMCA's direction and guidance for young men assumed an ever-more physical dimension in New York. The Industrial Revolution had wrought numerous changes in men's lives. Previously physical exercise had come naturally, without forethought, through men's daily labors, which often included farming and heavy lifting. Now, many jobs in the urban setting were sedentary.

As Association president, Dodge enthusiastically espoused the four-fold concept, which incorporated "physical work," as it was known. McBurney's enthusiasm had evolved more slowly. In the early 1860s he had shied away from physical work and games, stating that "Christ did not use the amusement plan." But he gradually came to see the physical program as a positive force in fostering a true Christian manhood, an important factor in "winning and holding young men in right paths."

Despite his early skepticism, McBurney had endorsed the inclusion of a gymnasium and even a bowling alley in the 1869 building on Twenty-Third Street. The gym, featuring simple equipment such as parallel bars, springboards, vaulting horses, punching bags, and tumbling mats, attracted a large following. The evangelist Dwight Moody also put aside his initial doubts about the four-fold work; his eventual endorsement gave the inclusion of physical work great stature.

The Twenty-Third Street building's gymnasium and bowling alley met with immediate popularity. The New York annual report in 1870 noted that "these have proved far greater attractions to young men than it was supposed

The Twenty-Third Street YMCA gymnasium quickly drew new members.

The gym relied on simple but sometimes dangerous equipment, such as parallel bars, springboards, vaulting horses, and tumbling mats.

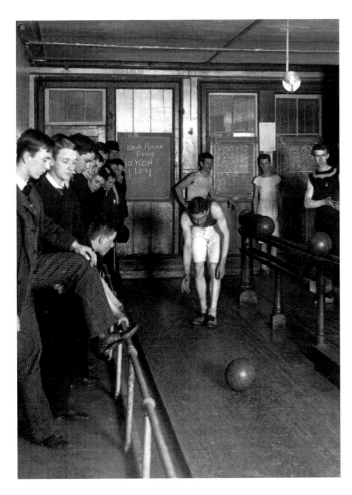

various apparatus, from parallel bars to punching bags, under the watchful eye of an instructor. Thus the New York staff developed the first systematic and organized plan for physical education.

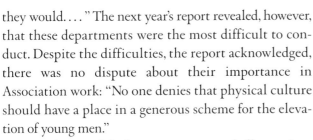

The new building had its own bowling alley, which by now was considered a suitable activity.

Men marched in formation around the Twenty-Third Street gym in a procedure called the Day's Order.

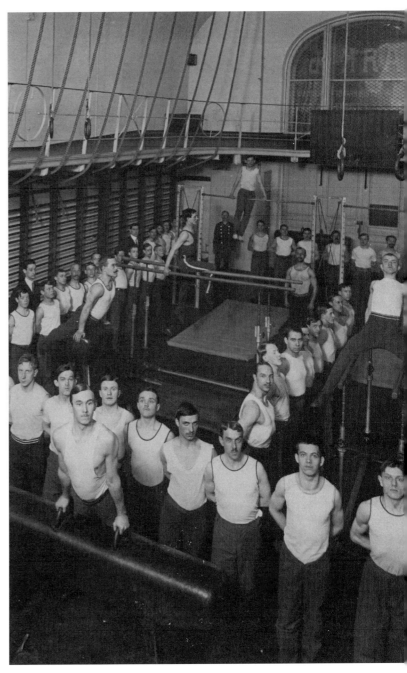

they would. . . . " The next year's report revealed, however, that these departments were the most difficult to conduct. Despite the difficulties, the report acknowledged, there was no dispute about their importance in Association work: "No one denies that physical culture should have a place in a generous scheme for the elevation of young men."

Finding qualified instructors was a challenge, since those who knew the equipment were circus performers and their questionable character would not buttress the YMCA's overall mission nor embellish its standing in the community. George M. Van Derlip headed a committee of twenty-four volunteers in 1870 whose charge was to supervise the gym. McBurney hired William E. Wood as the first YMCA physical director, and Wood organized a program around repetitions of a series of exercises—the precursor of "circuit training"—which continued for twenty years.

In a procedure called the Day's Order, men first marched around the gym to warm up, stopping at several calisthenics stations to exercise different parts of the body (this would become known as "body building"). Then they would break into smaller groups and work on the

The Colgate Connection

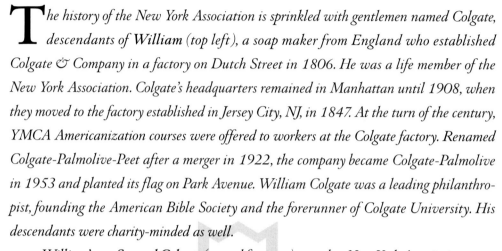

The history of the New York Association is sprinkled with gentlemen named Colgate, descendants of **William** (top left), a soap maker from England who established Colgate & Company in a factory on Dutch Street in 1806. He was a life member of the New York Association. Colgate's headquarters remained in Manhattan until 1908, when they moved to the factory established in Jersey City, NJ, in 1847. At the turn of the century, YMCA Americanization courses were offered to workers at the Colgate factory. Renamed Colgate-Palmolive-Peet after a merger in 1922, the company became Colgate-Palmolive in 1953 and planted its flag on Park Avenue. William Colgate was a leading philanthropist, founding the American Bible Society and the forerunner of Colgate University. His descendants were charity-minded as well.

William's son **Samuel Colgate** (second from top) served as New York Association secretary in the late 1870s and was president of the Society for the Suppression of Vice, which included fellow YMCA Board members. He joined his father's business and shared his Baptist religious benevolence, serving on the board of the American Tract Society. His brother **James** (left) was a Y member too. Samuel's son **Richard Morse** Colgate (second from bottom, to right of his uncle Richard C. Morse) was active on the International Committee for three decades.

Abner W. Colgate chaired the New York YMCA's Committee on Colored Association in 1867. The committee was charged with raising funds for the newly formed, independent YMCA for African Americans on Wooster Street.

Other Colgates who were life members in 1865 included **Edward, Robert, Charles C.** and **Bowles**, William's brother and partner in Colgate & Co. Bowles Colgate served as Association Board secretary in 1890. Among Samuel's six sons (bottom left) were **Gilbert** (second from left), a treasurer of the International Committee.

Later **S. Bayard Colgate** (below, far right), then chairman of the Colgate-Palmolive Company, was on the Seamen's YMCA advisory board when it turned to serving neighborhood youth groups in the 1950s. **Henry** (center) served on the International Committee.

2

1880-1898

Evolving Toward the Secular

BY 1880, THE formative period in the New York YMCA had drawn to a close. Policies and programs were now in place that would give the Association a solid foundation for years to come, and no insurmountable barriers remained to growth and expansion. While the YMCA's overriding interest was still the spiritual welfare of young men, "spiritual" had taken on a wider meaning. Despite the popularity of the previous decade's religious revivals, and the fervent Christianity of YMCA founders and leaders, the Association was quietly evolving as a

more secular institution. An internal survey later noted that beginning in the 1860s, "systematic religion. . . played less and less of a part in Association affairs."

The YMCA-sponsored revivals, with their nonsectarian religious character, had positioned the Association as a pioneer of interdenominationalism and the application of Christian teachings to "the practical problems of everyday life," the survey found. "What the leaders of the YMCA were. . . demonstrating to the world was the fact that the regulation of the social life of the individual is every bit as much a concern of the Kingdom of God as church attendance. . . and the discipline of repression was yielding to that of direction and guidance."

At the same time the YMCA's physical program was growing in importance and became a membership

boon for the primarily volunteer-led organization, which was highly dependent on dues. In 1875, the average daily gym attendance on Twenty-Third Street was estimated at 300, with 125 receiving instruction in several classes. By 1885, the annual report revealed rapid growth, noting that the full complement of 882 "dressing boxes" was in constant use, depriving some men admission "for lack of the needful supply of such boxes." Two years later the Association beefed up its gym facilities with 263 new lock boxes and shower baths, "the latter especially have given great satisfaction," the yearly report observed.

In 1883, the New York Association took the unusual step of sending a questionnaire to all participants to gauge the utility of the YMCA. It received more than 200 completed forms from the gymnasium users, including these intriguing observations:

> It has put me in first-rate trim, made me stronger both mentally and physically, and developed my muscles immensely. When I leave the Gymnasium in the evening I have an immense appetite, as the lunch-man in the neighborhood can testify.

> Instead of the flabby flesh which covered my bones before I placed myself under Mr. [William] Wood's instruction, there is now a certain degree of firmness in my muscles and a circulation of blood which fills one with a desire to tread on air; this may seem an exaggeration, but it is the fact.

> Being closely confined all day at my desk, [I] seldom exercise without having renewed my life and vigor. It has done much toward enabling me to cope with a busy business life.

Men enjoyed working out in the new gym at the Twenty-Third Street YMCA.

The survey also posed a broad question on the benefits the Association offered to individuals. Responses like this were typical: "the advantages offered in every department—physical, mental, social and spiritual—are warmly appreciated." Indeed, the survey vindicated the early proponents of the gym, as the annual report noted: "The number of replies which. . . refer to daily confinement at sedentary pursuits, shows that the Gymnasium is largely patronized by the class of young men that most need its benefits."

The gym was also beginning to attract non-traditional members to the YMCA. In 1884, the New York Association annual report noted that membership now included 125 Roman Catholics and 18 "Hebrews." The Association, it would seem, had come a long way from its early, narrow evangelical focus to a more sympathetic interdenominational outlook. And with that subtle shift it was set firmly on a course of welcoming all people, which defines its mission to this day.

A New Yorker Fathers Physical Education

TEAM SPORTS HAD just begun to appear in the United States when the YMCA was formed. The first baseball game was played in 1846 in Hoboken, New Jersey, and by the 1860s was considered the "national pastime." The first national boxing championship took place in 1849. For most men these were spectator sports, and the war's intervention slowed their progress. But in time the New York Association got involved. By 1887 it had formed a baseball club as an offshoot of its established outing club. Using the public grounds at 155th Street and Eighth Avenue, New York played its first game with the Hoboken Association and lost, but won all its other games that year. A football team was organized in the same year, followed by tennis and cricket clubs in 1888.

Significantly, the several New York YMCA Branches began interacting more through sporting competitions as well as their chess and checker clubs. Individual and team meets were popular. The New York Association sponsored a "gymnastics entertainment" on New Year's Eve in 1885, and in April a competition that included tests like the horizontal bar, Indian club swinging and running high jump. By 1887, an annual athletic contest might include swimming-only competitions or indoor and outdoor games. The first Inter-Branch Athletic Contest in June 1890 encouraged

Gymnastics competitions were a magnet for YMCA men citywide, such as this 1889 team from the Twenty-Third Street Branch.

"all-around bodily development, rather than the training of any one part of the body to accomplish some particular feat." Its events included a 100-yard dash, running broad jump and high jump, 220-yard hurdle, shot put and a one-mile run.

The Young Men's Institute, a YMCA Branch that opened on the Bowery in 1885, was the scene of much Association sports activity. In 1889, its lecture hall was filled to capacity for the Annual Gymnastic Contest, shutting out many would-be spectators. The evening's events included contests on the horse, horizontal and parallel bars, tug of war, fancy club swinging, running high jump and vaulting. Individual winners went home with gold medals, and winning Branches with banners.

The following year five Branches sent a total of twenty-two men to compete in the 1890 event, primarily in track competitions. In 1891 a two-mile bike race was added. "The games in June were the largest all-around games ever held under Association auspices, and as far as we can learn the largest of the kind in the country," the annual report noted. In 1892, the New York Association's athletic department claimed a YMCA State Championship. Moreover, its members had begun to compete in outside games, winning more prizes than any other club. This extramural activity promoted loyalty to the YMCA and prevented its men from joining purely athletic clubs.

With the popularity of athletic meets growing rapidly, the national YMCA had taken steps to standardize its competitions. In 1887, the International Committee appointed Dr. Luther Halsey Gulick, a New York physician and later a director of physical training in New York City schools, to the post of physical director. Gulick and James H. McCurdy, then physical director of the Twenty-Third Street Branch, proposed that these inter-YMCA programs should promote "a strong, sturdy Christian manhood."

Luther Halsey Gulick, M.D., the first national director for YMCA physical programs and the leading proponent of physical education, insisted on development of the "whole" man.

Eschewing expensive uniforms, travel costs and coaches' fees, Gulick devised a pentathlon that consisted of a 100-yard dash, 12-pound hammer throw, a running high jump, pole vault and a one-mile run. He developed a standardized scoring system, using objective performance criteria. Urged on by Association secretaries, Gulick also formed an all-YMCA athletic league to encourage general excellence and more interest in amateur sports. McCurdy led the International Committee in forming such a league in 1895 with oversight by a six-member committee, four of them New Yorkers.

At this early stage, the YMCA already saw sports as an important component of character-building in young men. "The athletic field photographs a man's true character as accurately as a detective camera, and affords to Christian men, who take a leading part in these sports, unequalled opportunity and responsibility," the 1888 New York annual report stated. "The officers of our

Rowing was one of the YMCA's earliest physical programs, and these young members formed one of New York City's leading teams in the early 1880s.

Outing Club aim. . . constantly to 'live up to and urge right views' in competitive sports especially; a high-minded generosity toward opponents; a 'gentlemen's game' at baseball, an 'honorable game' of football rather than 'anything to win.'" That lofty statement of principle, articulated so early on, still holds true today in YMCA sports. From youth leagues to adult sports, everyone plays and winning is never the overriding goal.

Dr. J. Gardner Smith, physical director at the Young Men's Institute on the Bowery, addressed the issue of training quite creatively. In the winter of 1886 Smith assembled a Leaders Corps, Christian laymen whom he instructed in the various gym apparatus, calisthenics, and dumbbell drills. The laymen also studied anatomy, physiology, and first aid under the tutelage of volunteer physicians. Lectures on Bible study and morals as well as prayer meetings were part of the training, which lasted at least two years. Forbidden to drink alcohol, smoke, or to visit questionable establishments, these volunteers eventually became section leaders who provided instruction and supervision in the gym.

In a move that would forever change American sports, Gulick took up residence in 1887 at the Springfield (Massachusetts) Training School, a college founded to train YMCA secretaries. Based in its gymnasium department, he provided leadership for YMCA physical work at a national level, taking it to new heights and fostering the creation of two of today's most popular sports.

At Springfield College, Gulick developed a comprehensive curriculum for training professional physical directors. The NYU Medical School graduate based his philosophy of exercise on the Christian concept of a unified spirit, mind and body, an idea that not only formed the basis of physical education in the YMCA but one that continues to provide the underpinning for all YMCA programs. Gulick's program of "physical culture" incorporated modern medical knowledge, a highly innovative approach in this era. He instituted physical examinations in which men were measured and charted, and their diets and habits corrected if it seemed necessary.

In 1891, Gulick urged one of his Springfield instructors to create a game that could be played indoors and would be easily learned and interesting to play. James Naismith responded by developing a set of rules for two teams to move a ball toward a goal, aiming for a half-bushel wooden peach basket installed overhead. The game, called "basket-ball," caught on quickly, although some opponents within the YMCA felt it would disrupt individual and team competitions by introducing pure play. But eventually the game succeeded, and when the Amateur Athletic Union held its first basketball tournament in 1897, New York's Twenty-Third Street Branch emerged the winner. Spurred on

James Naismith, an instructor at Springfield College, invented the game of "basket-ball" in 1891.

by basketball's success, a YMCA director in Massachusetts invented another recreational game, volleyball, in 1895.

With the rise of the YMCA physical program, interest grew in the culture of body-building and manliness. Concurrently, the YMCA ventured into another new field. Gulick developed a companion program in sex education, drawing upon concepts from medicine and psychiatry, which had lately achieved prominence. The YMCA's approach to sex education was consistent with the organization's emphasis on morality and the "whole man." The program emphasized sexual self-restraint and vigilance against "immorality" by espousing chastity, marital fidelity and family life. With men newly exposed to one another and encouraged to admire each other's prowess in body-building, the curriculum also warned against homosexual activity.

The New York Association introduced sex education in its program in 1885 by forming a league of the White Cross Army, a national movement for "the promotion of personal purity among young men." The White Cross Crusade admonished men to treat all women with respect; to discourage the use of indecent language and "coarse jests"; to maintain the law of purity as equally binding upon men and women; and to "keep thyself pure." The New York Association promulgated this teaching and also aided the White Cross in distributing its literature.

Gulick also conceived of the YMCA's universally recognized inverted red triangle, which was adopted in 1897 as the official Association symbol and is still used in the YMCA logo in New York, nationwide and worldwide. The equilateral triangle's three points symbolize unity of spirit, mind and body. Thus Gulick reconciled the YMCA's Christian purpose with the new value of physical culture. Through his leadership in advancing that program, Gulick is revered in the YMCA—and by many others—as the father of physical education.

The Brooklyn Association, too, made an early contribution to this work when the physical director of its Central Branch, Dr. George J. Fisher, was appointed national physical director by the International Committee, to spread the precepts of physical work throughout the national YMCA. Long before private health clubs would proliferate in the latter part of the twentieth century, the New York and Brooklyn YMCAs were respected leaders in physical fitness, health and wellness, promoting the holistic approach in physical education that is so widespread today.

By the twentieth century, the YMCA's physical program had surpassed religion as its primary means of outreach and attraction for members. Ironically, YMCA physical work, intended at first to lure young men to its religious programs, now largely attracted those who were indifferent to the Association's religious focus.

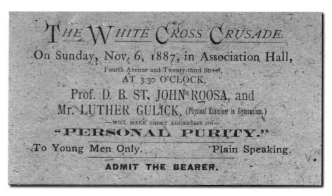

The YMCA sponsored an early sex education program in a joint effort with the White Cross Army Crusade, which urged sexual abstinence.

Buildings with a Purpose

THE FOUR-FOLD program would greatly influence the architecture of new YMCA buildings. As interest in physical work grew, the New York and Brooklyn Associations were challenged to design quarters that could adequately house those programs. Except for the Twenty-Third Street YMCA built in 1869, the New York Branches had been renting facilities, and they were increasingly unsatisfactory. When new Branch structures took shape, they would need to include gyms. By the end of the century, swimming pools were also a must-have, as were large courts for newly popular team sports like basketball. In 1885, following great fund-raising efforts, the Brooklyn and New York Associations would each open a fine new building, whose overhead costs would require the sale of memberships to ever wider audiences.

The legacy of jeweler Frederick Marquand allowed the Brooklyn YMCA to build its Central Branch in 1885.

A permanent edifice for the growing city of Brooklyn had been envisioned for some years in the Brooklyn Association. In 1867, the Rev. Stephen Tyng had challenged Brooklyn businessmen to match the New York Association, which raised $250,000 for its Twenty-Third Street home. But the Brooklyn community raised only an inadequate $70,000 toward the building goal.

Frederic Marquand, a prominent businessman from modest origins who rose to head New York's leading jewelry house, Marquand and Company, had pledged $100,000 to the Brooklyn Association but died in 1882 before he acted on his promise. In a stroke of good fortune, his legatees offered to buy land for a YMCA building at Fulton and Bond Streets and to donate $150,000 toward its construction if the Association would raise a $150,000 endowment fund. The Brooklyn YMCA achieved this goal by 1885, despite an economic depression, with F. Fulton Cutting making the largest individual gift of $15,000.

Brooklyn's Central YMCA, comprising three buildings that totaled nearly 20,000 square feet, opened two years after the Brooklyn Bridge made its debut. Its main entrance was at 502 Fulton Street. The Bond Street building housed an auditorium and the Hanover Street structure a gymnasium, with a swimming pool in the basement. At the time Central was considered to be the best YMCA building in the country. William E. Dodge Jr., president of the New York Association, spoke at the Brooklyn building dedication. "I fear it would make our members envious to go over to this magnificent building," he admitted.

The Brooklyn Central YMCA on Fulton Street, opened in 1885, boasted the first swimming pool in an Association building in the nation.

Central's novel swimming "bath" (below) provided pleasure as well as problems in keeping water comfortable and sanitary.

Within the imposing structure was a YMCA "first"—the only indoor pool, or "bath," to be found in any Association. The swimming bath, predating the Brooklyn public water system, was a 50-foot well circulating 100 gallons of water per minute. In addition to swimming, members could indulge in tub, sponge, foot, douche, shower, breast and hand baths with hot and cold water. The pool "liberally provided for the comfort and pleasure of our members," the Association proudly noted.

The new YMCA was an immediate success. Membership grew so rapidly that an expansion was called for within two years. The 1887 male membership of 2,517 was the largest in any Association, and member fees now provided 50 percent of the Brooklyn YMCA's income. Moreover, Henry Ward Beecher's vision of a mingling of classes had apparently been achieved: 57 percent of members were clerks, 19 percent mechanics, 10 percent students, 7 percent merchants, 4 percent professionals, and 3 percent laborers.

In the end, the building's total cost was $300,000. Popular evangelist Dwight Moody, speaking at the building's dedication, appealed to all gathered there for more funds. In the YMCA's pitch to prospective givers, a fact sheet drew attention to the Association's competition: the nearly 2,600 licensed saloons, 14 theaters, 490 licensed pool tables, 40 bowling alleys, and 10 shooting galleries in Brooklyn. The vast majority of their patrons were young men, of whom less than 10 percent could be found in churches or Sunday schools. Young men were clearly trouble-prone: the average age of state prisoners at this time, the fact sheet pointed out, was between 24 and 26.

However, some Brooklynites, viewing this grand new embodiment of the YMCA, misperceived the Association's financial situation. If it could erect such a structure, they thought, the YMCA must be a wealthy corporation with officers who made lofty salaries and backers who reaped handsome profits. In reality, the large building was consuming ever greater sums for maintenance, and a growing membership required hiring more staff. The non-profit Brooklyn Association clearly needed outside support to keep pace with those demands.

Even as its new building opened, the Association was hatching plans for development of Branch buildings that would be as solid as Central. With Brooklyn's population now topping one million, the eight existing Branches were outgrowing their memberships. Association General Secretaries Thomas J. Wilkie (1880–1886) and Edwin F. See (1886–1906) had devised a far-reaching plan for 20 Brooklyn Branches which would deliver the desired programs and services to the mushrooming city's many young men. But the financial crisis of 1893 put a crimp in their ambitious projects, pushing the Association's debt and financial straits to the top of its concerns.

Edwin See, general secretary of the Brooklyn YMCA from 1886–1906, presided over the Association's ambitious expansion of the early twentieth century following the success of the Central building, which some called "Lake Central."

A Modern Y for the Working Man

THE NEW YORK Association also dedicated a new five-story building in 1885, the Young Men's Institute, at 222 Bowery. It was not the first YMCA on that avenue, however; the Bowery Branch been a presence there since 1872. Association leaders had been upset by the neighborhood's unsavory conditions and the throngs of young men living and working in the area. Many were homeless, and the Bowery was rife with temptations to which they were easy prey. The New York Association had offered programs for the fallen and destitute since 1866, when it opened a free reading room at 76 Varick Street where McBurney taught a Bible class. (It had also added programs at Bellevue Hospital and Charity Hospital on Blackwell's Island after the Civil War.) But Morris Jesup, then president of the New York Association and an ally of moral crusader Anthony Comstock, insisted on permanent quarters to house this relief work.

The Young Men's Institute, at 222 Bowery, opened in 1885 to reach young working-class men, as opposed to the less fortunate already served by the Bowery YMCA. Its programs were primarily educational.

Jesup and McBurney joined with the New York Mission Society in 1872 to rent rooms at 134 Bowery in a once-notorious gambling house, the Crystal Saloon. William E. Dodge Jr., who was also president of the Evangelical Alliance and National Temperance Society, readily financed the necessary alterations. The Bowery YMCA offered Bible classes, temperance meetings, baths, clothing, and job leads. It also served meals, for which it issued tickets at $4 per hundred so that men would not squander their food money on drink in saloons. Following the Panic of 1873, the Association fed and lodged the destitute there for a short time , as it closed its Eastern Branch on Grand Street. After 10 years, the operation moved to 243 Bowery, with lodgings for 60 men, then to a purchased site at 153 Bowery in 1888.

HELPING THE POOR—THE BOWERY BRANCH OF THE YOUNG MEN'S CHRISTIAN ASSOCIATION.—From Sketches by C. A. Keetels.—[See Page 110.]

The Bowery Branch, established in 1872 as a rescue operation for destitute young men, afforded them dormitories, dining facilities, an employment bureau, and all-important baths to make themselves presentable for work. The library, reading rooms, and chapel provided for their mental and spiritual uplift.

The Association took pains to separate its Young Men's Institute from the Bowery Branch. Only Institute members could enter its premises, except for the Sunday evening service. "This was an imperative necessity," the Association noted. "Otherwise the building would have been crowded with the class of young men who frequent the Bowery lodging-houses—the very class our other Branch in the Bowery cares for. [There] we have found it impossible to reach the young apprentices, mechanics and clerks of the neighborhood; the two classes would not mix. Our work in our old Branch is largely one of rescue, while that of the Institute is almost wholly a work of prevention."

Constructed purposely in an infamous district populated mostly by derelicts, the Institute was designed as a beacon to better comportment, a more upright alternative to the neighboring bars and dance halls. It was meant to reach a "larger class of hard-working independent young men" from ages 17 to 35 who were "not yet hardened" like the destitute young fellows on relief at the nearby Bowery Branch. The new Institute, built in Queen Anne style by architect Bradford L. Gilbert, responded to "a need in that part of the city for an attractive building, in which to help this latter class to a full and wholesome development." Gilbert, best known for his railroad buildings, had made renovations to Grand Central Station. Some observed that the Institute also resembled a train station.

This new YMCA's programs were predominantly educational, built around a library, classes, lectures, discussions and a music program. Practical industrial courses, such as typewriting, engineering, electricity, penmanship, bookkeeping and architectural drawing, were added for the many mechanics joining the Institute. In 1886 a trade class was offered for carriage builders, a course unique in the nation at that time. Classes in English grammar for immigrants were added in 1887, and redesigned as English for Italians after the turn of the century. A steam engineering class was introduced in 1888 and civil service exams were given, in particular for firemen and police officers.

The Institute was not all seriousness. An annual report noted that, "There is a bright, manly social life in the Institute. It is alive with good feeling. There is no stiffness. The receptions are informal. There are checkers and

The original Branch on the Bowery moved to another building at 153 Bowery, in 1888.

chess clubs, and plenty of singing around the open fire-place—jolly war and college songs. The entertainments given by the subscribers are full of go and snap. With all this, lots of hard work. A jolly place, but with every incentive to self-improvement and work for others."

For $4 in yearly dues, the Institute gave young men the use of a 1,000-volume library, a reading room, bowling alleys and a gym. "The gymnasium is very popular," an annual report noted. "The drill classes are full, and Dr. J. Gardner Smith, in charge, has a manly Christian influence on the gymnasium members."

Weekly cultural events, gym and calisthenics classes, and "entertainments" by the Institute's own orchestra and glee club enlivened the place. Sunday spiritual meetings were non-sectarian, as specified in the Institute's act of incorporation, although they were frequently attended by the evangelist Ira D. Sankey. By the end of the century many Institute members were Roman Catholics, especially those of Italian origin. Devotional meetings encouraged abstinence from drink and narcotics, and lectures by prominent men such as Theodore Roosevelt and Henry Ward Beecher were frequent.

Thrift was a particular value espoused by the YMCA at this time. In 1888, the Institute organized a savings fund. Members could deposit small sums there and when their savings reached a certain amount, the funds were deposited in their name at the Dry Dock Savings Bank. One hundred men initially opened accounts. By 1890, two New York Branches sponsored savings funds, with 192 young men keeping a total of $2,818 on deposit.

William E. Dodge Jr., with his son Cleveland H. Dodge, helped finance the Young Men's Institute. Along with Percy Pyne Sr., then president of the City National Bank, the Dodges and Cornelius Vanderbilt II provided 42 percent of the building funds. Cleveland, along with his Princeton classmates Moses and Percy Pyne Jr., served on the management committee of the Young Men's Institute and he became its first chairman in 1881.

Cleveland H. Dodge, son of William E. Dodge Jr., helped to finance the Young Men's Institute, and became its first chairman in 1881. He became president of the New York Association in 1890 and served until 1903.

Police Commissioner ROOSEVELT *Recalls a Night at the YMCA*

"**I**n the spring of 1895 I was appointed by Mayor Strong Police Commissioner, and I served as President of the Police Commission of New York for the two following years. Occasionally I would myself pick out a man and tell him to take the examination. Thus one evening I went down to speak in the Bowery at the Young Men's Institute, a branch of the Young Men's Christian Association, at the request of Mr. Cleveland H. Dodge. While there he told me he wished to show me a young Jew who had recently, by an exhibition of marked pluck and bodily prowess, saved some women and children from a burning building. The young Jew, whose name was Otto Raphael, was brought up to see me; a powerful fellow, with good-humored, intelligent face. I asked him about his education, and told him to try the examination. He did, passed, was appointed, and made an admirable officer; and he and all his family, wherever they may dwell, have been close friends of mine ever since. Otto Raphael was a genuine East Sider. He and I were both "straight New York," to use the vernacular of our native city. . . Otto's parents had come over from Russia, and not only in social standing but in pay a policeman's position meant everything to him. It enabled Otto to educate his little brothers and sisters who had been born in this country, and to bring over from Russia two or three kinsfolk who had perforce been left behind."

—Theodore Roosevelt, *An Autobiography*, 1913

Course enrollment doubled in the New York Association between 1886 and 1887. Young men age 14 and older could enroll in commercial courses.

THE NEW YORK Association was reorganized as a metropolitan YMCA in 1887, with a headquarters office overseeing separate Branches. It kept its headquarters in the Twenty-Third Street building, which became the parent Branch. Future Association growth would come through adding new Branches, and in New York they nearly doubled from 1884 to 1898. Not only gym programs but educational offerings were now drawing young men to the YMCA for self-improvement and career growth through the acquisition of new skills, and who preferred Branches near their home or place of work. Between 1886 and 1887 course enrollment doubled, to 1,127, and the Association library, which by 1896 would be centralized on West Fifty-Seventh Street, boasted more than 7,000 volumes. The metropolitan form of organization would come to prevail in city Associations across the nation.

In New York, Association operations were primarily sustained by member dues. Members joining any New York Branch except the Institute enjoyed reciprocal privileges at the main Association building. Branches were generally expected to be self-sustaining, except for the Branch Secretary's salary which the Association paid. However, the New York YMCA provided the sole financial support for work at three Branches: Twenty-Third Street, Bowery and the Young Men's Institute.

The Association had only one endowment at this time, the Niblo fund, which was exclusively for the library, and net income from the Association building of $6,000 a year. Leaders were seeking more endowment funds for special departments such as coursework, lectures, gymnasium and relief work, since they were strongly against taking on debt, considering it "criminal" to jeopardize properties by borrowing to meet current expenses.

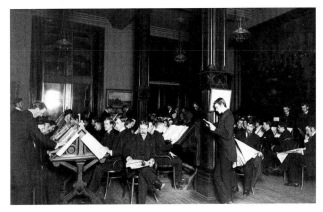

The 7,000-volume Association library offered many possibilities for men looking to broaden their knowledge in Branch reading rooms.

Branch requirements, however, only continued to grow, although they did their best to keep programs up-to-date in often limited settings. By 1884, three major Branches were all in need of new buildings: the Bowery, Harlem, and the German YMCA, formed in 1881. By the time the Statue of Liberty was dedicated in 1886, nine New York Branches had more than 7,700 members and were trying to raise money for new structures or improvements to those they occupied. The Yorkville Branch, started in 1884, had installed a bowling alley for physical improvement but discovered it had social benefits: "It

The Yorkville Branch on East Eighty-Sixth Street installed a bowling alley and later, a gym.

Bowling alleys were de rigueur in YMCA Branches, for socializing as well as physical improvement.

also leads us to a more intimate acquaintanceship with each other." In 1890, both Yorkville and the German Branch managed to open gyms.

Beset with inadequate facilities, the Yorkville Branch acquired a lot on East Eighty-Sixth Street in 1886. The rental structures there would generate income for a new building, which opened a decade later. The 20-year-old Harlem Branch inaugurated a new home on West 125th Street in 1888. The Branch moved again in 1897, to a building designed by Bradford Gilbert, the Institute's architect, on Third Avenue at 122nd Street.

William H. Vanderbilt helped purchase the site at Fifty-Seventh Street and Eighth Avenue for the initial West Side YMCA building.

source of income to the YMCA over the years as well as a needed community service.

Two educational programs, the Association Business Schools and a Day Business Institute for Young Men, begun in 1895, were housed at Twenty-Third Street. Young men at least 14 years of age could enroll at the YMCA for $10 in monthly tuition. The Twenty-Third Street Branch offered instruction in languages (French, Spanish, German, and English), business, phonography, drawing and art, elocution and Bible Literature. Evening classes at the new West Side Branch included commercial courses, drawing and art, physiology, English and music.

The Yorkville and Harlem Branches added educational programs on a smaller scale in 1888. Harlem also offered commercial and drawing classes. The Washington Heights Branch, opened in 1891, offered courses in German and English for beginners, emphasizing grammar and conversation. The French Branch, established in 1889, gave instruction in English and singing. The YMCA International Committee administered exams for students at YMCAs, and awarded certificates that were honored in many leading educational institutions in the nation.

As the first YMCA to be constructed as a Branch of the New York Association, the Young Men's Institute was an innovator in programs and services. Its Leaders Corps, devised to train young Christian leaders who would help in the gym, provided a concept that lives on today in Leaders Clubs for teens at YMCA Branches, who focus on community service. In the year the Institute opened, the Association surveyed its Twenty-Third Street members about classes and self-improvement programs, resulting in new courses and program features. Building on this knowledge the Institute, as the first manifestation of the modern YMCA in New York City, would offer a model for urban Branches there and elsewhere.

In particular the West Side YMCA, which opened in 1896 on Fifty-Seventh Street at Eighth Avenue, drew on the Institute's example. The edifice, built on a site purchased by William H. and Cornelius Vanderbilt for $165,000, was known as "McBurney's folly" since it was considered to be too far uptown to attract members, and because construction commenced before funds were fully in hand. In its own way it was a trendsetter, since it included a dormitory wing for the first time in a general YMCA. After referring countless young men to boarding-houses in the city, McBurney made sure that this new Branch building had two floors of rooms for overnight guests, as many other Branches subsequently would. His farsighted move would provide an important, continuing

Seeking Shelter at the
YMCA

"**M**yself and probably another young man will arrive in New York on Monday morning. . . . Could you secure two single rooms in a boarding-house, nice Christian family. . . I am a member and have been for some years of the local Y.M.C.A., was converted in a Y.M.C.A. building, and am therefore a Y.M.C.A. man. . . I am going to work for Dow, Jones & Co., 42-44 Broad St. and would like a place convenient. Of course, I would not mind a little distance for a nice place. About $5 a week."

—Letter from Fred H. Wood,
Norristown, Pennsylvania in 1899
to Henry Dickson, secretary,
Twenty-Third Street YMCA.

Young men could also enroll in public-speaking courses at the Twenty-Third Street building.

The Association elevated the importance of instruction in 1895 by appointing a permanent Council on Educational Work with representatives from each Branch, a milestone in the YMCA educational program. This Council coordinated the popular day and evening classes for young men, and entered into a partnership with the Horace Mann School, then on University Place, where YMCA classes were offered in the mechanical trades. By 1898, Association-wide, 1,700 students could choose among twenty-three classes in thirty-five fields of study. Board President Cleveland H. Dodge (1890–1903) and McBurney took pride in their large enrollment, which ranked behind only eight U.S. colleges and universities.

The Brooklyn Association also adopted the metropolitan structure in 1896, and its Fulton Street building became the Central Branch. It had added four other Branches in this period: Eastern District in 1888; Bedford in 1889; the Twenty-Sixth Ward, later called East New York, 1890; and Prospect Park, 1891. Existing Branches included New Utrecht, 1869; New Lots and the German (1878) YMCAs. The independent Greenpoint Association was reorganized in 1885 after its earlier brief life from 1869 to 1874.

All of these Branches would expand in coming years. The Eastern District YMCA planned a building that would cost nearly $400,000 and take 15 years to realize. The Bedford Branch, already serving 700 adults

The Brooklyn Association added a Branch near Prospect Park in 1891.

Talk of the Town, 1882

The New York Association's public lecture series, aimed at self-improvement, counted 40,300 attendees in 1882. Its Literary Society, with 110 members who focused on reading aloud, debates and declamations, took up a wide range of current issues. Discussion topics ranged from weighty political concerns ("Is it good public policy to allow the Socialists recently expelled from Europe to find asylum in this country?" "Should the General Government encourage foreign immigration?") to moral concerns ("Should the whipping post be revived as a punishment for wife-beaters?") and the purely esoteric ("Does culture promote happiness?"). Lively deliberations ensued on topics of popular interest, including Mormonism, the Monroe Doctrine and the Panama Canal, marriage and divorce, and women in the professions. The New York Literary Society held annual challenge debates with the Brooklyn Association—and often won.

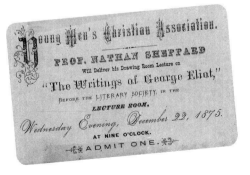

and 200 boys by 1891, was fast outgrowing its walls and considering options for future expansion. Prospect Park, whose physical program in a rented building featured chest weights, dumbbells, rowing machines and a basement swimming "bath," purchased property on Ninth Street in 1893. Another Branch, formed in 1891 by the Long Island College League, was launched in Long Island Medical College. It was the first YMCA program for students in Brooklyn.

Forging Strong Ties to Business

THE NEW YORK and Brooklyn Associations were created by and for businessmen, and from the outset served to sustain their interests. The YMCA was possibly the earliest business networking organization. The Associations aimed their first membership recruitment efforts at young men aspiring to positions in business. At the same time, business owners were worried about the caliber of a labor force made up of young strangers. How could they ensure that the character of their hires would be an asset, not a liability, to the enterprise?

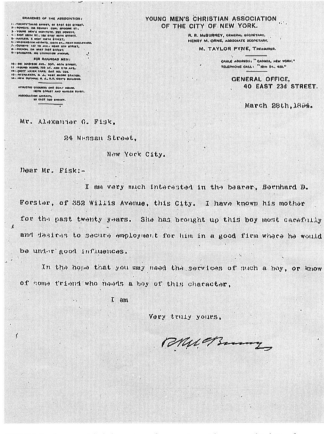

YMCA leaders provided character references to employers, as this letter from McBurney attests.

Since both YMCAs provided new arrivals a home away from home in an atmosphere conducive to self-improvement and good character, they came to be a trusted source of young Christian men for the city's employers, many of whom were staunch Protestants. The Brooklyn YMCA was a pioneer in employment efforts by urging its members to help newcomers in securing work. In times of widespread financial distress, like the depression of the 1870s, the Association helped men, women and children alike to find jobs, and in 1880 fully revamped its employment program.

The New York Association saw a steady stream of applications for help in finding work by 1860, and applicants joined a long waiting list. After a formal Employment Bureau was established, the Association recorded 400 job placements in 1865. The annual report noted its leaders' satisfaction: "Nothing during the year has been more gratifying than (our) success... in finding positions for so large a number of unemployed young men."

The long business depression that followed the Civil War put many young men out of work as establishments reduced their clerical forces. A Committee on Employment counseled the unemployed on how to search for work and avoid frauds, and how to live economically while seeking a job; it also checked on the young men's character with their former employers. YMCA members were encouraged to report job openings they knew of, in what was thought to be "the true principle of reduplicating good."

By 1867, the annual report noted that "the Employment Committee has been severely taxed to provide places for the great number of applicants." Nevertheless, the efforts had a secondary benefit in attracting new men and helping the depleted Association rebuild its membership. In the waning days of the Civil War, a Committee of Invitation, formed to make a more aggressive outreach, enlisted merchants and manufacturers "who employ large numbers of the class we design to reach." More than 2,000 young men received invitations in their places of business or boarding houses to visit the YMCA. President Dodge, drawing upon his business acumen, had instructed the committee to visit establishments systematically in lower Manhattan.

Following the post-war slump and depression in the following decade, Association job placements dwindled to 140 young men in 1874 and only 75 out of 566 hopefuls the next year. With little else to offer them, the YMCA helped many return home or sent them to seek "honest work" out West. Of the situation on the Bowery, the Association reported in 1875, "Thousands of worthy and intelligent men are idle, and, failing to find work, some become destitute and disheartened, gradually drift downward, and swell the ranks of paupers or criminals. Many come to the city, deceived by the false advertisements, calling for men.... They reach here only to find the places filled, or not worthy of their notice. With money gone, they apply at the station-house for lodging and in a day or two find their way to our rooms.... We persuade many of these to return home on foot, or write to friends to pay traveling expenses back."

The New York Association set up a "co-operative employment bureau," open daily from 9 A.M. until noon and 1 to 3 P.M., intended to "correct abuses" by both employers and employees. The bureau maintained a free

registry for job-seekers who would furnish references and postage to have them investigated. Once satisfactory referrals were obtained, the applicant received a certificate for 30 days of privileges at the bureau, such as directing potential employers to his references on file. When the YMCA located an appropriate situation, the job-seeker received notice by mail and if he was hired, the employer paid $1 to the YMCA and the new employee repaid half. "The result has been a falling off in the number of situations procured, but the character of the situations has been better, and the reliability of the employers and the employees whom we have been enabled to benefit cannot be doubted," stated the 1875 annual report.

By 1882, applicants in New York were searching for positions in a wide range of occupations: salesmen, clerks, porters, collectors, correspondents, teachers, trades, traveling salesmen, watchmen and stenographers. YMCA members were in a good position to help them: their businesses included law, manufacturing, dry goods, printing, groceries, cigars, printing, drugs, and medicines as well as railroads. Among those who stated their occupations were 519 clerks, 240 employees, 96 bookkeepers, 87 salesmen, 81 principals, 55 clergymen, 47 apprentices, 43 journeymen, 13 managers, 13 foremen, and 11 secretaries (91 members were students).

Thus the New York and Brooklyn YMCAs quickly became a favorite cause of business leaders, who saw them as ideal partners in perpetuating the Protestant ethic by which they ran their enterprises and prospered. As employers, they could come in search of young men who spent their non-working hours in approved pursuits, steering clear of the seedy lures of the metropolis. The YMCA's reading rooms and educational courses added luster and guaranteed that their new hires would have a means for self-improvement and the emphasis on prayer meetings and Bible study would ensure their uprightness.

In this gilded age of industrial progress, the New York YMCA's backers were a veritable roster of the city's prominent and influential businessmen, including William E. Dodge Jr. and his son Cleveland H., the Pyne family, J. Pierpont Morgan, Morris Jesup, Cephas Brainerd, and Cornelius Vanderbilt II. These aristocrats of industry and civic leaders, who brought prestige and fund-raising prowess to the YMCA and shaped its programmatic directions as well, heartily endorsed the Association's molding newcomers to the city into Christian manliness.

They formed a tight circle, bound by overlapping interests in the nation's rail system, banking and finance sectors, metals and oil. William E. Dodge Jr.'s company, Phelps Dodge, was the leading dealer in copper and metals. Dodge was one of the largest shareholders in the Erie

Cornelius Vanderbilt II immediately saw the usefulness of establishing a Railroad YMCA in the Grand Central Depot, and became its primary benefactor.

Railroad; his son Cleveland eventually became its chairman. William Dodge and Percy Pyne each had a large stake in the Farmer's Loan and Trust Company, where their sons eventually became officers. Their interests in philanthropy overlapped as well; Dodge and Pyne were also important figures in the new American Museum of Natural History, where Jesup was president of the board.

Jesup, a founding member of the New York YMCA at age 22, became a wealthy railroad man and banker. For years, he was one of the Association's most loyal and generous supporters. Jesup "(gave) away money as fast as he made it," *The Nation* observed in 1911, and believed that charity must "[aim] to remove the causes of poverty." His leadership also extended to the national YMCA, where he served on the International Railroad Committee. Measures he advocated for railway workers in the YMCA would eventually be applied to miners, lumbermen, cotton-mill hands, factory workers, and government employees in the Panama Canal Zone and in construction camps, military camps, and naval stations.

Cornelius Vanderbilt II rose from a clerk's position on the Harlem Railroad to chair the powerful New York Central Railroad built by his grandfather, "Commodore"

Vanderbilt. The Commodore, a Staten Islander who had gained control of the Harlem and Hudson Railroads in 1863 and the powerful New York Central in 1867, merged the latter two in 1869 and forged an empire. Also on the New York Central's board were Cornelius II's brother William Kissam, J. Pierpont Morgan, and William Rockefeller, brother of John, who would later play a major role in building up the YMCA. Morgan's company backed the electrification of lower Manhattan in 1882, bringing the gaslight era to a close, and financed a $10-million syndicated bond issue for the New York Central in 1897.

The Brooklyn Association's membership had waned by 1875, and the YMCA sought help from local businessmen to buy memberships for their employees. Starting in 1878, the Association reached out to specific industries by holding monthly trade receptions that brought in new members. Brooklyn was teeming with workers, with its arriving vessels in 1890 having doubled since 1855, exceeding arrivals in New York's port. Brooklyn's sugar plants were refining half the nation's sugar. Workers began to gain strength through unions that were forming.

During this period labor problems were emerging, with troubling implications for YMCA lay leaders in both Brooklyn and New York who commanded business enterprises. The increasing concentration of ownership, especially in the nation's railroads, was frustrating its employees. As they banded together in unions, their dissatisfactions were building to a point of confrontation. The Central Labor Union of New York Central alone counted nearly 10,000 members in 1883. Here was an industry where the YMCA could, and did, play a major role in employer-employee relations.

Serving Men in Specialized Industries

IN THE 1870s the YMCA had begun to focus on men in a specific sector of industry. The national growth in railroads, which fueled the expansion of modern industry, had reached a dizzying pace, with 80,000 miles of track in place and 800,000 men employed. Trainmen with layovers in unfamiliar cities had great need of clean lodgings and tasty food in good company, and their bosses were eager to mold a cadre of trustworthy, loyal workers. The first Railroad YMCA had opened in Cleveland, Ohio, in 1872 in hopes of promoting harmonious relations between owners and employees.

With missionary zeal, the Cleveland railroad men traveled to New York to convince the YMCA to establish

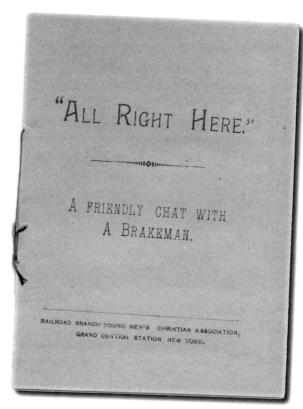

The Association sought to provide services to hard-working men in specific industries, starting with railroad workers.

its own Railroad Branch. McBurney introduced them to YMCA Board member Cornelius Vanderbilt II, the railroad scion and heir. Upon his grandfather's death in 1877 Cornelius II became vice president of the Harlem Railroad and head of finance at the New York Central and Hudson River Railroads; when his father William Henry retired in 1883, he became chairman of the board of directors of the New York Central. Vanderbilt, who had recently been elected to the Board of the New York YMCA, listened to the Cleveland men with interest and agreed to establish rooms for a Railroad YMCA in Grand Central Depot, the world's largest rail facility, which had opened in 1871 on the site of the present-day Grand Central Terminal.

The Railroad Branch formally occupied two basement rooms in the Depot in November 1875, with Cornelius Vanderbilt II serving as Branch chairman. There, railway workers found clean accommodations with baths in the rooms and recreation in a religious milieu. Not content just to support this YMCA, the devout Vanderbilt, a member of St. Bartholomew's Church, personally led Sunday Bible classes for the railway men and their families, where attendance averaged 325. His devotion and involvement with the Branch continued until his death in 1899; he also served the New York Association Board as vice president.

Railroad work opened an ideal avenue for YMCA outreach. The Branches were supported financially by employees and their companies. All railway employees were welcomed whether YMCA members or not. The New York Central Railway Company donated the reading and meeting room which was open daily, except Sundays, from 9 A.M. to 10 P.M. The Association only had to furnish staff and program, which included concerts, lectures and first-aid classes. The 1883 annual report noted that "Many of the men look upon the rooms as their head-quarters during their 'lay off,' and often the grateful exclamation is heard, 'Where could I spend my time, if it was not for these rooms?' " The circulating library and a publication entitled "Our Library" drew the men's attention to newly acquired books.

The early success of this work spawned another Railroad YMCA, opened in 1879 at the Thirtieth Street Depot between Ninth and Tenth Avenues, for the large number of freight men and others working there for the New York Central and Hudson River Railroads. By 1880 the work had hit its stride, and the Railroad Branch reported a "year of marked prosperity." Attendance at the Grand Central Depot rose to 32,396, a gain of 3,508, while the rooms at Thirtieth Street posted an attendance of 21,944. Entertainments were presented by railroad employees and Thanksgiving and Christmas dinners served to them, fueling the YMCA's popularity. The Branch at Grand Central welcomed 55,424 workers in 1886, up from 50,885 the previous year.

Off-duty railroad men enjoyed a buffet of activities, including reading, talks, musicales, socials, and religious meetings.

To better accommodate the burgeoning attendance, Vanderbilt decided that year to finance, at his sole expense, a new Railroad Branch on a site nearby provided by the New York Central Railroad. In 1887, the Branch dedicated its new building at 361 Madison Avenue (at Forty-Fifth Street), where the Roosevelt Hotel now stands. The building's lunch room and dormitories made it a model Railroad YMCA. By 1893, "Old 361," as it was known, doubled in capacity through another addition, which again was fully financed by Vanderbilt.

The railroads were happy to help the YMCA "feed'm and sleep'm," considering what was at stake: the nation's safety. Vanderbilt and his colleagues also found value in persevering with this work as they faced growing labor unrest and political radicalism. The YMCA philosophy could help counteract those trends with its considerable influence among both skilled and semi-skilled workers.

Chauncey DePew, president of the New York Central Railroad and a trustee of the Railroad YMCA, spoke to those themes at the new building's opening. "To many of these men are entrusted the lives of the hundred million passengers who annually travel over the railways of the country," he declared. "The demand for speed constantly increases the danger of carriage. The steady hand and clear brain of the locomotive engineer, of the switchman at the crossing, of the flagman at the curve, of the signal man at the telegraph, alone prevent unutterable horrors, and this Association does more in fitting men to fulfill these duties for the safety of the public, than all the patent appliances of the age."

DePew, who was known as a great orator, had some pointed words for the attendees: "There are two ways of getting on in the world; one is to work cheerfully all day and devote the evening to getting into that higher intellectual

As thousands of railway men flocked to YMCA programs, Cornelius Vanderbilt II financed a new Branch building at 361 Madison Avenue, which opened in 1887. There, employees could partake of meals and socialize with co-workers.

THE YMCA AT 150

Chauncey DePew, a Railroad YMCA trustee and President of the New York Central, preached the value of hard work.

socialistic meeting and howl all night." After a round of applause, DePew continued by making an example of Commodore Vanderbilt, "who, when he was nineteen years old, started out in the world without a dollar, formed an Anti-Poverty society of one, and the result was that he took in enough dividends to leave the largest fortune ever accumulated in a life-time."

On a more personal note, DePew reflected that he belonged to "five of the best appointed clubs in New York, and there is no clubhouse in the city as well appointed as this...." Few of his five clubs, he noted, had a bowling alley and not one had a gymnasium. "There are only three which have rooms where their members can sleep, and none of them has as many as this...the library downstairs has twice as many books as the University Club possesses."

The West Side Railroad Department at 30th Street grew briskly, reporting its best progress in 1886, with a membership of 476 up from 320 a year earlier. It also opened new rooms at 60th Street and Eleventh Avenue, in a New York Central and Hudson River Railroad building, to serve freight transportation employees who used the yards between Sixtieth and Seventy-Second Streets. In 1887 it moved to more convenient rooms, in the West Seventy-Second Street roundhouse. The Mott Haven Railroad Department was organized in the Bronx in 1891, and passenger cars were refitted for workers' recreational use.

condition which puts a man in a position where he can take the better place, if it comes to him, as surely it will—where he closes a satisfactory day's work by spending the evening with his family, and in the morning, starts again with a clear head and conscience; or he can go to the anarchists' picnic and drink beer all day, and then go to the

The Seventy-Second Street Railroad YMCA served freight transportation workers at the yards between West Sixtieth and Seventy-Second Streets.

At the Mott Haven Railroad Department in the Bronx, passenger cars were refitted for recreational use in 1891.

The Association underscored the effect of its religious meetings for rail workers in relating this incident: "One Monday morning a certain foreman who had attended the meeting, when his men came together for roll-call, said... 'Men... I have been trying to get work out of you by driving and searing, but I have been led to see that this is the wrong way, and I am going to try a new plan in the future. I intend to see what kindness will do. Now let's go to work on the new plan.'"

Not all of the YMCA's sector outreach efforts were as successful as the railroad initiative. The nation's rails transported legions of traveling salesmen, or "commercial travelers," and the YMCA sought to reach them with a Commercial Traveler's Ticket. "This large, intelligent, and intensely active class of our citizens, obliged to lead a nomadic life, opens up to us a very important source of mutual good," observed the New York 1880 annual report. But Sabbath services held for them were not well attended and were soon discontinued. Still, the Association kept on trying to reach traveling salesmen by placing 100 "neat wall-pockets" with information about YMCA work in business establishments and hotels where commercial travelers were habitués in 1882.

The New York Association opened a storefront reading room in 1878 for the "more than six hundred bright, intelligent, active boys" employed by the telegraph companies of the city. But this, too, failed to catch hold. In retrospect, leaders understood that "these boys are on duty some ten hours a day, and at night are glad to go home and rest."

Although the Brooklyn YMCA had begun cultivating men from specific trades, the Association initiated railroad work later than New York. The Brooklyn Association organized a Railroad Branch only in 1894, when it took over rooms at the Long Island Rail Road (LIRR). The next year the Branch quarters were destroyed by fire and a new building at Borden and West Avenues replaced them, with the entire cost of construction funded by the LIRR.

The teeming ports of the two cities offered the YMCA another promising population of workers. Transient seamen from far and wide, some of them quite young, arrived daily and departed when they found more work on ships loaded with cargo. By 1888, the Twenty-Third Street Branch had made "boys" on the training ship St. Mary's a regular part of its religious outreach, with services held for them on Sunday mornings and Tuesday evenings. "The boys manifested great interest," noted the annual report that year. This laid the groundwork for a New York YMCA dedicated to seamen. Brooklyn, by the 1880s the fourth largest industrial city in the nation, handled even more waterfront tonnage than New York. Work for seamen was at that time in the hands of a Scandinavian Methodist Church in Brooklyn, but would pass to the YMCA in 1918.

An Association
Caught in the Middle

THE YMCA, OF course, concerned itself with the quality of men's lives, in spirit, mind and body, apart from their jobs. But new and troubling concerns would not go away. Among the employed there was growing unrest around issues ranging from pay rates to working conditions. Concerned with the welfare of working men, the YMCA tried to advocate for them wherever possible.

In 1886, the New York Association formed an outing club with "rambles" on Decoration Day and on Saturdays through September. But numerous members were compelled to work on Saturday and could not join them. "The agitation which is now going on cannot but result in the establishment of the Saturday half-holiday throughout the entire year, but public opinion needs to be awakened yet more generally to the advantages which would follow its becoming a permanent institution," the Association stated. "It is believed by those who have studied the question... that the men and women employed in business avocations would not only be greatly benefited in body and soul, but would render more and better service to their employers, if they had this needed relaxation from business on every Saturday afternoon of the year."

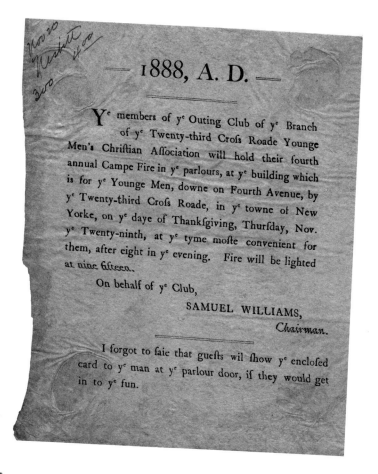

The New York Association formed an Outing Club in 1886, but numerous members could not participate in Saturday excursions because they were obliged to work.

But the issues were much larger than half-holidays, and pitted workers against employers—the YMCA's very backers. The disparity between owners and employees was increasingly apparent to the laboring classes as extravagant mansions sprang up along Fifth Avenue. At Commodore Vanderbilt's death, for example, his estate of $100 million, mostly in stock and property of the New York Central and Hudson lines, passed to his son, William Henry. By 1883 it was worth $194 million. William's wife, a striving socialite with a penchant for $1,000 party frocks, inhabited a world far different from immigrants who were working 10-hour days on the railroad for $1 a day.

By the 1890s, the American labor movement had taken shape, beginning with efforts to organize rail workers. To give them power and protection against the gathering

strength of corporations, Eugene Debs, the charismatic union organizer and socialist advocate, led a tumultuous strike of workers against the railroads in 1894, the largest in history, which paralyzed the nation's rails. Violence ensued following federal intervention to break the strike.

The YMCA, with allegiances both to young working men and business leaders, was caught in the middle of the growing labor-management conflicts. Somehow the Associations managed to toe a fine line, providing services to strikers and non-strikers alike, offering them forums for discussion and sometimes acting in a mediating capacity.

In a widely lauded move, the Brooklyn Association's Edwin See commissioned a series of social-economic lectures in 1894, nobly hoping to resolve "the social problem of the day." Topics included "Rights of labor and rights of employers," "Duty of the employer and the employee toward each other," "Moral obstacles to economic progress" and "The good and bad in strikes." The roster of speakers included Samuel Gompers of the American Federation of Labor and Jacob Riis, author of *How the Other Half Lives,* a widely read 1890 revelation of the desperate conditions of the poor. These highly praised lectures were attended by a large number of working men and bosses, and both were encouraged to speak their points of view.

Labor leader Samuel Gompers spoke at a Brooklyn Association series designed to bring working men and bosses together.

One of the lectures, "Moral and Economic Value of Industrial Education," summed up what was to be perhaps the YMCA's largest contribution to the aspiring working class. The Associations had, of course, been furnishing libraries and providing educational classes since their early days, but at the end of this century and the dawn of the new, the YMCA strengthened its emphasis on practical studies designed to help young men advance in industries where demand for skilled labor was great. Again, New York and Brooklyn would lead the way.

Ethnic and Racial YMCAs

THE YMCA'S SEGREGATION of men was not only by race. Ethnic groups were deliberately separated in the nineteenth century into affinity groups within the New York and Brooklyn Associations. These distinct YMCAs offered their members, who shared a common culture and language, a place to fraternize with their countrymen apart from dance halls and beer gardens. Some of the earliest Branches in both Associations were French and German YMCAs; briefly, there was an Italian Branch. New York's German YMCA was initially a separate Association, organized around 1850 but short-lived. In 1852, the New York Association reported, "we have had close relations with the interesting German Association of this city, which has need of our sympathy and aid." When the New York YMCA vacated its rented rooms in Bible House, the German Association took them over.

Clannishness and ethnic residential enclaves were prevalent in the mid- to late-nineteenth century. Half of Brooklyn's residents in 1855 were foreign born; of those, half were Irish and less than a quarter each were German and English. The Irish in particular had borne the brunt of rampant anti-foreign sentiment in the two preceding decades. The predominantly German Eastern District established a YMCA in 1866 and consolidated it with Brooklyn's German Branch in 1895. At that time the Brooklyn YMCA regularly hosted National Nights, offering Swedish, Scottish, Irish, British, and American members a separate time to socialize with one another. As immigration transformed the metropolis, the Brooklyn Association came to be viewed as a dynamic social force in a changing community.

A full-fledged German Branch of the New York Association was organized in 1881, after two precursors had failed; it occupied quarters on East Second Street, in the heart of the main German district, in 1884. Two years

THE CONTRIBUTION OF ONE MAN TO THE YOUNG MEN OF EUROPE

James Stokes Jr., a cousin of William E. Dodge Jr., spearheaded the New York Association's French and German Branches and was the master builder of YMCAs in other countries.

The German Branch was one of several YMCAs for ethnic groups in nineteenth-century New York.

later the new Branch acquired a building at 142 Second Avenue, at Ninth Street. This structure—the home of former Governor Hamilton Fish, who shaved his asking price—became the first YMCA building dedicated to German work in the nation. Association President William E. Dodge Jr. and his cousin James Stokes Jr., head of the YMCA's German Committee, headed a group that raised the necessary funds from American friends and German businessmen.

Stokes, a New York and national Executive Committee Board member from 1866–93, was also the moving force behind a French Branch established on West Twenty-Third Street in 1889. Its membership was comprised of Swiss and Belgians as well as Frenchmen. Of 116 members, 35 were Roman Catholics. Most who joined had no religious training, and nearly half had been in the United States for only a year. This Branch would remain active until 1929. Stokes, an independently wealthy lawyer, believed that his good fortune brought great obligations, and the YMCA, he said, gave him an ideal way to "do the most for the Church of Christ" and "the largest opportunity for service" to others. He also supported the Railroad and African-American Branches. Stokes' lifelong passion was the national YMCA's relations with Associations abroad. He gave substantial sums for YMCA buildings in Paris, Rome, Berlin, and other cities, and singlehandedly supported early Christian associations for young men in Russia.

By 1887, some remarkable shifts had taken place: Some African-American members were now taking part in activities at the Twenty-Third Street Branch, although they did not use the gym. One African American who wanted to study mechanical drawing at the Young Men's Institute was refused admission, and a dismayed McBurney offered him membership instead at 23rd Street. Just as the Association was quietly ignoring its own strictures on religious requirements, it apparently was selectively waiving some racial restrictions as well. But this seemed to depend on who was in charge: for example, the West Side YMCA's Education Committee later rejected a "colored boy's" application to its Mechanical Dentistry School because "it would have a bad effect on the school."

Societal strictures against the intermingling of races were exacerbated in the 1890s, when the Supreme Court condoned "separate but equal" accommodations—including public education, parks and libraries—in the *Plessy v. Ferguson* decision. In 1890 the YMCA International Committee appointed its first African-American secretary, William A. Hunton, to head the Colored Work Department. Jesse E. Moorland was hired to assist Hunton in 1898, and their work would greatly expand the participation of African Americans in separate YMCAs. When Hunton was hired, none of the nation's fourteen Colored Ys had its own building, or even a gym. By 1896, the country counted sixty Colored YMCAs, with forty-one located in colleges. New York Association founder Cephas Brainerd, who led the national YMCA movement for twenty-five years, wrote to a friend that the YMCA "ought to transcend the race issue," and that he hoped the Association would "keep clear of the idea that the black race is to be dominated and perpetually advised by the white race."

Women's Place in the YMCA

IN BROOKLYN, WOMEN had been welcomed as YMCA members with full privileges as early as 1859. It was the first Association known to admit the opposite sex. In a city renowned for its liberal religious thought (one founder, the influential abolitionist Henry Ward Beecher, was also outspoken on women's suffrage and rights), female members were seen as a positive force in the fledgling YMCA.

Having first invited the "ladies" to its monthly meetings in 1855, the Brooklyn Association did a fair amount of proselytizing among other American YMCAs to follow their lead. At the 1857 national convention, Brooklyn's

William Edsall introduced a resolution: "Resolved, That experience has demonstrated the fact, with some of the Associations connected with this Confederation, that the attendance of ladies at their society meetings has given increased interest to their exercises: and we recommend to such Associations as have not heretofore adopted this arrangement, to try the experiment."

While the Brooklyn advocates did not sway many others, their own female membership grew, and the Association continued to admit ladies for more than 25 years. The library and lectures were a major attraction for women, and by 1869 the Association counted 1,200 female members.

That year, however, the national convention barred women from YMCA membership and vowed to refocus Association work on young men. Women's auxiliaries were permitted, but they were largely limited to social and decorative functions and fund raising. As the national Association tightened its ranks, Brooklyn was one of the last YMCAs to withdraw female memberships. Women remained on the Brooklyn rolls, but their numbers declined over the next decade. By 1880 the national YMCA established a policy that women seeking membership be referred to the Young Women's Christian Association (YWCA) for membership.

Women's participation was limited to certain programs in the nineteenth century YMCA, as in this musicale at the Twenty-Third Street Branch.

Sunday evening teatime was for men only on Twenty-Third Street.

In this Victorian era, when same-sex friendships were the societal norm, it was not surprising that most YMCAs did not rush to admit women to their club-like men's societies. Leaders were split on the issue, however, with Dwight Moody saying the YMCA was "all wrong" to exclude women, while Cephas Brainerd argued that the movement "by young men, for young men" had no place for women. Siding with Brainerd, J. P Morgan remarked that "it is difficult to unscramble eggs." Women, however, participated in various aspects of the New York YMCA program. Certainly they were not ignored in religious outreach efforts. In 1874, New York's Eastern Branch on Grand Street reported the conversion of two young women at a YMCA service at Mariners' Church.

The Harlem Branch involved women in various ways. It sold tickets to ladies for $2 per year, entitling them to use the reading room two afternoons a week and to attend lectures and readings at no charge. Women also participated in Glee Club concerts, Sunday afternoon coffee-and-biscuit receptions for out-of-work and homeless young men, open-air and Sabbath praise services, and prayer meetings at the Ward's Island Hospital. They enrolled for lectures and classes in German, French and book-keeping. The Branch also housed weekly temperance meetings "chiefly under the management . . . of the Women's Temperance Society of Harlem."

By 1883, however, the women were relegated to a supporting role as this Branch followed the national trend and formed a Ladies' Auxiliary Committee of Management with 44 charter members "to co-operate with the Harlem Branch in its work for young men." Auxiliary members could still use the circulating library and enjoy lectures and entertainments, but their presence became notably decorative: "The ladies have also secured a new set of furniture for the parlor, a cooking stove, a full set of dishes, a cover for the new piano, decorated the rooms with Christmas greens, provided simple refreshments for the members' meetings and Sunday tea, and kept 'Open House' on New Year's Day," stated a report that year.

The German Branch adopted Harlem's practice in its new Second Avenue building, forming its own Ladies' Auxiliary Committee in 1885 "with the special aim to attend to the furnishing of our new house." The women held a fund-raising fair and netted a little more than $2,000. "The Ladies' Committee has since been formed into a permanent Auxiliary," the Branch reported. "This promises great good for the future, not only for the direct assistance rendered by the ladies, but by the increased interest created by their taking an active part in the work." The Twenty-Third Street YMCA had noted a general upswing in attendance at its lectures, to 800 on average, perhaps because they were free to members who were "entitled to the privilege of bringing a lady without extra charge."

Men could purchase tickets for women to attend certain YMCA programs.

The Century Draws to a Close

THE YEAR 1898 was a significant one for New York, the nation and the YMCA. With urbanization, trade and transportation growing apace, consolidation held the key to successful cities as well as companies, which were rapidly merging into corporations. On January 1, Manhattan and Brooklyn, along with Queens, Staten Island, and the Bronx, officially united to form the metropolis of Greater New York, and instantly created the largest American municipality. Brooklyn's standing as the fourth largest city and its character as the "city of homes and churches" were receding, with one-third of its churches having closed their doors since 1860. Its Anglo-Protestant aristocracy was overwhelmed by legions of new immigrants, and the borough would shortly be linked inextricably to Manhattan by new tunnels, bridges and subways.

Despite the city's consolidation, the Brooklyn and New York YMCAs would remain separate entities for another sixty years. But on their strong foundations, both

YMCAs would grow and flourish in ways their forefathers never imagined, spreading throughout the city's five boroughs and serving an unimaginably wide spectrum of people in new and innovative ways as great changes swept through American society.

On April 25, 1898, the United States went to war with Spain and the nation again turned to the YMCA to minister to the social and spiritual needs of soldiers, as it had done so effectively in the Civil War. Traveling soldiers found welcome accommodations at the new West Side YMCA. As soon as President McKinley declared war, the YMCA International Committee sought and received authorization from the administration to begin work in soldiers' camps and at naval posts, for the first time outside the country's borders. The YMCA drew upon the in-depth expertise it had developed during the Civil War and the service it had rendered to state militias following that war.

Although the Spanish-American War ended in a matter of months, it marked the beginning of sustained Army and Navy Work in the national YMCA. A permanent department would be established the following year,

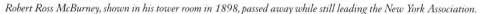

Robert Ross McBurney, shown in his tower room in 1898, passed away while still leading the New York Association.

organized along the lines of the summer tent work the YMCA had been conducting for the National Guard in peacetime—providing reading and letter-writing supplies and social, literary, musical, and religious exercises and meetings, "to help create an effective opposition to the saloon and other demoralizing agencies which infest and infect a camp of soldiers."

This YMCA work would be greatly expanded after the war. It was already underway in the New York Association, which had provided religious services at the U.S. Marine Barracks and Forts Hamilton and Schuyler since 1881. At frequent evangelistic meetings, the Association obtained pledges of abstinence and occasional conversions. Army and Navy YMCAs would be added rapidly in the coming decades.

On December 27, 1898, Robert Ross McBurney passed away in his tower room at the Twenty-Third Street building, marking a symbolic end to the Association's early history. The New York YMCA's first general secretary was eulogized as a master builder and the movement's greatest leader. McBurney had defined its purpose, principles, and the metropolitan association; set the standard for YMCA secretaries; and given shape to its classic buildings locally, nationally and internationally. For generations to come, he would stand as the "personal embodiment" of YMCA work, after his thirty-six years of service. William E. Dodge Jr., who presided at McBurney's memorial service, said: "I never knew anyone whose life I envied so thoroughly... working day and night for his Master... he was the discoverer of the value of young men to themselves. He believed there was a power in their lives, if only it could be turned in the right direction."

The statesman Elihu Root, who was appointed U.S. Secretary of War in the following year, praised McBurney in his memorial address. "The secret of his wonderful success lay in the quality of his sympathy with the best in every man's nature," said Root, who won the Nobel Peace Prize in 1912 while a senator from New York and credited the YMCA Literary Society for his preparation in public speaking. " He accomplished a work the like of which has never been seen in our modern civilization among all the people of Christian lands."

McBurney's legacy to New York encompassed all that and more. He left behind a ground-breaking 15-Branch Association, including five Railroad YMCAs, with nine Branch buildings worth $2 million, 149 full-time employees and an overall yearly attendance of two million in YMCA programs. The bold genius of his 1869 building made New York an innovator in YMCA facilities and inspired the International Committee to develop national standards and open a Building Bureau in New York City. Under the leadership of Robert Ross McBurney, the New York Association was widely acknowledged as the single most influential YMCA of the nineteenth century.

McBurney's vision created a loyal following. This man's membership spanned his lifetime.

New York Branches in 1884

Twenty-Third Street, 52 East Twenty-Third, at Fourth Avenue
Bowery, 243 Bowery
Yorkville, Third Avenue and Eighty-Sixth Street
Harlem, 2317 Third Avenue
Young Men's Institute, 222 Bowery
German, 6 East Second Street
Railroad, Grand Central Depot
Railroad, Thirtieth Street (between Ninth and Tenth Avenues)

New York Branches in 1898

Twenty-Third Street, 52 East Twenty-Third Street
West Side, 318 West Fifty-Seventh Street (including Association Library)
Harlem, 5 West 125th Street
East Side 158 East Eighty-Seventh Street
Young Men's Institute, 222 Bowery
Washington Heights, 531 West 155th Street
Students' Branch, 129 Lexington Avenue
German Branch, 140 Second Avenue
French Branch, 112 West Twenty-First Street
Bowery Branch, 153 Bowery
Railroad Branch, 361 Madison Avenue
Railroad Branch, Seventy-Second Street and Eleventh Avenue
Railroad Branch, Mott Haven, Bronx
Railroad Branch, Weehawken, N.J.
Railroad Branch, New Durham, N.J.

Brooklyn Branches in 1898

Central, 502 Fulton Street
Eastern District, 131-33 South Eighth Street
German, Graham Avenue and Debevoise Street
Bedford, 420 Gates Avenue
Twenty-Sixth Ward, 142 Penn Avenue
Prospect Park, 362 Ninth Street
Long Island Medical College, Hoagland's Laboratory

Greenpoint Association (independent),
752 Manhattan Avenue

3

1899-1929

A T THE START of the twentieth century, New York City was expanding its transportation infrastructure to link its five boroughs and building railroads and shipping facilities to reach the nation and the world. At Manhattan's southern tip, millions of immigrants from Europe were streaming through Ellis Island. By 1907, 40 percent of the city's residents were foreign born.

New York City's population would bulge over the next two decades, climbing from 3.4 million in 1900 to nearly 4.8 million in 1910 and more than 5.6 million in 1920. Brooklyn in particular would swell with hundreds of thousands of eastern and southern Europeans and African-American migrants from the south. The semi-pastoral Bronx was about to balloon exponentially.

With its concentration of the nation's largest corporations, and with its Wall Street firms financing their astonishing growth and creating wealth, the newly consolidated city led the country in business, politics, education, philanthropy, and the arts. Enhanced by a populace bringing their talents, skills, and labor from the world over, Gotham assumed a key position in the "American Century."

The YMCAs of New York and Brooklyn, each nearly 50 years old, stepped up to these remarkable changes in the city and in society, including the looming World War. Through their hearty and creative response, new areas for growth would open up and professional staff would be added to complement an emboldened volunteer leadership. In 1924, the Brooklyn Association would be renamed the Brooklyn and Queens Association, reflecting rapid expansion in the neighboring county. As YMCAs added bricks and mortar to house expanding programs and services, membership in the New York Association alone more than tripled, from 9,100 in 1900 to 31,300 in 1920.

At the turn of the century New York City teemed with traffic, both vehicular and pedestrian, as its population ballooned. Brooklyn was newly linked to Manhattan by bridges spanning the East River.

The years leading up to and through World War I saw the greatest period of growth in the New York YMCA's history. Building on its base of expertise in physical fitness, the YMCA would become closely identified with athletics in the 1920s. Programs would also fan out of YMCA buildings to local military bases, factories, train depots, schools, and neighborhood centers, involving many New Yorkers who were, unlike the YMCA's founding fathers, neither young nor male, Christian nor Caucasian.

A Building Boom in the New Century

THE TURN OF the century brought a building boom in the New York and Brooklyn Associations and for the New York–based International Committee, which united all North American Associations. New members, needs and programs meant that the YMCA was constantly outgrowing its quarters, in need of space and popular new amenities such as swimming pools, basketball gyms, and rooms for overnight stays as well as important necessities like fireproofing. Dormitory rooms were in great demand, especially among transient military personnel in both war and peacetime. The two YMCAs stepped up to the challenge, ambitiously putting up new buildings that were often touted as the "biggest" or "best" of their kind.

In 1904, the New York Association departed from its historic 1869 building to move several blocks west. The new Branch it constructed on Twenty-Third Street near Seventh Avenue occupied a ten-story fireproof building. This $850,000 structure continued to be called the Twenty-Third Street Branch until 1943, when it was renamed for Robert Ross McBurney. Said at the time to be the finest YMCA building in the United States, the Branch contained many appealing features: a 112-room dormitory, a top-floor gym, a hot-air bath, a cork running track on the eighth floor, and a roof garden for open-air handball and socials. The marble-lined swimming pool was a marvel of engineering in its day since it was suspended on the sixth floor. Its library, with capacity for 20,000 volumes, and classrooms would enhance its day business institute and evening courses.

Dedicatory Services of the New Building of the Twenty-third Street Branch of the Young Men's Christian Association of the City of New York Monday evening, March twenty-first, 1904, at eight-thirty o'clock

The new Twenty-Third Street YMCA housed a 112-room dormitory.

Among the innovations on West Twenty-Third Street were a top-floor gymnasium and a cork running track around the upper perimeter.

They Made Financial History at the YMCA

The new Twenty-Third Street Branch spawned a famous financial pairing in 1907, when Charles E. Merrill, newly arrived in New York and employed by a textile firm, met Edmund C. Lynch, a soda-fountain equipment salesman. . . some say in the swimming pool. Merrill left two years later to run the bond department of George Burr & Company, a commercial paper firm. In 1913 he became sales manager of another Wall Street firm, Eastman, Dillon & Company, and backed Eddie Lynch as his replacement at Burr. The next year Merrill founded Charles E. Merrill & Company, renting space and phones from Eastman and persuading Lynch to join him. Once settled in their own rented quarters, the young men renamed their firm Merrill, Lynch & Company in 1915.

Unable to attend the dedication, Morris K. Jesup cabled an offer from Washington to double his subscription to the building fund if the remaining $25,000 of a $30,000 deficit was raised that afternoon. Cleveland H. Dodge, who was presiding, later announced that the amount had been raised. Although the donor remained anonymous, The *New York Times* reported that Miss Helen Miller Gould, daughter of "robber baron" Jay Gould, arrived with an automobile party of friends. When calls for donations were made, she filled out a card. No one would say how much she pledged, but YMCA officials did admit that "the sum surprised them."

Nobel Prize winner Elihu Root helped to fund the new Twenty-Third Street building. The year it opened he served as U.S. Secretary of War, and would be named Secretary of State the following year. Root chaired the YMCA Committee on Devotional Meetings in 1868 and later, the Literary Society, which he credited with giving him the confidence to speak in public.

The Brooklyn Association, whose quarters at 502 Fulton Street had grown increasingly inadequate, raised capital for new buildings through the 1903 Jubilee Fund, a drive that marked its fiftieth anniversary. Between 1904 and 1907 the Association completed three new buildings: Eastern District in Williamsburg; Bedford, on Bedford Avenue between Gates and Monroe Streets; and Greenpoint, which became a Branch in 1903. The Jubilee Funds also allowed for retirement of mortgages totaling $800,000 on its Prospect Park and Twenty-Sixth Ward Branch buildings.

The new Eastern District YMCA occupied a six-story structure of 70,000 square feet, with a swimming pool, running track, two gyms, club rooms, lounges and 157 residence rooms. The Branch raised $275,000 of its $379,000 cost through the Jubilee fund. The smallest of the three new Branches, Greenpoint, was a compact red-brick building that nevertheless contained a swimming pool. The Bedford Branch featured a swimming pool, gymnasium, and rooms for meetings and classes. Its theater-style auditorium featured an early moving-picture projection booth, made of metal and cantilevered over the front entrance to reduce the danger of fire from the highly flammable celluloid films. In 1905 a fire destroyed its gym, which was promptly rebuilt with insurance proceeds.

The Greenpoint YMCA opened its new building shortly after becoming a Branch in 1903.

Entertainments for the Community

The Bedford YMCA, well known for its trade courses, nonetheless appealed to all segments of the community. Each year this Branch staged a season of "entertainments" in its auditorium. In 1905, its annual bill included the costumed *Royal Gypsy Concert Company*, the *Rutgers College Glee and Mandolin Clubs*, the *Brockway Jubilee Singers* (billed as "the leading colored concert company of America"), scientific lectures, scenes from comic operas, and *Lyman Howe's Moving Pictures*.

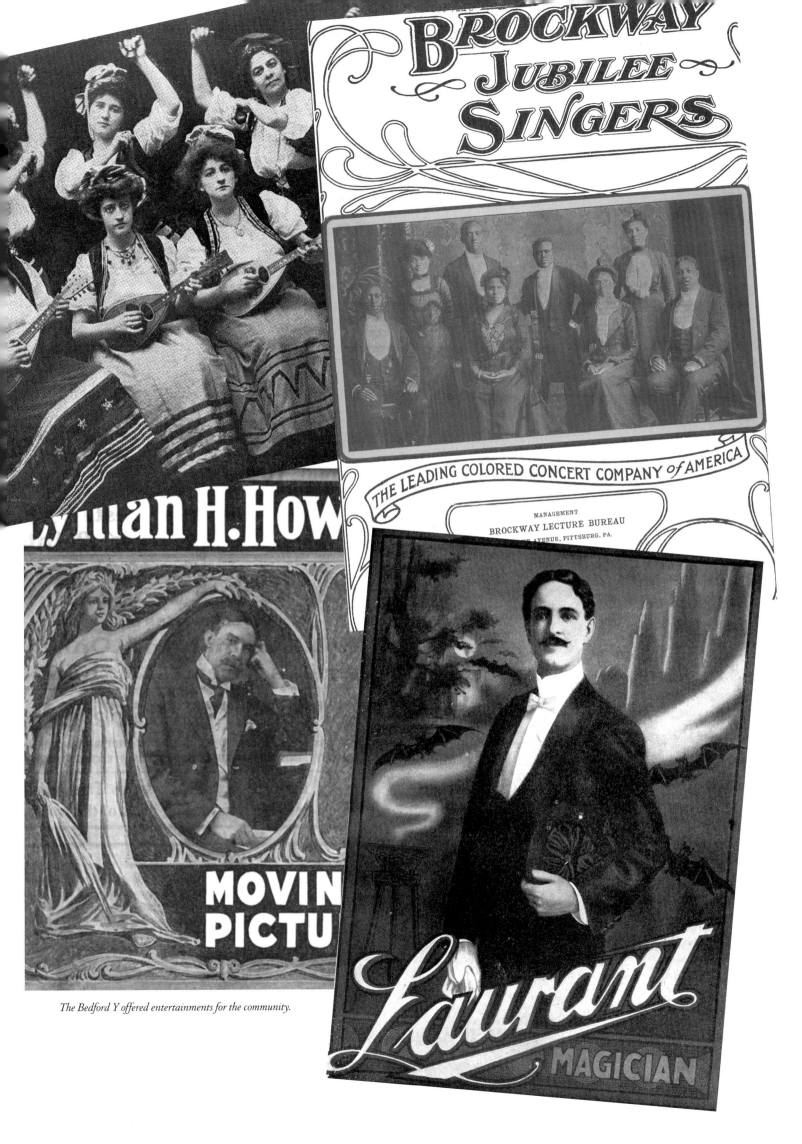

BROCKWAY
JUBILEE
SINGERS

THE LEADING COLORED CONCERT COMPANY of AMERICA

MANAGEMENT
BROCKWAY LECTURE BUREAU
AVENUE, PITTSBURG, PA.

Lyman H. How

MOVIN
PICTU

The Bedford Y offered entertainments for the community.

Laurant
MAGICIAN

Association Buildings in Brooklyn.

Brooklyn's existing YMCA Branches were soon to be joined by a raft of new buildings.

The Brooklyn YMCAs had a major benefactor in John D. Rockefeller, who gave the Association building fund two gifts of $100,000. The second was a challenge grant available to the Association if it completed its Jubilee Fund Drive for $700,000. Members of the Pratt family, fervent supporters of the Brooklyn Association, were officers at Rockefeller's Standard Oil Company. Charles Millard Pratt, from a modest family in Massachusetts, had come to New York and joined Astral Oil, rising to become its owner and merging the company with Standard Oil in 1874. Well before the company's court-mandated breakup in 1912, Rockefeller was largely devoting himself to philanthropy guided by his son, John D. Rockefeller Jr.—they established the Rockefeller Foundation in 1913—and the YMCA was a fortunate recipient.

Two New York Association Branches were added in the Bronx in 1904: Bronx Union and Williamsbridge. That expansive borough, previously annexed in part to Manhattan, had been settled in 1848 by Irish and German immigrants and was still primarily farmland even as New York and Brooklyn became vast urban centers.

The Bronx Union YMCA's predecessor was the Young Men's Christian Union, organized in 1888 at 148th Street and Willis Avenue. Two years later the group began

The Williamsbridge Branch, in a former Bronx saloon and dance hall, joined the New York Association in 1904.

The Bronx Union Branch also opened in 1904.

The 1896 West Side YMCA on West Fifty-Seventh Street added a much-needed residence wing in 1912, something Cleveland H. Dodge, YMCA president from 1890–1903, and Seth Low, past president of Columbia College and former mayor of Brooklyn and New York City, had been promoting for years. The Frederick H. Cossitt Memorial Dormitory, named for Mrs. A. D. Juilliard's late nephew who died while on honeymoon in England, opened on West Fifty-Sixth Street as an eleven-story fireproof annex to the Branch. Mrs. Juilliard funded most of its $500,000 cost. The building provided dorm beds for 308 men and some very modern features: "plunger-type elevators," marble-lined bathrooms, hot and cold water at all hours, telephone booths on each floor and buzzers in every room.

The New York Association sought $317,000 to expand other Branches early in the century. Funds would enable the Harlem Branch at 5 West 125th Street, which had an all-white membership at the time, to provide dorms and expand work for boys in adjoining buildings it had purchased. A fund-raising booklet, "Social Centers for the Better Sort of Young Men," noted that Harlem had a population as large as Buffalo and that the 1,500-member YMCA could not handle any more.

discussions with the New York YMCA, resulting in the 1904 merger. Bronx Union founder Charles B. Lawson influenced its move to the remodeled Wheelock Piano Factory at 149th Street and St. Ann's Avenue. Lawson, who headed the Branch for 27 years, worked for William E. Wheelock and Company, the borough's first piano makers. The Williamsbridge Branch was organized in a three-story former saloon and dance hall at 215th Street and White Plains Avenue. Its reading room and bowling alleys attracted young men who had not darkened the doors of the former establishment—and perhaps some who had. This Branch ceased operating in 1918.

By 1915, Bronx Union moved into a new, four-story building at 161st Street and Washington Avenue with a capacity of 3,500 members. At a cost of $450,000, the edifice boasted two gyms, the "largest swimming pool in New York," dormitories for more than 800 and a motion-picture auditorium for educational films. Some 5,000 people attended the building's dedication, where choirs sang Handel's "Hallelujah" chorus as the cornerstone was leveled. In one year Bronx Union enrolled 2,400 in educational classes, 2,900 in Bible classes and religious meetings and 7,600 in physical classes. This YMCA, along with West Side, Twenty-Third Street and Harlem, was designated one of the four "general" Branches of the New York Association.

The West Side YMCA, opened in 1896, added a 300-bed residence on West Fifty-Sixth Street in 1912.

The East Side (formerly Yorkville) Branch at 153 East Eighty-Sixth Street, with more than 1,000 members in that predominantly German-American community, had purchased two brownstones on Eighty-Seventh Street to provide dorms for 101 young men; fees from the rooms would help finance the extension of its work. The former German YMCA, now called the Second Avenue Branch, occupied an old building at 142 Second Avenue in a neighborhood "densely populated with foreigners" with members representing seventeen different nationalities. Its twenty-nine dorm rooms were constantly filled and needed improvements such as better sanitary facilities.

The Colored Men's Branch sought $30,000 for better quarters. With 424 members and a twenty-two-bed dorm, its rented space at 252–254 West 53rd Street was inadequate to the demand. "With the exception of the churches, there is no agency of importance in the city besides this Branch which works for the elevation of the young Colored man," the fund-raising brochure stated. "The Colored people themselves," it noted, had already raised $5,000 of the sum needed.

Following Cornelius Vanderbilt II's death in 1899, his brother William Kissam, son Alfred Gwynne and grandson Frederick W. Vanderbilt each gave the New York Association $100,000 in 1913 for the Cornelius Vanderbilt YMCA Memorial and its Railroad companion. Their gifts ensured that the New York Central Railroad Branch, then on Madison Avenue, could build anew at 309 Park Avenue between Forty-Ninth and Fiftieth Streets under a 21-year property lease from the New York Central. A seven-story building, where the Waldorf-Astoria hotel

The new Railroad Branch building, at 309 Park Avenue, was financed by the Vanderbilt family.

stands today, was constructed of white brick and Indiana limestone to harmonize with the nearby Grand Central Terminal. The *New York Times* called the new Railroad YMCA "thoroughly modern in its generosity of window space" and admired its roof garden where most activity took place in warm weather. The New York Central and New Haven Railroads gave $175,000 to complete the project. The Branch would remain at "Old 309" until 1929.

Brooklyn's Central Branch left its Fulton Street building in 1915 to occupy "the largest, most complete Y in the world," reported the *Brooklyn Eagle*. The new thirteen-story building on Hanson Place between South Elliott and Fort Greene Places, with capacity for 8,000 members, cost $1.6 million and was said to be the world's priciest YMCA. Mrs. William Van Rennselaer Smith donated $500,000 for the building in memory of her son, Clarence E. Smith. Prominent residents of Brooklyn flocked to the dedication, where John Raleigh Mott, the pre-eminent YMCA leader who was at this time general

The 1915 Brooklyn Central Branch building on Hanson Place, containing two swimming pools, was said to be the largest YMCA in the world.

secretary of the International Committee, and the Reverend. Lyman Abbott were principal speakers.

The Hanson Place YMCA housed two large swimming pools, a roof garden with three handball courts, and an auditorium seating 1,000 that featured a pipe organ. Seventh-floor rooms were devoted to the educational department and the Marquand School for boys during the day. This YMCA was a small, self-contained city with restaurants, bowling alleys, a pool room, and 900 dorm rooms that accommodated some 1,500 young men daily. A running track spanned the gym gallery. Membership quickly shot above 10,000, with a long waiting list. The fellowship among members of this YMCA was said to be comparable to that of a big school or college.

Brooklyn's Twenty-Sixth Ward Branch sought to follow the population which was moving east, but its fund-raising for a $110,000 building was slowed by the war. Renamed the Highland Park Branch in 1921, this YMCA gathered donations from prominent citizens in East New York and Cypress Hills, Queens, to purchase a full block on Jamaica Avenue, the old Albert H. W. Van Siclen homestead running from Shepherd Avenue to Highland Place. In 1926, it opened a four-story YMCA with a nearly 100-bed residence and the capacity to serve 7,000 men and 500 to 1,000 boys.

In 1918, the Greenpoint Branch added two stories of dorm rooms to its Meserole Avenue building with gifts

from the John D. Rockefeller Fund and the Pratt Fund. That year the Brooklyn Association also saw the opening of a new three-story building for the Carlton YMCA, its "Colored" Branch founded in 1902, at Carlton Avenue and Fulton Street.

The Brooklyn Association's Carlton Branch opened its new building in 1918.

In 1920, when the Brooklyn Association formalized its expansion into Queens, it made plans for two new YMCAs in that borough. Citizens in Flushing broke ground for a Branch in 1924 on Northern Boulevard to serve residents of Bayside, Douglaston, College Point, Whitestone, and other nearby communities; the building opened in 1926. Individuals in Jamaica subscribed $20,000 for community YMCA work, which took place for two years on playgrounds, in athletic leagues, at father-and-son banquets, and summer camps. They also helped to fund the new Central Queens YMCA building that opened in 1928 on Parsons Boulevard. The black population of Queens had grown to more than 10,000 people, many of whom were settling in Jamaica, and this YMCA would soon welcome them as members.

The International Committee, the New York–based steering body for national YMCA work, needed better quarters as well. In 1900 Mrs. Russell Sage added $100,000 to her previous gift of $250,000 to construct an eight-story building for the YMCA International Committee at 124 East Twenty-Eighth Street. Her gift defrayed the entire expense of erecting and equipping the fireproof structure. Mrs. William E. Dodge Jr. donated the property, a gift worth $135,000. The new building devoted a floor to the YMCA Publications Department, which published five periodicals and books for Bible study, religious work and character building. It was dedicated in 1908 by Brooklyn's Theodore L. Cuyler, a minister and one of the last living YMCA founders. (In 1918, the International Committee would move to quarters at 347 Madison Avenue.)

A "clock" on Jamaica's Town Hall tallied building fund contributions in 1926 for a new community YMCA, Central Queens, opened in 1928 (facing page).

The Flushing YMCA was the first Branch in Queens with its own building, opened in 1926.

Mrs. Sage and Mrs. Dodge also wanted to house the new National Board of the Young Women's Christian Association in the Twenty-Eighth Street building. "Their wishes will be followed," the New York Association annual report noted tersely. The YMCA establishment was not entirely welcoming: the YWCA would use a separate entrance on Twenty-Seventh Street and separate elevators. Miss Grace Hoadley Dodge, sister-in-law of Mrs. Dodge and the YWCA's president, was steering her organization in ways she had observed her father and brother lead the YMCA. She and her brother jointly gave $625,000 to the combined YMCA-YWCA building drive. She also acted as a mediator between the two organizations, chairing a joint committee that briefly considered, then rejected, a merger. Gender integrity was reaffirmed, at least for the moment.

New York City YWCA members joined the YMCA in fund-raising work around 1912, including Elizabeth W. Dodge, daughter of Cleveland H. Dodge, bottom left; above, to her right, Mrs. Edwin Gould; Mrs. William Fellowes Morgan, seated, third from the right.

Early Supporters of the
NEW YORK ASSOCIATION

I n 1927, the New York Association reported that member dues and fees accounted for 88 percent of its operating revenues. "Interested friends" made up the 12-percent deficit. In its appeal for donors to an endowment fund, the following significant gifts were listed:

Abner W. Colgate, $5,000 for water fountain,
	Young Men's Institute, 1905
Cornelius Cuyler, $25,000 bequest, 1910
Miss Grace Hoadley Dodge,
	$25,000 bequest, 1915
Mrs. Morris K. Jesup, $250,000 bequest, 1915
William Douglas Sloane, $10,000 bequest, 1915
Mrs. Margaret Olivia Sage,
	$100,000 bequest, 1919
Miss Mary Roberts, $430,000 bequest, 1919
James Stokes, $90,000 bequest, 1920
Mrs. Helen Juilliard, $50,000 bequest, West Side
	Branch, 1920

YMCAs for "Special Classes"

IN THE EARLY twentieth century the New York YMCA categorized Negroes, seamen, military men, students and "strangers" as "special classes." In what the Association called the "group principle," specific industry units like railroad workers had their own Branches. Certain Branches served primarily clerks and mechanics and others, shop men; six Branches organized boys apart from men. College students had their own Intercollegiate Branches. In 1884 "work among the Chinese" was also cited in New York.

By the turn of the century, many African Americans were living in more affordable Brooklyn, including new arrivals from the south. Leading black citizens there worked in business, the medical professions, the clergy, education and the public sector, among them Arthur Alfonso Schomburg, organizer of the Negro Society for Historical Research. Their churches formed the hub of African-American social and community life. A group of young black men from the community petitioned the Brooklyn Association to establish a Branch for young men "of their own race," indicating that they had promises of financial assistance. The Association employed a temporary secretary to secure more support.

Accordingly, in 1902 the Brooklyn YMCA organized a "Colored Men's and Boys' Branch" with 200 members in a brownstone on Carlton Avenue, which was given to the Association by banker and philanthropist George Foster Peabody, a Brooklyn Association director and trustee since 1895. Peabody, who retired from business in 1906 to be a full-time philanthropist and public servant, served as Association chairman from 1906 to 1911. He made education for African Americans his personal cause. From an impoverished family, Peabody had quit school at 14 to go to work but educated himself through reading extensively at night in the Association library. He considered this the equivalent of a college education, and many considered him among the best informed men of the time.

Ten years later the Carlton Avenue Branch obtained funding for the first of two "Rosenwald Y" buildings in New York City, thanks to another backer of education for black Americans. Julius Rosenwald, a top executive of Sears Roebuck and Company in Chicago, had offered the Branch $25,000 in 1912 to fund the new structure if the Brooklyn Association would raise another $75,000. During this period Rosenwald gave a total of $600,000 in challenge grants to build YMCAs and YWCAs for African Americans in many North American cities.

The Brooklyn Association succeeded in raising the money, and the Carlton Branch, slowed somewhat by World War I, was dedicated in 1918. The building and equipment cost nearly $230,000, with $22,000 coming from African-American donors, $25,000 each from Julius Rosenwald and John D. Rockefeller, and the balance from the Brooklyn Board of Directors. The Carlton Y had seventy dorm rooms, a swimming pool, fifteen showers, bowling alleys, a billiards room, a boys' game room, a gymnasium, a social lounge, and five meeting rooms. It was, observed the *Brooklyn Eagle,* the world's second largest "Colored YMCA."

Members of Brooklyn's Carlton YMCA enjoyed musicales and literary society meetings in a brownstone donated by Association director George Foster Peabody, a benefactor of education for African Americans.

Seventy rooms like the one below were available in the 1918 Carlton YMCA building, financed by Julius Rosenwald (right).

Unfortunately, by 1924 the Carlton Branch had problems. Built by a local architect, its first-floor plan was inadequate, its gym gloomy and the underground pool too damp for comfort. Locker rooms, also underground, were freezing in winter and the roof did not have space for a single handball court. Even janitorial service was lacking. Carlton's general lack of efficiency and effectiveness contrasted starkly with the other Rosenwald YMCA, the new 135th Street Branch in Harlem, where everything was going strong. That Branch's membership had more than doubled from 210 to 535 from 1917 to 1918, when the building opened, and by 1926 it topped 1,000, mirroring the extensive growth in Harlem's black population during that period. Between 1920 and 1940, it would double again.

The 135th Street YMCA traced its roots to the summer of 1900, a year that was marked by racial disturbances in the still predominantly white Harlem and Manhattan's Tenderloin district over the growing inequality of black citizens. Dr. Charles T. Walker, minister of the

The twentieth-century YMCA in Manhattan for black Americans first occupied two brownstones at 132 West Fifty-Third Street. They included much-needed sleeping quarters.

Mount Olivet Baptist Church on West Fifty-Third Street, decided to initiate a young men's program focused on Bible study and lectures. In the fall the group of young men sought membership in the New York Association, with a $3,000 stake they had raised at a church fair. The Association accepted their proposal. This group, which had no apparent connection with the previous "Colored YMCA" downtown, was successful in establishing a new Branch that offered social, educational and religious programs and dormitory rooms for members. The new YMCA opened at 132 West Fifty-Third Street in the heart of San Juan Hill, an African-American residential area where fashionable clubs fueled artistic life and gave the district its reputation as "black Bohemia." An elegant hotel there, The Marshall, was a showcase for talent, especially jazz orchestras.

Three years later, the new YMCA acquired two three-story brick buildings at 252-254 West Fifty-Third Street for $28,000 and set up a reading room, a small gym and dorms in "an ideal location. . . furnished with all modern improvements," *Colored American Magazine* noted. More than $10,000 had been raised at a meeting in Carnegie Hall that year; the renowned educator and author Booker T. Washington was among the speakers.

In the early 1900s, numerous migrants from the American South were establishing homes in Harlem, rapidly creating the only large-scale, fully developed African-American community in the nation. Harlem's population had doubled in 1917 alone. Overall, New York City's black residents would increase by 154,000 between 1910 and 1930, as the white population fell by 633,000. Powerful organizations were forming in the city: the

The Manhattan "Colored Men's Branch" staff in 1911 consisted of John H.E. Elmendorf, assistant secretary; Thomas J. Bell, Branch secretary; and Abram B. Green, janitor.

Educator and author Booker T. Washington helped raise $10,000 for the 135th Street YMCA building by speaking at Carnegie Hall. "Money invested in a community where the Negro population has been elevated industrially, intellectually and religiously, is a safely invested dollar," he declared.

National Association for the Advancement of Colored People (NAACP) in 1908, followed in 1911 by the National Urban League. Harlem was the logical neighborhood for a new YMCA for African Americans, although the all-white Harlem YMCA formed in 1868 was still operating on West 125th Street. (That Branch closed in the 1920s, transferring its memberships to a new East Side Branch.)

In his offer for a "Colored YMCA" in New York, Julius Rosenwald wrote to William Fellowes Morgan, then President of the New York Association: "You say it gives you great pleasure to inform me that the Young Men's Christian Association of the City of New York anticipates including in its budget $150,000 for a new building for a Colored Men's Branch. I can assure you it gives me far greater pleasure to learn of this than it could possibly give you to impart the information. It may sound trite to say that nothing would give me greater pleasure than to have New York take advantage of my offer to give $25,000 toward such a building, but it is really a fact that I would rather see such a building in New York than in any other city in the country."

Writing in *Outlook* in 1914, Booker T. Washington noted that the gifts from his friend Julius Rosenwald and the YMCA "have been a help to the members of my race... in what they are doing to convince the white people of this country that in the long run schools are cheaper than policemen; that there is more wisdom in keeping a man out of the ditch than in trying to save him after he has fallen in; that it is more Christian and more economical to prepare young men to live right than to punish them after they have committed crime."

Henry C. Parker Sr., chairman of the Colored Y's Property Committee and a real estate broker and investor, was in charge of locating a site for the new Branch uptown. Parker, whose office was on West 135th Street, was pressed by Jesse Moorland to find a site without delay in order to qualify for the $25,000 Rosenwald gift. At a meeting in Parker's office, the committee was inspired by looking out

his window, and set its sights on a property at 181-183 West 135th Street, then in a primarily white neighborhood.

The New York Association argued that the 135th Street location was unsuitable. The committee, however, was determined, envisioning a six- or seven-story building there. It prevailed, and its vision proved correct. The new 135th Street YMCA opened in 1919, at a cost of $375,000. The *New York Times* called it "the most modern and largest YMCA building for Negroes in the country." The Branch quickly established itself as a pillar of the community in civic and social affairs, and of the Harlem Renaissance that began in the 1920s.

"Character-Building" at West 135th Street Branch
AN OUTSTANDING CENTER FOR COLORED MEN AND BOYS

BIG MEETING
Big in scope and results. Held every Sunday afternoon.

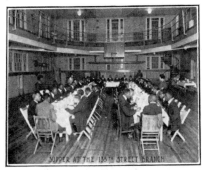

BEAN SUPPER
Followed by Bible classes. Given every Wednesday night.

The African-American Branch moved to West 135th Street in 1919, to a building financed in part by Julius Rosenwald.

A BEE HIVE IN HARLEM
One thousand pass between the portals each day.

LOBBY LECTURE
Practical courses are given in public speaking, advertising, newspaper writing, etc.

SWIMMING POOL
3392 used the pool last year. 734 taught to swim. 52,434 attended gymnasium activities.

By 1918 the Young Men's Institute was conducting work for Russian men, to give them an opportunity for physical training, "social enjoyment" and educational classes. A Japanese YMCA program was active in Brooklyn at 17 Concord Street in 1912 and in 1925, a Filipino YMCA club opened at 264 Hicks Street, primarily to serve students. Many felt a responsibility to the latter group following the Spanish-American War, which put the Philippines under U.S. governance. At the dedication of New York's Twenty-Third Street Branch in 1904, a Major H. W. Halford made a plea for the Filipinos, referring to them as "the dear little brown Filipino-Americans." America was responsible for their religious welfare, he asserted, and for giving to them "the best there is in American civilization."

A short-lived YMCA program for Japanese men occupied a building on Concord Street in Brooklyn.

The Filipino Club met in a center on Hicks Street in Brooklyn Heights.

From Christianity to Character Building

WITH THE CITY'S population swelling, the resolutely Protestant Associations were receiving a new cadre of young men, dominated by the first big wave of immigrants since the YMCA's inception. Many of these men held different religious beliefs. Those of the Jewish and Catholic faiths came in significant numbers, eager to find work in New York's thriving industries and factories, especially in Brooklyn, Queens, and the Bronx. Their needs for help and guidance, decent jobs and a place to socialize or to stay were great. Would the YMCA step up to serve so many men who were not Protestants?

The Associations seemed to have determined that an ecumenical attitude could enhance their success. The *New York Times* quoted Episcopal Bishop Henry Codman Potter, presiding at the dedication of an International YMCA building at 10 West Fifty-Fourth Street in 1905, as declaring: "I am meeting here on this platform... a rabbi of the Jewish Church [sic] and a priest of the Greek Church, together with ministers and representatives of all denominations. This building stands for the decay of creed animosity, for the passing of those theological wars that have been so destructive in the past." Following the

The Bible Class at the Twenty-Third Street Branch attracted many young men.

Bishop, Rabbi Joseph Silverman of Temple Emanuel "heartily" agreed, saying, "Today there is no difference between us. There is but one religion and that is of the heart. We are all working together for a common end and differ only in our methods."

On this occasion, Rabbi Silverman credited the YMCA for providing a model. He noted that members of his synagogue, concerned that they were losing young men, "looked at your work and founded a Hebrew Y.M.A. [at Ninety-Second Street and Lexington Avenue] and the result has been most satisfactory."

TAKE YOUR CHOICE

Despite a growing ecumenism, the YMCA was still closely identified with Christianity, as this cartoon attests.

The YMCA's desire to serve community needs was strong, and with the city's population changing so dramatically, this was not a time for exclusivity. The YMCA's Christian mission—at least by the book—remained essentially unchanged. The Portland (Maine) Convention of 1869 had imposed the evangelical church-membership basis upon North American YMCAs, overriding local autonomy. Not until 1925 would local Associations be officially allowed to accept, as an alternative to the evangelical requirement, a statement of personal belief in and loyalty to Jesus and to the Association's purposes.

While continuing to be primarily identified with the Christian religion, the New York and Brooklyn Associations had been quietly disregarding the evangelical stipulation by embracing non-evangelical Protestants and others in their programs since the era of Moody's religious revivals. An 1884 analysis of New York Association membership found 305 Episcopalians, 266 Presbyterians, 139 Methodists, 126 Roman Catholics, 116 Baptists, and 101 Lutherans. The remainder included Congregationalists, Reformed Dutch, Universalists, Unitarians, "Hebrews," Swedenborgians, and Quakers. This early ecumenism was nothing if not pragmatic, since it allowed the YMCA entrée into new, diverse groups for participation in its programs and for fund-raising appeals. President Theodore Roosevelt, a consulting member of the YMCA, remarked, "The thing I like about you YMCA people is the way you combine religion with common sense."

The Brooklyn Association, too, had tempered its religious barriers. Its Long Island College League, the first student YMCA program in Brooklyn, had a stated policy of no religious "fences." New York City's Intercollegiate Branch, organized in 1890 as the Students' Branch, sponsored five student centers in Manhattan in 1901 that counted large numbers of Jewish and Catholic students as members. Apparently the YMCA's religious orientation and programming did not discourage the involvement of non-Protestant students. In a sign of decidedly more secular times, a New York Association survey in 1926 found "more indifference toward the religious program of the Association than either approval or disapproval."

The mixture of spirit and body proved a powerful combination. In 1904, the YMCA spawned the Brooklyn Sunday School Athletic League, the first of its kind in the nation. Dr. George J. Fisher, the Central Branch physical director who devoted half his time to the YMCA International Committee as its physical work secretary, enrolled sixty-two Brooklyn Sunday schools in the league, which included five Brooklyn Ys with fully organized athletic associations.

Dr. George J. Fisher was physical director at Brooklyn's Central Branch and physical work secretary of the YMCA International Committee. He enrolled 62 Brooklyn Sunday schools in an athletic league, the first of its kind in the nation.

At that time, six out of 10 gyms in Brooklyn were conducted by YMCAs as "a place of body building and character building": the Central, Eastern District, Bedford, Prospect Park and Twenty-Sixth Ward Branches, and the Greenpoint Association. The YMCAs offered some of the few bowling alleys not associated with saloons. The Brooklyn Association introduced sex education in 1913 in its gyms, clubs, and church groups, where discussions stressed the importance of family life and cautioned against homosexuality.

Six Brooklyn YMCA gyms conducted programs for body- and character-building.

The Brooklyn Association sponsored sex education talks in YMCA gyms, clubs and church groups.

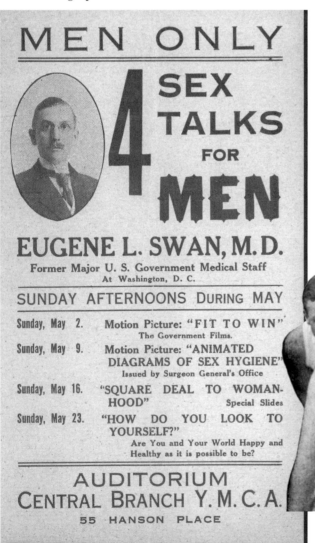

The Brooklyn YMCA was the site of the first National YMCA Volleyball Championship in 1922, and the first National YMCA Indoor Track and Field Championship in 1928..

Some Catholics may have hesitated to participate, however, after the Vatican asked bishops in 1920 to "watch" the YMCA, which it deemed an organization that instills "indifferentism and apostasy to the Catholic religion in the minds of its adherents." Rome warned in particular that the Association would corrupt the faith of Catholic youth. Monsignor Michael Lavelle, rector of St. Patrick's Cathedral in New York, made haste to observe that the Catholic Church and YMCA in America "had long maintained cordial relations."

Despite their new openness, the two Associations still firmly adhered to their Christian programs and purpose. The Brooklyn YMCA's link to local Christian churches was especially strong. In the nineteenth century Dutch-English Protestants and their great preachers had made the city a national center of liberal Christian thought, and the YMCA was frequently a conduit. Men's religious meetings at the YMCA sparked by the financial depression of 1893 continued well into the new century. At the Bedford YMCA, ministers addressed street-corner crowds from a soap box before marching, accompanied by a band, to the Central Presbyterian Church for a meeting.

Reverend S. Parkes Cadman, an outstanding pulpit orator, spoke at the Bedford Branch men's meetings for many years, drawing men from other cities as his programs were broadcast over six radio networks to half the United States and remote Canada. In Manhattan YMCA street preachers, notably Joel Nystrom, drew crowds in Times Square while holding forth from an automobile owned by the West Side Branch.

Rev. Parkes Cadman's pulpit talks at Bedford Branch men's meetings were broadcast throughout North America.

YMCA street preachers drew crowds in Times Square.

The Brooklyn Association also aligned with the Sunday Observance Association of Kings County, which met in its Fulton Street rooms in 1906. These Sabbatarians, primarily clergymen celebrating their suppression of professional baseball on summer Sundays in Brooklyn, turned their attention to an appalling increase in Sunday theater performances and hatched plans for a united public protest.

The religious emphasis was most prominent in five Brooklyn Branches—Bedford, Eastern District, Carlton Avenue, Army, and Merchant Seamen's. The focus was not exclusively evangelistic: Bedford and Eastern District united "religious fervor with real religious tolerance," a 1927 Association survey found.

In a second group, where membership was heavily immigrant and less susceptible to fervent Protestantism, "the religious program has been allowed to lapse into insignificance," the survey stated, citing Bush Terminal, Flatbush, Long Island City, New Utrecht, Greenpoint, and Highland Park. In the Central Brooklyn and Prospect Park YMCAs, religion exerted its influence only subtly in active club programs and dormitory activities. Bay Ridge, Flushing and Central Queens had "foregone any religious program in favor of coordinating and strengthening the work of local churches," the survey noted, remarking that whether their programs were religious or not, they were largely attended by non-YMCA members at all Branches.

In its 1905 annual report, "Things Old and New in the YMCA," the Brooklyn Association stated that its religious work was not essentially different than 60 years earlier, when the YMCA began in London. What had changed dramatically was its mode of outreach. YMCA Bible classes now took place not only in Association buildings but in numerous locations where men congregated: in gyms, boardinghouses, in shops at noon and midnight, in managers' homes, railroad caboose shops, roundhouses,

Bible breakfasts were standard fare at several Brooklyn Branches.

flagmen's shanties, on battleships, in soldiers' camps at army posts, in lunchrooms, camps, classrooms, dormitories, fire engine houses, police headquarters, street railway barns, and college fraternity houses.

The YMCAs' flexibility in accommodating a changing population illustrated the organization's strong desire to adapt to new times, circumstances and communities—and opportunities. This flexibility would prove essential to the Association's survival. By 1910 the Protestant Church in Brooklyn—once the "City of Churches"—was in rapid decline as immigration altered the borough's religious character, ushering in tens of thousands of Jews, Roman Catholics and Eastern Orthodox adherents from southeastern Europe.

The New York Association would witness a similar if less staggering influx. By 1926 its membership rolls revealed that only 54 percent were Protestants, followed by 33 percent Catholics, 4 percent Jews and 3 percent Greek Orthodox. In another sign of the times, as scientific Darwinism raised new questions about the origins of life, more than 5 percent claimed no religious affiliation.

In its efforts to embrace all, regardless of creed, the Association moved with the tide of changing social attitudes to serve the "less fortunate members of the social structure." A 1924 policy statement observed that the YMCA's "social emphasis may certainly be interpreted by members of all the great religious groups as itself essentially religious. Indeed it may well prove to be the basis upon which these groups can effectively cooperate. Yet this does not of necessity involve the great majority of them in any denial of the tenets of their own peculiar faith."

After World War I, outside voices were urging the YMCA to downplay its religious emphasis in order to serve one and all. An article in *The New Republic* of December 21, 1918 called on the YMCA, despite its "handicap" as a religious agency, for a new definition of religion. It noted that through the YMCA's "long service in undermining this system [of religious sects], and in generating the spirit of religious unity and active cooperation... with no sect qualifications... The Association has voluntarily shattered many of its sectarian traditions during the war emergency. It has with little economy discarded most of its 'tests' in the selection of secretaries and directors of its stupendous enterprises... if the newborn institution does not bravely cast off this self-imposed restriction its great opportunity will pass to other agencies...."

Stalwarts in the Associations were not prepared to surrender its Christian emphasis, even as it was receding in prominence. A 1926 survey recommended that the purpose of the New York City Association should be seen as two-fold: to develop Christian character through loyalty to the basic teachings of Jesus, and to serve men and boys regardless of their religious affiliations. The first aspect, the survey recommended, should get "far stronger emphasis."

In that statement of purpose, the word "character" was key. Over the years the YMCA had been refining its mission as one of molding character, based on its "spirit, mind and body" credo of developing the whole man. The motto coined by Luther Gulick in the late nineteenth century would become the article of faith by which the Associations, in all their diversity, could live. The physical program of the four-fold work had attracted countless young men to the YMCA, where they encountered its character-building philosophy.

Thus, YMCA programs began their subtle, practical shift from overtly religious to character education. The *Brooklyn Eagle* editorialized at the end of World War I that the YMCA buildings "swarm with the young men of the type which twenty years ago was to be found hanging about billiard rooms, barrooms, restaurants, and resorts at which 'life' was to be studied firsthand. The crowd in the Association does not look quite as its predecessors in the other places... but they are the same young fellows beginning to make their way in the world and wanting something to do in the evening. The Association has given them recreation under cleaner surroundings and it has made them like the new conditions better than the old... that change of attitude is a triumph of practical righteousness."

Building Boys into Men

ANOTHER IMPORTANT SHIFT was in the making: the YMCA's sole focus on young men was coming to include boys. The New York Association's objective as amended in 1907 was "the improvement of the spiritual, mental, social, and physical condition(s) of young men." By 1924, its purpose was stated thus: "to assist young men *and* boys in the attainment of Christian character and manhood." And its program sought "to demonstrate the value of a healthy body, a trained mind, a wholesome social life, a useful vocation, the right use of money, and unselfish service to others... to inspire young men *and* boys in the ideals found in Christ's teachings and exemplified by his life."

The policy adopted that year emphasized the "building of Christian manhood among the youth of this great city." The increased admission of boys that followed would further diversify the sects represented in the YMCA's membership. By 1926, 44 percent of boys who belonged to the New York Association were Protestant, 46 percent Roman Catholic, and 4 percent Jewish.

Walter Diack, then head of the West Side Branch, explained the rationale for boys' work in *Men of New York,* a national YMCA publication, in 1921: "The Association work is that of character-building. It has no other reason for being. It is manifest, of course, that character-building

Sometimes it was hard to sort the young men from the boys in YMCA programs, since so many went to work at an early age.

is a process for the formative stages of life. After a young man's life has 'set,' there may be some character transformations; but real building must take place in the plastic years. Not much can be done in building a man's character after he is twenty-five."

In the Associations' early years, it was often hard to sort the young men from the boys. Many came to the city seeking work in their early teens, forced to do so because of financial circumstances. Far from family to sustain them, or with no family at all, many working boys were well below the YMCA's stated minimum age for membership, although some efforts were made to help them. At the turn of the century, the YMCA was increasingly aware that younger boys needed the support that it could provide. Its leaders were coming to believe that "it is easier to build a boy than to mend a man."

One way to do that was to find and help boys where they worked. The New York Association formed a special Branch in 1919 for boys who worked in Wall Street as pages, clerks and messengers. Staffed by volunteers who worked in the area, this special YMCA occupied small offices at 56 Pine Street, and used the great hall of the New York State Chamber of Commerce and the New York Stock Exchange Educational Institute for large gatherings. This Branch disbanded during the Depression. In special Branches near the docks, both Associations also worked with boys, many of them orphans, who were casually employed on ships and otherwise left to fend for themselves when in port.

World heavyweight champion Gene Tunney told members of the Wall Street Boys' Branch that the harder they worked toward their goals, the happier they would be in the end.

Sumner Dudley, pictured holding a sledge at Camp Talcott in 1888, led the first organized camping excursion for the YMCA in 1885.

In 1901, the publication *Brooklyn Men* declared: "The surest way to redeem the world is to save a generation of boys." At the time, the borough had an estimated 75,000 boys ages 12 to 18. "Some have good homes... a large number lack them," the article noted. The YMCA was already providing physical exercise, play and Bible studies "which make an appeal to the boy's love for the heroic and manly." But it was also turning boys away, limited by the capacity of its buildings and equipment.

The Brooklyn YMCA had taken thirty boys on a first camping excursion in 1881. The New York Association formed Work for Boys, a new committee, the following year. The committee sponsored an organized camping program developed by a volunteer, Sumner F. Dudley, who took an initial group of boys for an eight-day camping trip in 1885 near Poughkeepsie, New York. Dudley is often referred to as the father of organized camping and the New York YMCA is acknowledged as its birthplace. The YMCA's Camp Dudley on Lake Champlain is the oldest resident camp still operating in the United States.

Camping caught on quickly in the two YMCAs, since city boys and young men had so few opportunities for rustic experiences. In 1904 more than 300 summer camp sessions hosted in excess of 8,000 campers from the New York Association. Of the many sports offered, swimming was the most popular, usually in a lake on or near the campsite, followed by diving, rowing, canoeing and sailing. Typical camp fare included baseball, tennis, running, jumping, climbing nearby hills and mountains, fishing trips, "jolly games," and amateur theatricals. Evenings ended with campfires, stories and songs.

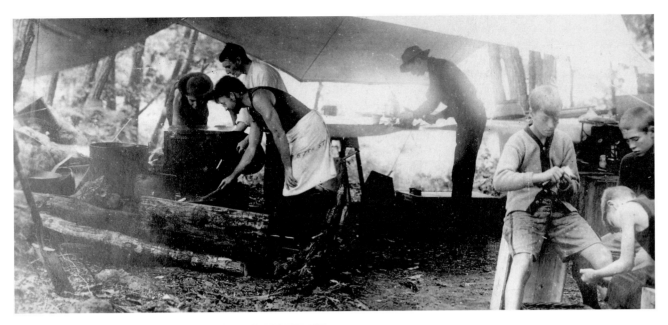

Outdoor cooking was a novelty for city boys at the turn of the century.

Songs around a campfire usually capped a summer evening.

By 1922, the Association was sponsoring six resident camps: Greenkill, five miles from Kingston, New York, operated by the West Side Branch; Camp Talcott, near Port Jervis, New York, conducted by the Bronx Union Branch; Camp Glenwood, under auspices of the Twenty-Third Street Branch, located in Sussex County, New Jersey; Camp Harlem, near Millerton, New York, run by the Harlem Branch; Camp Oscawana 10 miles from Peekskill, New York, conducted by the French Branch; and Camp Crumbie, five miles from Kent, Connecticut, belonging to no particular Branch. Today, the YMCA of Greater New York still operates Camps Greenkill and Talcott which share a site with Camp McAlister in Huguenot, New York. By 1930, a citywide Camping Committee was organized for New York Association boys.

The Brooklyn Association's summer camps for boys had attendance topping 2,000 in 1900. Its campers went upstate to Camp Dudley and to Camp Brooklyn in Purdys, New York. The Association also maintained a camp at Lake Waccabuc, fifty miles north of the city. From 1897 to 1899, it experimented with camps at Bath Beach and Bensonhurst, and considered establishing permanent summer headquarters there because young men were moving toward Coney Island, "especially toward its more demoralizing portions." With gifts from Herbert L. and George D. Pratt, the Association Board established Camp Pratt in 1914 on 17 acres of wooded waterfront land in Princes Bay, Staten Island, especially for use by working boys, a growing group in the community.

The French Branch sponsored a boys' camp at Lake Oscawana.

CAMP BROOKLYN

ON LAKE WACCABUC, NEW YORK

Conducted for the BOYS OF BROOKLYN by the
BROOKLYN YOUNG MEN'S CHRISTIAN ASSOCIATION
Monday, July 2, to Monday, July 30, 1906

Brooklyn Association boys enjoyed pitching tents by the lake at Camp Waccabuc.

The Bronx Union YMCA, which had welcomed boys in its programs since 1888, increased boys' memberships six-fold in its new building.

Work for boys had also begun early in Staten Island and the Bronx. On Staten Island, a second YMCA had been incorporated on the East Shore in 1883. Its Club House, containing a library and gym, primarily drew juvenile and adolescent parishioners from four nearby Protestant churches. After Staten Island became the Borough of Richmond of New York City in 1898, the East Shore YMCA continued its independent work for four or five more years. Eventually another Staten Island YMCA, known as the Port Richmond Association, followed but its tenure was brief.

A concerned father wrote to his son's camp director.

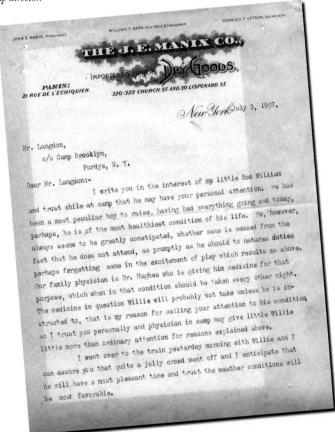

In the Bronx the Young Men's Christian Union, predecessor of the Bronx Union Branch, had been organized in 1888 to do work for boys and young men. By 1915 Bronx Union, with its move to a new building, was able to increase this work significantly and attract many more boys. In the first year boys' memberships leaped from 103 to 603. (Men's memberships also jumped in that year, from 220 to 1,567.)

Six Brooklyn Branches offered work for boys by 1904. Eastern District had a separate boys' department; the Twenty-Sixth Ward offered a program for working boys and a gym for their use; and the new Army YMCA at Fort Hamilton organized a boys' club for sons of officers living at the fort.

Brooklyn boys enjoyed a rustic setting in Prospect Park's log cabin room.

Bedford's boys' program was the most elaborate. The boys' clubhouse occupied its own four-story building at 416-20 Gates Avenue with an adjacent small outdoor playground. A 1906 brochure described in some detail its "Jolly 10" clubs "for wholesome fun." Activities, or "clubs," included gymnasium, athletics, swimming, baseball, basketball, handball, bowling, camping, a championship club, an outing club, and a social club, educational activities and entertainment. Annual dues were $6 for working boys at night, on Saturday afternoons and holidays, or $5 for school boys during the day. By 1906, Bedford boys had won Brooklyn and Greater New York championships in athletics, aquatics, and gymnastics.

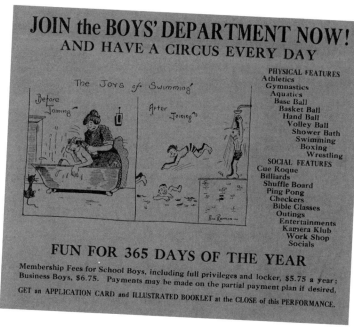

The Bedford Branch offered the most elaborate program for boys.

The Bedford boys' department appealed to their heroic and manly instincts through the Moral Muscle League.

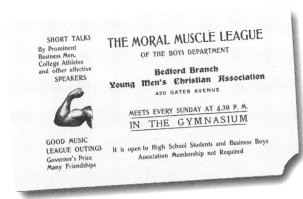

Bedford's Evening School for Employed Boys ages 14 to 16 charged $2 for a 12-week term.

In 1911, Bedford opened an Evening School for Employed Boys ages 14 to 16 who had abandoned grammar or high school for work. (Boys ages 16 to 18 could enter regular men's classes offered at the Branch.) There they could fill in gaps from an abandoned public school education, through individual instruction with teachers from nearby public schools. A 12-week term cost $2, and those who passed exams received a certificate.

From 1910–1933, Italian boys had their own program in an East Harlem extension of the Harlem Branch. In 1921 Philip Le Boutillier, an officer of Fifth Avenue merchant Best & Company, led fund-raising to bring in up to $200,000 for the West Side YMCA Boys Work Committee. The West Side Y proposed an eight-story clubhouse entirely for younger men, under age 21, which would house 200 working boys and offer play facilities for 1,500 others. The Branch's "territory" ran from 42nd to 125th Streets. In most of this area no clubs existed with a good atmosphere and surroundings for boys of this age. The proposed clubhouse would provide "everything to help them live clean in a homelike Christian atmosphere."

Head Work
for
BOYS

A Special Evening School for Employed Boys

Opening November 3d, 1911

BEDFORD BRANCH
Y. M. C. A.
1125 BEDFORD AVENUE,   BROOKLYN

Join Your Nearest Branch NOW

Great Sport fine exercise

Swim all Winter

YMCA

Aquatics soon became one of the YMCA's most popular offerings for New York City boys, with swimming pools available at Brooklyn's Central Branch since 1885 and at the Young Men's Institute in Manhattan since 1887. All YMCA buildings constructed after the turn of the century included indoor pools for recreation, games, and serious, competitive swimming.

Based on the gym model with graded steps and exercises, aquatics developed into a signature YMCA program nationwide. Eventually the Associations evolved a rational, systematic plan of instruction and certification in aquatics and an Aquatic Leaders Corps to train swimming instructors, including all-important lifesaving skills. The Brooklyn YMCA hosted the first national YMCA Swimming Championship in 1923.

Both Associations held learn-to-swim campaigns each year, offering free lessons to teach basic skills to as many young men as possible. (This popular annual program for youth and adults alike continues as Splash Week. In 2001, New York City YMCAs hosted 2,275 participants, among them more than 1,900 boys and girls.)

As aquatics grew in popularity, so did learn-to-swim campaigns and courses in lifesaving.

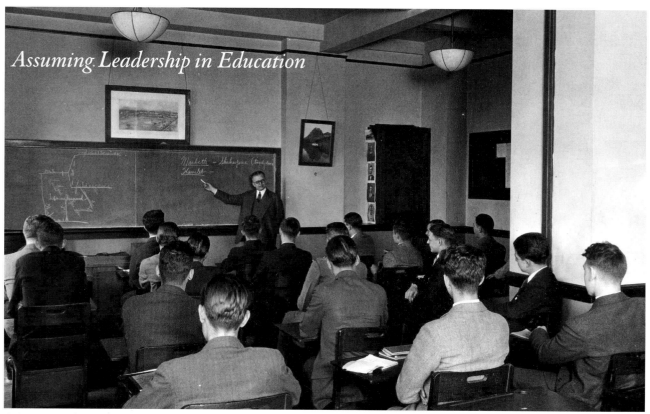

Cultural subjects, like this Shakespeare class at Central Queens, were less of an attraction than practical courses.

The YMCA viewed its educational courses as a means of molding character in young men.

THE YMCA HAD realized very early that education was essential in molding character and good conduct, if not Christianity, in young men who would staff the city's enterprises. "Mental improvement," a program goal since the 1860s, had begun with religious and ethical education through inspirational lectures, Bible classes and well-stocked libraries. Non-religious instructional classes, too, were among the YMCA Education Department's earliest offerings. The New York Association offered cultural subjects, mainly to attract young men to the Association, but these were not a large drawing card. Religious classes endured for decades but by the turn of the century it was the more practical educational programs that attracted members, and their value was widely acknowledged.

Vocational education gave young men an opportunity to improve their job prospects. In this era before night schools and community colleges were common, many young arrivals to the city had abandoned their education. Few had completed high school or even grammar school, and adults did not go to school. Those eager to get ahead found the YMCA's informal education program, with expert instructors in particular areas, to be an efficient, low-cost setting to fill gaps in general learning and culture, and to hone practical skills in business. YMCA classes offered skill-building courses for clerks, bookkeepers, machinists, carpenters, factory workers, draftsmen, stenographers, and more. In effect, this was the beginning of adult education.

Practical courses gained favor over religious classes in the early twentieth century.

As part of its work for boys, the New York Association operated two day schools: the Chelsea School, a college preparatory school at the Twenty-Third Street Branch, and the McBurney School at the West Side YMCA. McBurney, opened in 1916, was a six-year secondary school "preparing (boys) both for college and for the actual business of life." In 1924, the two academies were merged as the McBurney School, enrolling full-time students in an accredited program.

The years during and after World War I brought heightened interest in the YMCA's educational offerings. Enrollment in five New York Branches—Bronx Union, East Side, Harlem, Twenty-Third Street and West Side—doubled between 1910 and 1920, from 5,320 to 10,760 students. By that time ten Branch libraries contained 103,100 books and 1,070 periodicals. When the East Side Branch closed in 1927, the West Side YMCA, which was assuming the lead in New York Association educational programs, took on its educational work.

Edward L. Wertheim, Educational Director of the West Side YMCA for a decade, was appointed in 1920 to head an Educational Cabinet composed of Branch representatives to increase cooperation among the Branches doing educational work. In 1923, the New York Association turned to Teachers College of Columbia University for a thorough survey of its educational programs and recommendations for strengthening them. (Teachers College, founded in 1892 by Grace H. Dodge, sister of Cleveland H. Dodge, was a reliable resource for the YMCA.) The College recommended unifying administration and supervision of all YMCA programs under a City Secretary of Education; in short order Jerome H. Bentley was appointed the first citywide Educational Director. Course duplications were eliminated, and policies and objectives were formulated to guide and standardize the work.

The YMCA's leading role in education earned wide recognition by other institutions. In 1920, the the New York Law School took quarters on the third and fourth floors of the Twenty-Third Street Branch, becoming part of the Branch's education program and operating under its management. This arrangement continued until late 1933, when the law school departed. In 1927, the Evening High School at this Branch, which had enrolled many World War I veterans, was chartered by the State Board of Regents.

The New York Law School was a department of the Twenty-Third Street Branch from 1920 to 1933.

In this period public accounting was growing in importance and popularity. Two brothers, Homer St. Clair and Charles A. Pace, chose to offer their Pace Standardized Course in Accounting at the Brooklyn and New York YMCAs. In 1909, 300 candidates for state certification enrolled at the two Associations; by 1919, overall enrollment had mushroomed to 4,000. This course laid the foundation for the Pace Institute, which was chartered in 1933 to offer business courses as higher education. These courses laid the foundation for the educational institution now known as Pace University.

Charles A. and Homer Pace offered their accounting course at the Brooklyn and New York YMCAs.

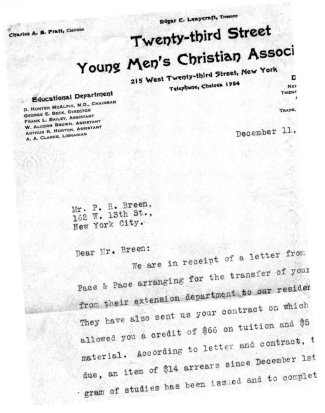

The New York Association operated two preparatory schools for boys, including the Chelsea School at the Twenty-Third Street Branch.

Dale Carnegie, a young man from small-town Missouri, began his career in public speaking in 1912 by teaching classes at the Harlem Branch on 125th Street, after several universities turned him down. His first book was published by the national YMCA Association Press. He expanded that vocation into an extraordinary career, going on to publish his perennial best-selling volume, *How to Win Friends and Influence People,* in 1936.

The Education Department was second only to religious work in the Brooklyn YMCA by 1900. Education had enjoyed a favored status from the outset. Initially the

The Brooklyn Association offered evening classes in twenty-one fields in 1900.

Dale Carnegie taught his first classes in public speaking at the 125th Street Harlem Branch.

Association's work was guided by two respected professors, Darwin G. Eaton and David H. Cochran, who established weekly scientific lectures in 1870. The best instructors in Brooklyn were recruited to teach evening classes in penmanship, mechanical and free-hand drawing, German, French, Spanish, and music.

However, some aspects of learning at the Brooklyn YMCA had brought about a dispute. In 1892 the literary society banned discussion of politics or religion and challenge debates. Half its members departed, and 40 of them formed the Lowell Literary Society of Brooklyn, sidestepping the YMCA and its reluctance to engage in controversial issues.

The Brooklyn Association benefited greatly from the leadership and influence of the Pratt family. YMCA board member Charles Pratt, the Standard Oil Company executive, was also a giant in the education of youth. A man of limited education, he founded the Pratt Institute in Brooklyn in 1887 and remained its president until his death in 1891. The renowned private institute, devoted to the teaching of practical vocations and skilled trades, was exceptional in its era: from the start, its student body was co-ed and interracial. It also offered the first manual training high school in New York City. Pratt's innovative ideas were also brought to bear on the education program of the Brooklyn Association.

Charles Pratt also founded the Pratt Institute Free Public Library, a first in Brooklyn or New York, and the Thrift, one of the first savings-and-loan institutions, in 1888. Thrift education was a Protestant virtue that ranked with honesty, temperance, industriousness and benevolence. Pratt, considered the wealthiest man in Brooklyn, brought those values to the YMCA in 1890 by opening a branch of the Pratt Thrift Institute Association there.

The Pratt leadership in the Brooklyn YMCA continued through Charles' five sons. One of his eight children, Frederic Bayley Pratt, who subsequently served as president of the Pratt Institute, headed the YMCA's education department faculty beginning in 1892. Under his leadership, YMCA admission standards and discipline were tightened and courses were standardized in five Branches by 1895. The Association offered evening classes in 21 fields and enrolled more than 1,100 young men in 1900. Its libraries boasted some 25,000 volumes, and the quality of education was so high that its students could sit for the State Regents examinations. The Association proudly touted the economy of its courses: the average cost per enrolled student was $4.12, compared to $35 in Brooklyn public schools, and YMCA attendance was nearly double that in the public system.

Frederic Pratt also chaired the YMCA International Committee's educational effort, which designed a uniform course of study for 26,000 students attending YMCA evening classes in the United States and Canada in 1900. YMCA schools offered international exams and diplomas, and sponsored a biennial exhibition of student work.

The Bedford YMCA established itself as an early leader in industrial education. In 1908, the year Henry Ford unveiled his popular model-T, the Branch introduced a course in auto mechanics, repairs and servicing, the first of its kind in the United States. As New Yorkers abandoned the horse and buggy, the course was in such high demand that the Branch had to rent new quarters within two years. Despite an economic depression in 1907–09, Brooklyn YMCA membership grew, thanks to the popularity and practicality of its vocational courses at Bedford.

The first auto mechanics course in the nation was taught at the Bedford Branch.

Learning To Run

An Automobile

After a four or eight-week course of shop lessons in its mechanism, operation and care—
IN THE
BEDFORD Y. M. C. A.
AUTOMOBILE SCHOOL
1125 Bedford Ave., Brooklyn   'Phone 6000 Bedford

The Bedford YMCA was a leader in industrial education, with a trade school adjoining its main building.

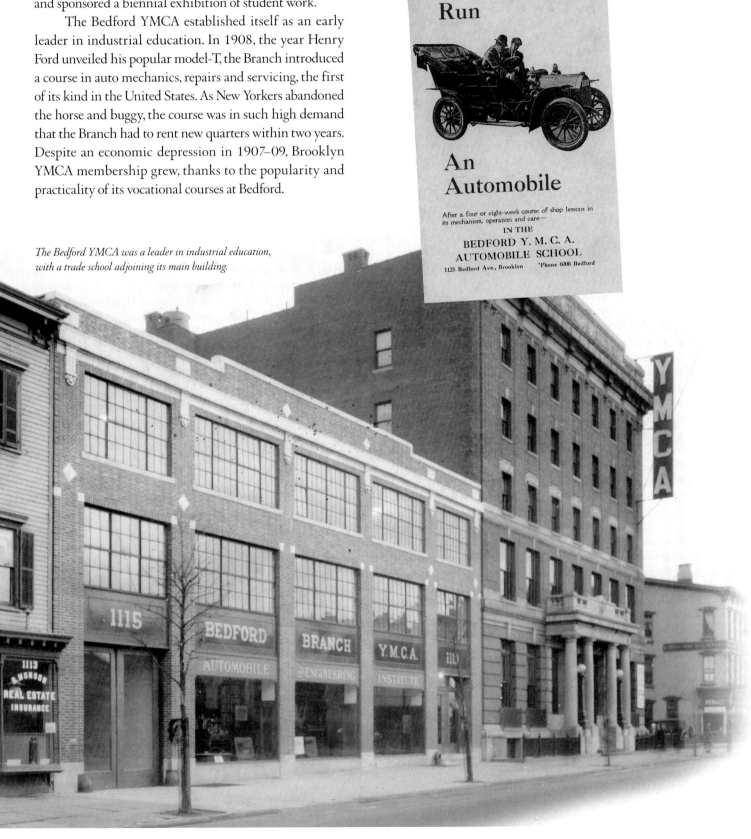

The Pratt
PARTNERSHIP

T*he influential Pratt family of Brooklyn figured prominently in that Association's history and leadership.* **Charles Millard Pratt** *Senior, a young man of limited education and modest means, went to work for the Astral Oil Company in Greenpoint, on Newtown Creek. He rose to be its owner and merged Astral with John D. Rockefeller's Standard Oil Company in 1874. In 1887 he formed the Pratt Institute for practical vocations and skilled trades. Pratt was a key member of the Brooklyn YMCA Board, inspiring the Association's education and thrift programs. His five sons also played important roles in the Association:*

1 **Frederic Bayley Pratt**, a Brooklyn YMCA director, vice president from 1893–1906 and subsequently a trustee, headed its Education Department faculty beginning in 1892, overseeing a tightening of admission standards and discipline and standardizing courses at Branches. As chairman of the International Committee's educational committee, Frederic outlined a uniform course of study for students attending YMCA evening classes in the USA and Canada. A businessman and an officer of Pratt Institute, Frederic secured an unconditional gift of $100,000 from John D. Rockefeller for the Association's 1902–1905 Jubilee Fund.

2 **Herbert L. Pratt**, a YMCA director elected Board vice president in 1920, served on the Brooklyn Association's first industrial committee. A vice president of Standard Oil Company of New York, he made a gift to the Association that established Camp Pratt in 1914 on seventeen acres of wooded waterfront land in Princes Bay, Staten Island, especially for use by working boys. He also chaired the Greenpoint Board of Managers beginning in 1908.

3 Charles M. Jr., senior partner in Charles Pratt and Company, and a civic leader in Brooklyn, was a director of the Association Board from 1884–89 and was elected a trustee in 1892. He was also a member of the YMCA International Committee. Like his father, he served as president of the Pratt Institute and as a vice president of the Long Island Rail Road, was instrumental in founding its Railroad YMCA Branch.

4 George D. Pratt served as chairman of the Central Branch from 1910–14, and a director of the Association from 1911–35. He donated $10,000 for an organ in the new YMCA auditorium.

5 Through the Pratt Fund the brothers, including *Harold I.*, made a $150,000 gift in 1914 to fund the site of the new Central Branch. They also donated money to the Greenpoint Branch in 1918 to add its dormitory floors.

Richardson Pratt (left), son of Charles Jr. and an officer of the Standard Oil Company of New Jersey, was a member of the Swift survey committee in 1927-28. He served on the Central Branch Board from 1920–37 and as its chairman from 1928–31, and was elected to the Brooklyn and Queens Association Board in 1923. He was also vice chairman of the 1930 building campaign and chairman, special gifts, and with his uncle Herbert, supported consolidation with the New York YMCA.

Other Pratts have been notable YMCA supporters: **Mary S. Pratt** *gave $25,000 to the YMCA in 1957.* **Francis DeWitt Pratt** *(bottom left), an executive with Time-Life Inc., chaired the YMCA Counseling and Testing Board in 1968–69.*

Bedford opened a Flying School in 1930 on the site of LaGuardia Airport.

In 1919, Bedford erected a trade school adjoining its main building at Bedford and Monroe Streets that would rise to national prominence. The school's three floors and basement housed a machine shop and automobile equipment. In 1923, to address a citywide shortage of mechanics in the building trade, Bedford conducted classes at night so students could work as apprentices during the day. Chasing another popular transportation trend, the Branch added aviation courses and a flying school in 1930 on the site where LaGuardia Airport now stands. The Brooklyn Association purchased a two-seater biplane, students came from far and wide, and Amelia Earhart paid a visit to inspect the YMCA equipment.

Other institutions recognized the Brooklyn Y's educational excellence. By 1910, Columbia University was offering extension courses for young men at the Central Branch. The borough's population was 1.7 million, and there the University could reach Brooklyn students who might not make the long commute to its Morningside Heights campus. The New York City Board of Education offered lectures at the Association, and YMCA methods and evening vocational training were influential in the public education system. The Brooklyn Association also promoted health education within the public schools by distributing thousands of manuals in their classes and gyms, at parent meetings, and through lectures.

In Manhattan as well, the YMCA led the way in industrial education, stepping in at a time when rapidly changing technologies demanded new skills. Though the need was great, neither private nor public educational institutions were meeting it adequately. The Association's large roster of practical courses included interior decorating, salesmanship, advertising, and wireless telegraphy, in addition to Regents and college prep courses. The West Side Branch developed an important trade school and the Association entertained the idea of a citywide Working Men's Institute at a university level.

The New York Association concentrated most of its courses at two Branches: West Side, for technical subjects, and Twenty-Third Street for business management and high school subjects. The East Side Branch provided training for radio operators, plumbing and drafting, and the latter was also offered at the Harlem YMCA.

The West Side YMCA had established a Trade and Technical School in 1903, and an Automobile School the next year. The popular Auto School soon had a waiting list and reorganized in 1907 to accommodate more than 300 students. It broadened its curriculum from automobile theory and principles to mechanics, due to the tremendous demand for trained auto mechanics. The Automobile Club of America donated $1,000 per year to the School, whose expenses included maintaining a 1911 Cadillac and a garage at 40 West Sixty-Sixth Street, bought for and leased to the School by the father of member William Sloane Coffin, who also invested $5,000 in alterations. In 1917, the Auto School purchased a building at 38 West Sixty-Sixth Street. Courses were added in trucks and motor boats; another, airplane mechanics, enrolled 1,090 men by 1918. A Radio School was added 10 years later.

West Side's real estate course ranked next to auto classes in popularity, with more than 100 enrolled, and courses were added in real estate law and insurance. In 1908, consideration was given to offering courses in psychotherapy, no doubt due to the growing influence of Sigmund Freud.

As new technologies were introduced, the West Side YMCA trade school offered courses in them, such as this class in operating motion-picture projectors.

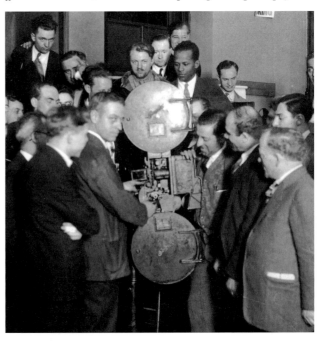

A sign-painting class was one of many practical subjects taught at West Side.

Bronx Union, in addition to numerous courses, offered an educational guidance service in 1926–27. YMCA Schools offered correspondence, or home study, courses in the 1920s. The Extension Division of the United YMCA Schools, based at 347 Madison Avenue, handled the correspondence courses for the entire nation. By 1925, the New York YMCA's total educational enrollment had grown to 5,334 students in seventy-four courses for nearly 680,000 student hours.

Although YMCA courses were not aimed at college men, the Associations took a strong interest in them. By 1926, the New York Intercollegiate Branch, whose Advisory Board included such prominent women as Mrs. John D. Rockefeller and Mrs. Edwin Gould, a daughter-in-law of Jay Gould, had programs at the College of Physicians and Surgeons, City College of New York, Union Theological Seminary, New York University (Bronx campus), and New York/Cornell and Bellevue medical schools. This work, consisting largely of religious programs and social action, traced its beginnings to 1865, when a Medical Students Christian Union had a brief life.

By 1882, a subcommittee of college graduates was enlisting other alumni coming to the city; in 1890 the YMCA student movement formally began as a Students' Branch at 136 Lexington Avenue. The Branch acquired a site at 129 Lexington in 1894 and added another in 1901 at 328 West Fifty-Sixth Street. In a related move, William E. Dodge Jr. erected the interdenominational Earl Hall at Columbia University in 1902 as a memorial to his late son William Earl III, to house religious groups on that campus. The Association purchased a six-lot property on Claremont Avenue near 124th Street in 1920 to provide social, recreational and living quarters for college students and to introduce foreign students to American customs. The twelve-story building housed 200 students.

William E. Dodge Jr. built a hall at Columbia University in honor of his late son Earl, to house religious programs for students.

Extending a Hand

AT THE BEGINNING of the new century, another compelling group of men was attracting the attention of YMCA educators. The years between 1900 and 1920 saw a vast population shift as immigration changed the face of New York City. Unlike previous waves, this generation of newcomers knew even less English. The New York YMCAs responded by offering "Americanization" programs for immigrants, focused on the English language, citizenship and customs. These programs and classes were designed to foster loyalty to the country and the culture among immigrants from eastern and southern Europe, Russia, and to a lesser extent, Asia.

Various Branches offered English classes for the new immigrants.

CAN YOU TALK FOR FIVE MINUTES

without committing grammatical errors or using slang; mispronouncing, misusing or mumbling words?

Mr. HORATIO N. DRURY will conduct a course in

Conversational English

which will help you to remedy such defects and to express yourself at all times with clearness, vigor, correctness, and grace. It will also help you to think straight first and to talk straight second.

¶ Mr. Drury's method is both sensible and practical, being based upon a minimum of theory and a maximum of practice. Moreover, he is possessed of a winning personality and an abundance of enthusiasm, these facts combining to make the course absorbingly interesting.

As the CLASS will be LIMITED to TWENTY-FIVE MEMBERS, SECURE YOUR PLACE AT ONCE.

Wednesday Nights, 7.30-9.30, Starts January 5, 1910
Cost, Five Dollars for Ten Sessions
To Members of the Y. M. C. A.

Educational Department
Bedford Branch Y. M. C. A.
1121 Bedford Ave., cor. Monroe St., Brooklyn, N. Y.

Americanization courses aimed to acculturate the new arrivals and foster loyalty; here, a class for workers at a Colgate plant.

The earliest indication of the YMCA's "Americanizing" young men was in 1888, when the leaders of the Young Men's Institute observed that the majority of their members were foreign born or of foreign parentage. This, in their view, constituted a problem to be addressed. "We cannot but feel, that in Americanizing these young men, we are helping to practically solve the troublesome problems which arise from the fact of the enormous foreign population in this city," the executive committee reported.

At Ellis Island and other ports of entry, YMCA secretaries awaited to present cards of introduction to incoming immigrants, to "insure them right companionship, a job and an opportunity to learn the English language and American life," noted Fred H. Rindge Jr., Secretary of the national YMCA Industrial Service

The YMCA established a Branch on Ellis Island around 1910 to facilitate work with immigrants.

Movement, writing in *The American City.* The Association opened a Branch on Ellis Island around 1910 to facilitate work with the new arrivals. The YMCA's International Committee went even further, deploying representatives at fourteen European ports of embarkation. As Rindge explained, "The Association believes that to adequately solve the problem of the foreigner in America we must begin with him before he embarks from the home port."

Rindge detailed the YMCA's solutions for the "problem": English and citizenship classes in day and evening schools, and "character-building" meetings. Nationwide, he noted, the YMCA counted more than 117,000 industrial men and boys as members, and reached more than 1.25 million workers annually in noonday shop meetings; many if not most were of foreign parentage. At least 600,000 others were reached through other kinds of social, educational, physical, and religious extension work.

The Industrial Service Movement in New York City, for the "uplift of industrial men and boys," centered on a strategy involving local college students. The YMCA offered lectures at NYU, City College, and Columbia especially for engineering students, offering them reading matter and studies in industrial betterment. In turn, students were enlisted to join the YMCA's outreach and welfare work in industrial communities. In one example, students signed on as paid census workers, which provided insight—for them, as future managers, and for the YMCA—into the domestic life of workers.

Some 100 other college students taught night courses in civics, history and English to foreign workers from Europe, Russia, China, and Japan. Most men who enrolled in the thirty-five English classes in New York were between the ages of 20 and 30, working on average nine and a half hours each day and representing forty occupations. College men also led boys' clubs, providing instruction in subjects like drawing and athletics. The YMCA advertised these classes in foreign language newspapers and through notices posted in clubs, in barber shops and saloons, and at subway and elevated rail stations. "Saloon keepers have been willing to assist even though it has meant our taking the men away from them," Rindge reported.

The work had a beneficial effect on instructors as well as students. One young man who taught Italians observed: "My whole viewpoint of life has been changed.

The religious emphasis was strong in Americanization courses; here, men singing at the end of a class at Prospect Park.

There has sprung up a sense of brotherhood which I had not conceived possible. Not long ago I had one desire in life—to make all the money I could, but now I don't care what position I get, where it is, or what the salary as long as I can get in some place where I can help other men. Nobody ever took an interest in me or gave me a chance to express myself before. I cannot tell you what it has meant to me."

The religious emphasis was strong in Americanization courses, even though fewer and fewer immigrants were of Protestant persuasion. The YMCA took great satisfaction not only in helping thousands of foreign working men and boys and seeing them become citizens and affiliated with churches, libraries and other American institutions, but in observing "that many lives have actually been transformed and souls completely won for the Master."

Most YMCA industrial work took place at various worksites. The West Side Branch offered eighty educational classes outside its building, and the Twenty-Third Street YMCA conducted Bible classes in nearby factories and shops as well as at the Branch. Several Brooklyn Branches were conveniently situated close to the borough's factories and adjacent to those in Queens. Notably the Greenpoint YMCA, in earlier days known as the Workingmen's Christian Association, devoted its program to the needs of employees in many nearby factories.

The Brooklyn Association initiated shop meetings where attendance averaged 300. Led by the Central Branch, those meetings took place weekly at noon in six factories, including Pioneer Iron Works, Mergenthaler Linotype Company and McNeill Last Company. By 1920, the program was established in eighty-seven industries, with 326,000 workers attending classes. The Association also

College students were enlisted to teach English to factory workers like these Italian boys at the S. Weil Company shoe factory in Brooklyn.

The Twenty-Third Street Branch conducted Bible classes in nearby factories, such as the Williams Brass Foundry, 1900, and Cornell Iron Works, 1905.

Most YMCA industrial work took place at the noon hour in factories.

conducted Americanization programs at eight Branches. Those six-to-eight-week citizenship courses encompassed American ideals and government and culminated with Branch secretaries personally taking candidates to file their papers for citizenship.

In 1918, the Brooklyn Association organized an Industrial Branch in Long Island City as unionizing efforts were gathering force. Its goal was to encourage a spirit of agreement between employers and employees, creating "an atmosphere in which the adjustments of differences become easy." Its policy was stated thus: "The Association is not partisan, yet it is more than neutral— it is mutual." To this end, it conducted both foremen's conferences and thrift clubs for workers.

The Industrial Branch in Long Island City included baseball and other games in its Americanization work, initiating an unbroken tradition of sports leagues in Queens.

The Long Island City YMCA put great stock in recreation, or "play," which it deemed critical for education, Americanization and general character building. The Branch initiated league play among teams in Queens in 1919–20, introducing many foreigners to new games and social customs. John W. Cook, general secretary of the Brooklyn Association, praised the initiative: "We sincerely believe that men are learning that there is recuperative power in short intervals of complete relaxation, and industrial leaders are recognizing that it has a genuine investment value. The increased output of energy, the happier spirits, greater endurance, and greater ease and pleasure with which tasks are accomplished, more than compensate for the investment of time and money." The popular sports leagues have continued to the present day.

Irving T. Bush, president of the Bush Terminal, provided the Brooklyn Association with "amply equipped, very attractive" rooms for a YMCA program in the

Terminal's Building 20 at fortieth Street and Second Avenue. For $3 a year, employees of any Bush Terminal Company could enjoy music, games, entertainments, socials and company nights. The YMCA offered a room and board directory listing homes in the neighborhood for workers who needed lodging, and four handball courts, gym classes and baseball leagues for individual recreation, company teams and athletic meets. For self-improvement it provided appropriate reading matter, vocational talks and the option of attending classes in commercial and mechanical subjects at other YMCAs. A special "Course in Personal Efficiency" promised to help members "learn to manage yourself with the same foresight and acumen as though you were a bank or a factory." Bush spoke to fellow businessmen of "turning over our welfare work" to the Association and encouraged them to do likewise.

The Brooklyn Association established a Branch for workers at the Bush Terminal Company.

The Brooklyn Association also mobilized hundreds of college men to fan out to factories and teach English under YMCA leadership. The organization hoped that engineering students would eventually be employed by factories where they would engage in "larger efforts for industrial betterment," according to Rindge, who predicted the advent of "human engineering," or human relations, in industry.

Promoting Progress

WITH IMMIGRANTS AND Americans alike, the Associations clearly perceived their role as elevating workers and also ensuring a stable and productive labor force. The YMCA hoped to promote progress by helping the city's employers to mold loyal and willing workers without strife and rebellion among the rank and file at a time when labor reform movements were gaining power. In taking on this role, the YMCA found itself in the middle of a dilemma. It professed a mission of helping all men to improve their lives, in body, mind and spirit, but its leadership was composed of some of the city's most powerful capitalists and industrialists. The aims of business leaders were quite different: to hold down labor costs and prevent what they feared would be anarchy if workers agitated for better conditions and pay. "The Association is identified with the capitalistic regime," declared the *New Republic* in 1918. "If it had antagonized American capital it would long ago have gone out of business."

In one difficult instance of loyalty, the West Side YMCA had supplied strikebreakers to a printing establishment, Schweinler Company on Hudson Street, in 1926. An editorial in the *New York Call* chastised the YMCA for furnishing "scabs" to break the strike at the printing establishment where seventy-five "flyboys" were demanding a weekly minimum wage of $12. An institution supported by "plutocratic patrons," the *Call* surmised, "can be expected to do their will." Members of the Railroad Branches sometimes were at loggerheads with Association secretaries over strikes. Striking members expected the YMCA to uphold them. Over time, YMCA staffs generally were supportive of workers' demands for industrial and social reform.

Such was the dilemma of the age, and the YMCA's predicament. The Protestant work ethic, whose proponents like Beecher and Moody viewed poverty and failure as tantamount to sin, had played a vital role in creating a successful industrial machine. In turn, industry relied on low-cost labor to maintain its dominance. Great amounts of capital were accumulating in these industries as they merged into powerful corporations, fabulously enriching their backers. The workers, however, continued to put in long hours for low wages. It was little wonder that laborers felt alienated from conventional Christian institutions and were inclined to put their faith instead in workers' unions.

Certainly, there were Protestants who were critical of this new industrial society and its ills; through the Social Gospel movement that arose in the nineteenth century, they sought to alleviate suffering among the lower classes. The horrors culminated in the 1911 Triangle Shirtwaist factory fire where 146 workers—mainly young immigrant girls—jumped to their deaths or perished in heat and flames. But while the YMCA engaged in a certain amount of relief work, it was never considered to be the Association's primary mission.

COLUMBUS, O., *Dispatch*

DR. GLADDEN—" You can't mix them, John, you can't mix them."

The YMCAs in New York City found their comfort level in matching would-be workers with employers. As Brooklyn's General Secretary Cook stated, "The Association is not only working for the members, it is setting members to work." In 1904, the Employment Department of his Association proudly reported placing 878 men and boys in jobs paying an average weekly salary of $6.

"When [the YMCA] has gone into industrial communities, it has, as a rule, entered by the door of the general manager's office," Ernest Hamlin Abbott wrote in *The Outlook* in 1919. But in a country concerned with coal and steel strikes, and a growing radicalism among its workers, said Abbott, the YMCA should work for democracy and the "exercise of the spirit of Christianity in industrial relations as well as in all others."

Neither the New York nor Brooklyn YMCAs could afford to alienate the captains of commerce among their leadership, who also brought their influential friends to the cause. A 1905 article in *World's Work,* "Our Financial Oligarchy," listed the seventy-six men who made up the U.S. "Business Senate," controlling and financing major industries. They included such YMCA benefactors as J. Pierpont Morgan; William K. Vanderbilt; John D. Rockefeller (the "richest man in the world"); and Morris K. Jesup, then president of the New York Chamber of Commerce. Russell Sage, who "commands more ready money than any other capitalist," would leave that fortune to his widow, who directed a good portion of it to the YMCA. The author observed that a number of these men were vying for dominance of the transcontinental railroad system, one of the most cherished prizes of the Industrial Age.

Labor reform movements were gathering force, and New York was a center of strike activity.

Broadening the
YMCA's Transport Work

THE NEW YORK Railroad YMCAs, initiated so successfully under Cornelius Vanderbilt II's leadership in 1875, had grown enormously, spreading from Manhattan and the Bronx to Brooklyn and Queens. The national YMCA, invited by railway companies to establish Branches at their expense, was operating 150 of them with 37,000 members by the turn of the century. In 1901, J.M. Dudley, national secretary for work among streetcar employees, also organized a Brooklyn Rapid Transit Railroad Branch. Installed in 1903 at the corner of Jamaica Avenue and Gillen Place, this work reverted to the company after a few years.

The Associations regarded work among railway workers as a high calling. In 1901, the Y publication *Brooklyn Men and their Doings* noted that the "railroad men of this country form one of most important classes of the population. . . a good-sized army, one million of them." The YMCA had a critical role to play in shaping this workforce to the advantage of their employers and the nation's rail travelers. "Great consequences to the corporations and to the public depend upon the steadiness, sobriety, morality and fidelity of these men," the article

J.M. Dudley organized a Branch for streetcar employees.

warned. The Railroad Ys also ensured that the men would make it to work by giving them a wake-up call.

One of the largest programs was based in Long Island City, in a building erected and supported by the Long Island Rail Road (LIRR). Its dorms, lunch room, reading and game rooms were "used to the limit." In 1908, the Brooklyn Association constructed a $150,000 railway building in Long Island City, which continued there until 1933 when it was condemned for a railroad tunnel; operations moved to Jamaica Station for five more years. As it happened, Association board member Charles M. Pratt Jr., senior partner in Charles Pratt and Company, was also vice president of the LIRR.

In 1911 the Pennsylvania Railroad YMCA, which had operated as a Branch with a residence since 1900, opened rooms in the Pennsylvania Terminal, a year after station operations commenced on Seventh Avenue and Thirty-Third Street. This Branch also maintained an annex at the Sunnyside Yards building in Long Island City.

Trainmen stopping over in New York could always count on the Railroad YMCAs for a warm place to sleep, good food in clean surroundings, and plenty of opportunity for recreation and camaraderie. But this population of men was one of the most difficult for the

Brooklyn Rapid Transit workers had their own reading room.

The Long Island City Rail Road Branch occupied the Brodel House in 1900.

Trainmen enjoyed recreation and exercise at the Grand Central Branch during their stopovers in New York City.

YMCA to handle. Railway workers didn't like Bible study, and challenged the Association's somewhat hostile attitude toward clubhouse games. While checkers, chess, and parlor croquet were approved activities at the Railroad Ys, billiards were not, since they were closely linked with drinking and gambling. But railway members eventually won, forcing an acceptance not only of billiards but of smoking rooms and bowling alleys in their YMCAs.

Another transport sector the YMCA served was the shipping industry. In 1920, the New York Association established a Merchant Seamen's Branch on West Twenty-Third Street at Tenth Avenue, aiming to reach one of the most transient populations of young men and boys. When they were in a strange port, these young men could

New York YMCA secretaries greeted merchant seamen aboard their ships.

depend on the YMCA for dormitory beds, a cafeteria and comfortable places to meet their friends, write letters and enjoy program activities, especially athletics. "At Home" hours on Sunday evenings and Wednesday afternoons were staffed by women of the Branch Social Committee.

Thrift was emphasized, given the many temptations for seamen to squander their wages in this port city. The area along the waterfront and the Branch vicinity was "infested" with 445 houses of ill repute and "speak-easies" after Prohibition in 1920. Sailors were urged to save and to deposit their savings with a bank paying them 5 to 6 percent interest. Again, the YMCA ventured into employment, acting as matchmaker for some fifteen steamship companies by placing 300 to 400 men every month on their ships.

The Branch also concerned itself with bellhops and deck-boys. Special activities for these boys included at-home hours, theater parties, afternoon teas, and educational trips. "The problem of the sea boy is the largest one this Association has to face," Branch officials stated. "Great numbers of these boys have no fathers and frequently no mothers. They are largely the byproduct of orphanages which, because of their lack of funds, find it cheaper to place them in sea service than to keep them on land. These boys are allowed to wander at large (when ashore) with no definite plans for their spare time. They pal with older men and frequent houses of ill repute along the water front."

By 1925, daily attendance at the Merchant Seaman's YMCA mounted to 1,100, far too many for the building's capacity. Many seafarers were turned away from the sixty-bed dormitory; the kitchen could only serve 100 meals daily, and programs accommodated just 200. "Men are nightly refused hospitality because of lack of sleeping quarters and the building is often too crowded for comfort," noted the annual report.

Brooklyn established its Bethelship Seamen's Branch in 1918 on Sullivan Street, carrying on work begun there in 1844 for Scandinavian seaman by the Bethel Ship Norwegian Methodist Episcopal Church. The YMCA remodeled the existing building and in 1922 added a new six-story brick structure on the site. The new edifice offered ninety-five bedrooms, a restaurant, a gym with a stage for entertainments, mail service, and a trust fund. This YMCA served more than 1,000 seamen of all nationalities annually until 1948.

Seamen could catch up on the news from home in the reading room of the Brooklyn Seamen's Branch.

Relief Efforts and War Work

THE YMCA HAD performed relief work since its inception, but outside of war work had not created a department dedicated to those efforts. Social service to the disadvantaged was never seen as the primary mission of the Association. The 1926 New York annual report emphasized that the YMCA was "not primarily for welfare work, charity or reform; not for abnormals or subnormals."

However, YMCA volunteers had long done their share in this domain. One, S. J. Wertheimer, had worked since 1884 with boys in prisons who had landed there due to "bad companions and also in living beyond their means." Over more than two decades, Wertheimer

involved numerous young YMCA members on these visits to help the imprisoned boys. Other charitable efforts, such as the Brooklyn Central Branch's Thanksgiving and Christmas dinners for 100 poor families, were not uncommon. In the depression of 1875, the YMCA collected cast-off clothing to give to the needy.

Before the turn of the century, New York Association relief work centered on the Bowery Branch, located in the epicenter of New York's downtrodden and destitute since 1872, in a series of rented rooms. By 1903 the Branch was ready to erect its own large building. It would provide small, comfortable rooms at nominal cost, "principally to meet the need of the young man of limited means and provide a congenial home and helpful influences which would counteract the evil effects of the cheap lodging houses." A quiet campaign for $400,000 succeeded, and enabled the purchase of a site at 8-10 East Third Street in 1910. Five years later William Fellowes Morgan, Association President, laid the cornerstone of the new Bowery Branch.

At the opening, the *New York Times* reported that the completely fireproof 300-bed "hotel" was "full of light and fresh air" and noted some intriguing novelties: an electric potato peeler, telephones on every floor, washing machines, a resident doctor and a physical trainer. In the basement a fumigating plant treated each newly arrived man's garments, which were washed, pressed and mended while he slept to assure him "good appearance for his future employer."

As at all Branches, helping young men find jobs was paramount, and the new Bowery YMCA instituted a job placement service. As long as men there were unemployed, however, they could utilize a clever credit system. Once they were vetted for admission, residents could sign for all services and pay for them once they had secured employment. Lodgings, in dormitories or private rooms, cost 25 cents per day. A self-service dining room provided free meals for the jobless; behind a glass partition was another dining room for the employed, where waiters served meals for a tab of 10 to 15 cents. The *Times* observed that this YMCA was for all "who are having hard luck"—professional men as well as unskilled laborers and immigrants—"regardless of their past, creed or color." Nor did their religion matter: By 1930, 46 percent were Protestants, 42 percent Catholics, and 8.5 percent Jewish.

The 1920 law prohibiting alcohol sales did not address all ills on the Bowery; in that year, the Branch counseled 2,000 drug addicts. Even so, they did not represent the

New York Association relief efforts had been focused on the Bowery Branch, which occupied a new building (right) on East 3rd Street in 1915.

majority of men served by the YMCA. In 1921, the Bowery Branch accommodated 6,000 men in its $286,000 operation, 96 percent of which was financed by the men themselves.

After the Spanish-American War, the YMCA International Committee had decided to make army-navy work a permanent program. The Association considered itself the most effective volunteer agency in linking churches and communities with the military in order to "to diminish at all points the abuses and evils of army life."

The Brooklyn Association established its Army Branch in 1899 at Fort Hamilton. This YMCA operated in an overcrowded building in "pernicious environs... the city vices and allurements follow the soldiers, but few of its opportunities for improvement," noted its annual report. When the program began, one soldier reportedly said: "Glad you have come; I'm sick of the saloon." The New York Association opened its Army Branch on Governors' Island in the same year, and William E. Dodge Jr. later gave $5,000 for a 1927 Georgian-style building. In 1928 it was named the Fort Jay Army Branch; in 1941 it would merge with the Fort Slocum Army Branch in New Rochelle, New York, as the Governor's Island Branch. The New York YMCA also initiated army work at Fort Wadsworth on Staten Island in 1900, which continued until 1918.

The New York Association opened its Army Branch on Governors Island in 1899, where soldiers could relax with a game of billiards.

The New York YMCA's army work extended to Fort Slocum in New Rochelle, NY.

Responding to the Navy's request for the YMCA to continue its work in peacetime, the Brooklyn Navy YMCA opened in 1899 near the Brooklyn Navy Yard, in rented quarters at 167 Sands Street. Under direction of the International Committee, it was the first permanent Branch of the Navy YMCA, and remained its bulwark for sixty-six years. "It provides the men ashore, on liberty, with a safe refuge from the land shark, and a harbor where he can bid defiance to his worst foes," one speaker noted. "Its door swings wide open to him, but closes tight to the leeches that fatten on his blood." The Port was rife with "hazards of the day—the saloons, the 'con' artists, the temptations that lure a young sailor down the prim-rose path." The YMCA stepped up to protect them.

Cleveland H. Dodge and John D. Rockefeller Sr. were significant contributors to work for military men, with Dodge encouraging the YMCA and American Red Cross to cooperate in serving them. Rear-Admiral John W. Philip, Commandant of the Brooklyn Navy Yard and a member of the YMCA International Committee, also recruited a group of wealthy New York women, forming a Ladies' Auxiliary of the International Committee to raise funds. Among them, Miss Helen Miller Gould gave land and $500,000 to erect a handsome YMCA at the Navy Yard in memory of her late mother and father. Opened in 1902, the seven-story edifice was one of the largest ever constructed for YMCA purposes, with all the conveniences of a club. It comprised 200 bedrooms, four dormitories, an auditorium, pool, banking facilities, and a roof garden.

Opening ceremonies were attended by the Secretary of the Navy; various admirals; William Sloane, who chaired the national YMCA's Army and Navy Department Committee; Miss Gould; Mrs. E.A. McAlpin, Auxiliary president; and Mrs. Russell Sage, first vice president.

Miss Gould, who brought magazines and other literature on the dedication day, was the first to dine in the new building's restaurant, partaking of "probably her first and only ten-cent meal," observed the YMCA's *Armed Services News*. Sailors paid nominal fees for stays there, and average daily attendance was 420 in the first year. The facility was often overcrowded; sometimes air mattresses had to be used in hallways and other available spaces. In 1905, Miss Gould made another gift of $10,000 so the Branch could purchase the adjoining building and add fifty-four beds.

Mrs. Sage donated $350,000 for the extension, dedicated in 1909, which doubled the capacity of the plant at the Brooklyn Navy Yard and added a gymnasium. Margaret

Sailors turned away temptation with wholesome pursuits at the Navy YMCA, such as writing letters on Mother's Day.

Miss Helen Miller Gould financed a seven-story Navy YMCA building on Sands Street in Brooklyn, which was dedicated in 1902.

Sage was the second wife of Russell Sage, partner of Jay Gould. Sage was a great capitalist and a notorious skinflint, but Mrs. Sage changed that. The former teacher began giving away his millions around 1890 and became a prominent philanthropist after his death in 1906, when her inheritance of $75 million reputedly made her the world's wealthiest woman and the city's single largest taxpayer. Miss Helen Gould and Cleveland H. Dodge were directors of the Sage Foundation, established in 1907 to help Mrs. Sage handle up to 900 requests per day. Mrs. Sage also gave $85,000 to the Long Island City YMCA.

The Brooklyn Navy YMCA became a hub of great activity in World War I. Led by the now-married Helen Gould Shepard, a committee of 100 volunteer women staffed the mail room and provided supper daily for fifty men. In 1917, when the New York Naval Militia, Second Battalion, was sent to guard the three East River bridges, it used the Brooklyn Navy Y as its headquarters. By the time of its closing in 1964, when Defense Secretary Robert McNamara shut down the Brooklyn Navy Yard, this YMCA had served an estimated 47 million military personnel with its plant and services.

When World War I began in Europe, the YMCA jumped in—well before the United States declared war. Calling on its experience in addressing human needs in two earlier wars, plus its peacetime Army-Navy program, the U.S. government asked the national YMCA to undertake a massive war work effort on behalf of its forces. Eventually the YMCA conducted 90 percent of welfare work among American enlisted forces in Europe. It ministered to 19 million Allied soldiers and helped more than 5 million prisoners of war on all fronts. The national YMCA established 1,500 canteens and 4,000 respite huts, and eventually raised $235 million in public support for fighting men. The Association also provided 80,000 educational scholarships to war veterans, which became the basis for design of the G.I. Bill after World War II. A New York army sergeant, Irving Berlin, commemorated the Y's contributions in a song composed during his military service—"I Can Always Find a Little Sunshine in the YMCA."

The YMCA's work in World War I focused on the welfare and morale of uniformed men by providing rest and recreational (R&R) activities, troop education, canteens and overseas exchanges. A YMCA Eagle Hut for servicemen opened in 1918 in Manhattan's Bryant Park. Building on what it started for troops in the Spanish-

Sgt. Irving Berlin commemorated YMCA war work in his 1918 song.

The YMCA staffed 4,000 respite huts in World War I, including one in Manhattan's Bryant Park.

American conflict, the YMCA provided even more overseas entertainment during the Great War. New York Association member William Sloane retired temporarily from the Sloane family carpet firm to chair the YMCA War Council, and Cleveland H. Dodge served as its treasurer. Sloane, at the time in his early 40s, was well qualified since he had chaired the International Committee's Army and Navy Committee for fifteen years. He spearheaded fund raising of $3 million for YMCA buildings in military camps. In one month New York raised $1,090,000 of that total and Sloane quickly determined to raise another million, putting muscle to the YMCA's slogan "Follow the boys that follow the flag."

The New York Association raised more than $1 million for YMCA work during World War I, primarily for troops overseas.

Before the War the Brooklyn Association had been expanding its services to all classes of the population, while wondering how it could maintain its leadership in a declining Protestant community. World War I provided a distraction from this burning issue, as the Association stepped up services both abroad and at home. Brooklyn leaders had recommended creation of the YMCA War Work Council at a national meeting in Long Island, which would provide direct services to prisoners of war and men in training camps overseas. Now the Association accelerated efforts with Brooklyn men working nearby in the war industries, and supported a war secretary at a military base in Pharr, Texas.

U.S. troops in Brooklyn enjoyed free use of Branch buildings, where they partook of social and recreational programs like billiards and bowling. Some 10,000 recruits also found lodging there; when beds were full, cots were set up for them. Soldiers who were not Y members could freely use the gyms, pools and showers, and, for 5 cents, could obtain soap and towels. Brooklyn YMCA enlisted men benefited from extended memberships without dues for the duration of World War I; more than 20 percent of its senior membership was in the service.

YMCA staff made "doughnuts for doughboys" in France.

Military personnel were welcomed at New York and Brooklyn YMCAs during and after their service.

Some 250 Brooklyn members worked in overseas YMCA programs. At four army work sites—Forts Totten, Tilden, Hamilton, and Camp Bliss—work was stepped up considerably and additional books and periodicals brought in. New buildings were planned for Fort Totten and Fort Jay. Unlike the Navy YMCA, overseen by the International Committee, these Army YMCAs were all under leadership of the local Associations. Brooklyn's General Secretary Cook worked full-time leading YMCA fund-raising efforts for war work in the Middle Atlantic States—the national goal was $35 million—and a number of other Brooklyn secretaries worked full time in the war effort.

The Bronx Union YMCA took part in Three Liberty Loans and allowed the Red Cross to set up headquarters in the Branch for sixteen months. The Branch served thousands of uniformed men coming through New York, and raised funds to provide a respite hut and a secretary to work among prisoners of war in Europe.

The YMCA's International Committee also supplied a New Yorker as its leader in the national effort. John R. Mott, an outstanding figure in relief work with prisoners of war in various countries, was appointed general secretary of the YMCA's new National War Work Council in 1917. Mott had led the Intercollegiate YMCA for twenty-seven years following his student involvement at Cornell University and founded the World's Student Christian Federation.

The "Y," a nickname that caught on during the war, was not invulnerable to criticism for its efforts. Ironically, in its successful appeals to the nation for support, it had both enhanced its power and public image and exposed its evangelical underpinnings to closer scrutiny. The YMCA's continued insistence on evangelical ties in its officers was beginning to hamper its work. The government, despite the YMCA's magnificent war efforts, could hardly sanction keeping work in the hands of an overtly religious organization.

In 1919, the YMCA was withdrawn from the U.S. Department of War and every army camp and center. The military assumed responsibility for human services for its forces, patterning its program and activities on the YMCA's pioneering work. However, there were questions about the Association's religious and gender exclusions and, in some cases, narrow-minded staff. In this new day for democracy, the YMCA would have to rethink its requirements for personnel.

One more voice raised for diversity in the YMCA came from *The New Republic* in 1918. The magazine noted that the YMCA "emerges from the war the dominant religious force in American society. It has met a great emergency magnificently." It also expressed the hope that the Y could lead America out of the "confusions and pettinesses of American religious sectarianism" toward a "larger religious unity." The magazine called for the YMCA to play an inclusive role in community building for the post-war era: "There are women and children and old men. There is family life to be fostered. The home is to be rebuilt as the security of our civilization," the publication declared. "A sectional agency cannot lead in that task. It must be an agency as broad in its sympathies as the whole people, and it must think with the mind of the whole people."

By the late 1920s, the YMCA was challenged as

never before to keep pace with the changes in society. In 1919, women had gained the right to vote, after decades of passionate struggle, and were asserting themselves as never before in public life. Around 1920, in the Great Migration, thousands of African Americans began moving from the Jim Crow South to what they hoped would be better opportunities and quality of life in northern cities. That same year the prohibition era began, handing

YMCA programs a great opportunity to replace the cheerfulness and camaraderie of saloons. The New York Association opened a lunchroom in a former saloon on West Twenty-Ninth Street, and the Brooklyn YMCA operated a "temperance bar." After a decade of punch-drunk prosperity, the eventful period would end with a startling stock market crash in 1929, the prelude to the Great Depression of the 1930s.

Well Done Men
America Greets
YOU
YMCA

STATUE OF LIBERTY, NEW YORK CITY

tatue of Liberty on Bedloe's Island in New York ay 1¼ miles from the Battery, a colossal figure of iberty enlightening the World. It lights the harbor ith an electric torch held 306 feet above the water, he highest beacon in the world. Was presented to merica by the French nation.

Brooklyn and Queens Association Branches, 1929

Camp Bliss
Bay Ridge, Fourth Avenue and Senator Street
Bedford, 1121 Bedford Avenue
Brooklyn Navy, 167 Sands Street
Bush Terminal, Fortieth Street and Second Avenue
Central, Hanson Place (between South Elliott and Fort Greene Places)
Carlton Branch, 405 Carlton Avenue
Eastern District, 179 Marcy Avenue
Flatbush, Church and Kenmore Avenues
Greenpoint, 99 Meserole Avenue
Highland Park (formerly Twenty-Sixth Ward), 570 Jamaica Avenue
Bethelship Seamen's, 56 Sullivan Street
New Utrecht, 1841 84th Street
Prospect Park, 357 Ninth Street
Central Queens, 89-25 Parsons Boulevard, Queens
Flushing, 138-46 Northern Boulevard, Queens
Long Island City, 41-23 Academy Street, Queens
Long Island Rail Road, Long Island City, Queens

New York Association Branches, 1929

Bowery, 8-10 East Third Street
Bronx Union, 470 East 161st Street
East Side (formerly Yorkville), 153 East Eighty-Sixth Street
Intercollegiate Branch, 55 Washington Square
Merchant Seamen's, 525 West Twenty-Third Street
135th Street Branch, 181 West 135th Street
Pennsylvania Railroad Branch: Penn Terminal; Sunnyside Yards, Long Island City
Railroad Branch, 309 Park Avenue
Second Avenue (formerly German), 142 Second Avenue
Twenty-Third Street Branch, 215 West Twenty-Third Street
Wall Street Boys' Branch, 24 Broad Street
West Side, 316 West Fifty-Seventh Street; dormitory annex, West Fifty-Sixth Street

4

1930-1960

A Time of Taking Stock

THE YEARS FOLLOWING the Great War were challenging ones for the two Associations in New York. The stock market crash and ensuing Great Depression brought misery on a grand scale to the city. Prayer revivals were no longer the panaceas for New Yorkers' pain, as they had been during hard economic times of the nineteenth century. By 1931, city churches were increasingly turning to the Bowery YMCA to handle their share of relief for homeless men. That year the Branch served 1,345,000 meals in its restaurants and provided 144,540 lodging nights. The Bowery Y was not just giving hand-outs, however; it managed to secure jobs for more than 1,500 men. In this very difficult time, some of the largest YMCA buildings also opened, symbols of progress for a crestfallen city.

For many years the Bowery YMCA had been an important charity in New York. Indeed, it was deemed the "Ritz-Carlton of lodging houses." But changes brought about by the New Deal undercut and even supplanted its mission. Having lost business in its restaurant and 5-cent cafeteria to government food programs, the Branch was running a $75,000 annual deficit by 1938. Its room rentals were also declining, a result of lower demand on the now less densely populated Lower East Side. The public had grown less inclined to support mission-style services for the poor, preferring to fund hospital and medical services and advanced education. "Nobody likes to pay for a dead horse," a Branch memo noted. The Bowery Branch revived somewhat during the war years. In 1940 its Penny Cafeteria, opened with help from the New York Community Trust, served more than 9,000 meals in its first week of operation, and nearly 50,000 the first month, but the Branch closed for good after World War II.

The New York City YMCAs were also coming face to face with a challenging new spirit of freedom, self-government and social justice sweeping through society and industry. As the YMCA's early evangelical emphasis, once considered the "very life-blood of its existence"

Breadlines were common in the city during the Great Depression.

Homeless men could find clean, comfortable lodgings at the Bowery Branch during the Depression.

The Bowery YMCA served more than one million meals in 1931, at an average cost of 9 cents each.

develop a ten-to fifteen-year comprehensive improvement plan.

In 1926, the New York YMCA Board hired Professor Arthur L. Swift Jr. of Union Theological Seminary to direct an extensive survey of its growth since 1880. Board members personally footed the $45,000 bill for the project, which consumed a year and a half. The "Swift survey," as it was known, was the first of its kind ever conducted by the Association and would influence its work for decades to come. The blue-ribbon survey committee included eminent men such as George D. Strayer, chairman; Galen M. Fisher, of the Institute of Social and Religious Research; Shelby M. Harrison, of the Russell Sage Foundation; and Herbert N. Shenton, a Columbia University social scientist. Cleveland E. Dodge, now president of the Association Board of Directors, following in his father's footsteps, and Walter T. Diack, its general secretary, served as ex-officio members.

By design, the survey report focused more on the Association's problems than its strong points, but it observed that the YMCA's social assets exceeded its liabilities: "Its effect upon the community is beneficial and sufficiently great in value." The major constructive finding was that the YMCA's activities were not focused enough on meeting community needs, nor were its relationships with other organizations clearly articulated.

John D. Rockefeller and his son, known as "Mr. Junior," were pivotal figures in funding the YMCA building boom of the 1920s and 1930s, but imposed certain conditions.

according to President Howard Crosby, gave way to a social service orientation, the YMCA was urged to become more of a community builder. This was a logical time to take stock of YMCA work and its effectiveness in New York City, and to reconsider its course for the future. A powerful philanthropist effectively brought that about by his demand for long-range planning from the Associations—none other than John D. Rockefeller Jr.

Rockefeller's father had been famously intense, requiring thorough analysis in his many business dealings. He held charities to the same exacting standards, examining their purposes, programs and value before agreeing to fund them. In 1924 the New York Association had approached John D. Rockefeller Jr., who was directing his father's philanthropic activities, to help with an ambitious building program it was crafting. True to his father, Rockefeller suggested that Association leaders

THE YMCA AT 150

The current program consisted mainly of physical and educational work, and the provision of living accommodations. Those three areas, the report stated, were "almost entirely unrelated to each other." Furthermore, the YMCA was operating like an aggregation of Branches rather than a thoroughly integrated organization.

The Swift report suggested that the Association analyze more precisely its position and function in the community and reinterpret its aims for the future. Its current membership was too highly concentrated in men over age 25, the average term of membership was less than two years and most members participated in only one activity. Single men made up 75 percent of the membership, and two-thirds were involved mainly in the physical work program. Members were, on average, 30 years old; 63 percent of them were over age 25. The largest occupational category was "low-paid white collar workers" (clerks, salesmen, office workers) at 37 percent, with mechanics, artisans and machinists next at 18 percent of the total. Despite the YMCA's avowed interest in their involvement, boys accounted for only 12 percent of membership.

Swift recommended that the YMCA's priority should be young men between 16 and 30, helping them to adjust to the city and to develop a balanced personality with a keen sense of social responsibility—in short, a program of personal guidance for individual young men. It also suggested "early and extensive cooperation" with the YWCA to bring women into its work.

The Swift report concluded that the Association's spontaneous, sometimes confusing growth and overlapping programs and authority had hindered its efforts and efficiency. But it acknowledged that the dislocations of World War I and the city's stunning population increases, averaging 31 percent in each decade surveyed, had compounded this confusion: "No wonder the YMCA lost its breath in its efforts to keep up with that frantic pace. There was no time to stop and think where it was going, when the expanding field called with such relentless insistence for immediate action on all sides. To anybody who knows New York City that state of mind ought to be familiar enough."

With the Swift survey as its guide, the New York Association took a number of steps that set the pace for remarkable changes in the 1930s and beyond. It began to professionalize and train staff and to focus on group work in its programs. It would develop a program focus on youth as that age segment came to dominate the population. But the lasting legacy of the Swift survey, and the leaders who implemented its recommendations, would be the remarkable YMCA building expansion it inspired in New York City.

[?]AL ACTIVITIES . .

TEN CENTERS

[cl]asses enrolled 2,015 dif-
[ferent] in practical, technical,
[p]opular subjects. Reading
[?]es, educational lectures
[?]s were provided for addi-
[?]ls.

SOCIAL ACTIVITIES . .

TWENTY-TWO C[ENTERS]

Each *weekday* 2,905 young peo[ple]
[?] [ac]tivities, includi[ng]
[?]l events and
[?]ls and other
[?]nt for young [people]

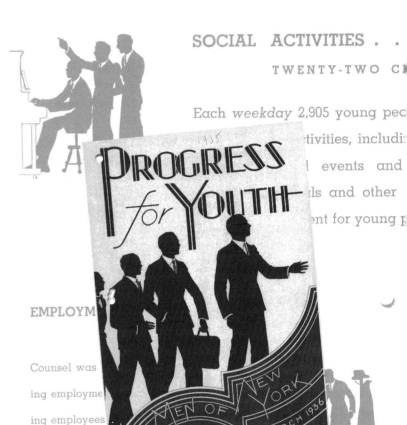

EMPLOYM[ENT]

Counsel was [?]
ing employme[nt] [?]
ing employees [?]
16,537 plac[ed] [?]
30,410 seamen reassigned to ships

*The New York Association touted
its youth programs in 1936.*

PHYSICAL EDUCATION

TEN CE[NTERS]

An average of 2,716 men and bo[ys]
[par]ticipated *each week day* in gym[nasium]
classes, swimming, boxing, wr[estling]
handball, volleyball and ind[oor]
workouts.

The Second Building Boom

DESPITE THE RAPID erection of YMCA buildings in the late nineteenth and early twentieth centuries, most were now inadequate in light of New York City's ever-increasing population. By the 1920s both the New York and Brooklyn and Queens Associations had outgrown their facilities. Most buildings were too small and equipment was worn out and obsolete. To keep pace with community needs, the Associations sought funds to expand. The 1920s were a very prosperous decade in New York, and the time seemed right to mount building campaigns. Thus President Dodge approached Rockefeller for funding and agreed to his prerequisite survey, which provided the Association with a detailed blueprint for action.

The survey's recommendations regarding buildings were quite specific: replace the YMCA on Fifty-Seventh Street with a modern plant in the same area; greatly enlarge the 135th Street building currently serving only "colored" men; thoroughly renovate the Bronx Union and Bowery Branch buildings. Work should be discontinued at the East Side Branch on Eighty-Sixth Street and the Harlem Y on 125th Street; these buildings should be sold as soon as membership could be transferred to other YMCAs. The Young Men's Institute Branch and the French Branch, Swift concluded, should also cease work and the properties be sold within five years. Remarkably, the survey advised building a community YMCA on the West Side near Fourteenth Street, to address needs and special opportunities in downtown New York. (In 2003, the McBurney YMCA will finally fulfill that suggestion by opening a Branch facility in a new complex on West Fourteenth Street.)

Heeding most of the report's recommendations, the New York Association began raising money for its vast

construction program in 1926, laying out its plans in a booklet entitled "Give Boys a Chance... Modernize the New York YMCA." The appeal stated upfront that the "organization that builds character by direction rather than by repression... is seeking to enlarge and improve its facilities so that many more thousands of the 'youth which lives alone' can find cheerful surroundings, healthful activities and true companionship."

Some 100,000 young men per year, it said, came to the New York YMCA looking for "the home they have left behind. Just as many are turned away, due to lack of accommodations." Playing to current concerns, the appeal noted that 28 percent of these young men were foreign born, and mentioned the past decade's "crime wave," alluding to the younger age of criminals. The YMCA had not made a pitch for buildings since 1913, it noted, and New York City had made tremendous strides since then. The Association was "seriously incapacitated" by the demands of strained, worn, antiquated and meager facilities but was nevertheless was doing its

The Association's capital campaign appeal, "Give the Boys a Chance... Modernize New York's Y.M.C.A.," stressed that "live-wire American boys" needed guidance in finding good wholesome fun in order to become "the guiding minds of the city."

best to mold young men into the type of which the city could be proud. The appeal closed by emphasizing the YMCA's character-building work, a tenet popularized by the new field of educational psychology.

The Association's request focused on five new buildings, not all of which were emphasized in the Swift survey. The Merchant Seamen's Branch needed to be modernized; 1,000 mostly foreign seamen and cabin boys signed in each week for recreation at the outmoded facility. Each day, 30 arriving vessels at the West Side docks deposited thousands of seamen, who stayed in the city on average six days. The Bowery Branch needed an overhaul, having borne "hard wear due to its intensive use and overcrowded condition." The West Side YMCA had turned away 167 young men seeking dormitory rooms in just one day. Its land was worth a great deal, but 25 percent of the building was wasted space. The Association proposed to sell it and build a $3.25 million home that would accommodate a record 10,000 members.

The YMCA proposed another colossal Branch in the Pennsylvania Terminal area, primarily to serve the thousands of soldiers, sailors and marines who came through midtown. To be called the William Sloane

Memorial, in honor of the Army YMCA's late champion and well-known furniture merchant, the building would also provide a temporary home for 100,000 civilian young men and boys seeking their fortunes in the city each year. Its Army-Navy clubrooms, cafeteria and 1,600 sleeping rooms would cost $3 million to build.

Finally, the brochure appealed for funding for "one of the liveliest and healthiest of the branches," the 135th Street YMCA for "colored men and boys," which it described as "suffering under the strain of its success." The Association proposed a $750,000 addition that would double its housing capacity to 192 dormitory rooms and provide better exercise and social facilities.

New York's President Dodge wrote to Rockefeller in 1926, formally requesting his contribution before publicly launching the building campaign. But Rockefeller demurred, saying that the Association had not had time to adopt and implement the new policies suggested by the survey that he thought necessary.

The 1,600-bed Sloane House, opened at the outset of the Depression, accommodated thousands of service men and transients.

The Dodge Dynasty

O ne New York family has figured more prominently than any other in the formation and continuation of the YMCA of Greater New York. Descendants of **William Dodge** (above left), a young man of modest means from Connecticut who built a business in New York City, have been continuously associated with the Association's lay leadership since its inception in the city. The family is well known and respected for its important public philanthropy, including the Metropolitan Museum of Art, the Museum of Natural History, Teachers College of Columbia University, and many other causes. **Reverend Theodore L. Cuyler**, a founder of the Brooklyn YMCA, called the Dodge family "the most illustrious in the religious history of New York." Over the years, the family has generously and consistently supported YMCA endeavors, providing $1 million for a Youth Trust Fund in 1992 and $2 million a decade later for a much-needed YMCA in Brooklyn.

William E. Dodge Jr. (above right) set the standard for YMCA lay leadership in New York and the nation. He reorganized and revitalized the New York Association after the Civil War. Twice its president (1866–72; 1875–77), and an advisor to the International Committee for 36 years, William Dodge Jr. was the leading proponent of adding "physical" as the fourth dimension of the YMCA program. He was pivotal in financing the first YMCA building in 1869, and the Association's revival meetings featuring Dwight Moody and Ira Sankey. William Dodge Jr. presided over the YMCA's American Jubilee Celebration in 1901. Whenever funds were needed locally or nationally for the YMCA, this unfaltering supporter could always be counted upon.

William Junior's sons, **William "Earl" III** and **Cleveland H.** (below left), organized the YMCA at Princeton University in 1876 and took the Student Volunteer Movement to other colleges. Cleveland H. Dodge was elected president of the New York Association and served from 1890–1903, then as chairman of its Executive Committee for many years. (Earl died in 1886 from typhoid fever.)

William Fellowes Morgan, a member of the New York Association Board since 1886, assumed its presidency from 1903–19. Morgan's daughter Pauline was married to Cleveland E. Dodge, son of Cleveland H. Dodge. She was a benefactor of both the YMCA and the YWCA.

Cleveland E. Dodge (below right) followed his father and father-in-law in serving as New York Association president, from 1925–35, and presided over the Association's largest period of growth through construction of new Branch buildings. A major leader and benefactor, he was elected honorary chairman for life of the YMCA of Greater New York in 1963. He chaired the International Committee of YMCAs from 1935–60, and later its Executive Committee. Through the Dodge Foundation, his charitable initiative, the YMCA has been munificently supported over the years. Cleveland E. Dodge was the first recipient of the Order of the Red Triangle, the Association's highest award for volunteer leaders.

Alfred H. Howell, whose wife Ruth was a Dodge family member, served on the YMCA Board of Directors for many years, and was chairman from 1963-66. Howell, a recipient of the Order of the Red Triangle, was also president at the metropolitan, state and national levels. He was a director and vice president of the Bronx-based Cleveland H. Dodge Foundation.

William Dodge Rueckert has served on the Association Board of Directors since 1991. President of Rosow & Company, a private investment firm, Rueckert was instrumental in obtaining the $2 million gift from the Cleveland H. Dodge Foundation which will allow construction of a new YMCA in downtown Brooklyn. The new YMCA will be named for the Dodge family.

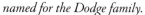

The philanthropist eventually selected some projects he would fund: new buildings for the Colored Men and Boys Branch, the Merchant Seamen's Branch and the YMCA's Central Laundry facility; improvements to the Bowery Branch; and a two-year pilot program in personal guidance. His total pledge was $900,000, over and above his yearly $5,000 donation for operating expenses. Rockefeller also wanted the YMCA to enter a joint program with the YWCA in the Grand Central Terminal area, and proposed that the YMCA defer any extensive building until an experiment could be conducted in work involving both men and women.

Dodge countered his idea by proposing the West Side Branch as the venue for the two-gender experiment and promoting the need for a new building for the Association's most important Branch and one of its greatest assets. In 1926, West Side accounted for nearly 42 percent of Association memberships, more than twice that of the next largest Branch. A new West Side building could be "readily adapted to work for both men and women," Dodge assured him, suggesting that land adjacent to the proposed site could be used for joint YMCA-YWCA programs if the experiment proved successful, "as we hope it will."

Dodge also made the case for the William Sloane Memorial YMCA. The Swift survey made clear the need for a men-only building, he emphasized, given the general housing shortage in New York that particularly afflicted young men. Moreover, the proposed housing-transient hotel combination would allow the Sloane YMCA to be self-supporting.

But Rockefeller stood firm. When the New York YMCA overran its estimates in 1927 by spending $2 million more than projected and taking in $2 million less, it had to cover the $4 million gap with bank loans, a solution that distressed the Rockefeller team. An internal Rockefeller report later observed that "the basic financial problems of the YMCA stand little chance of being solved through large-sized financial campaigns." Despite his demurral, the New York Association managed to raise $4 million in its special building campaign.

In 1930, within a month of each other, two massive YMCAs opened in the city: the West Side YMCA on West Sixty-Third Street, with a 500-bed residence, and the William Sloane Memorial YMCA on West Thirty-Fourth Street, boasting 1,600 rooms for transient men. Sloane House, as it was called, would quickly attain prominence among New York and national YMCAs.

The 14-story West Side YMCA, designed by architect Dwight James Baum with an Italianate exterior, was billed as "the largest YMCA in the world." Its Spanish-style interior was adorned with iron grillwork and hand-painted tiles made in Spain and donated by that country's government. Spanish tiles lined one third-floor swimming pool, and Pompeian tiles the other. This grand YMCA also featured a large gymnasium with a running track suspended above the floor, two smaller gyms and a jewel-box Little Theatre, where occasional resident Tennessee Williams's play *Summer and Smoke* was presented in 1952. Three theme rooms on the boys' side of the building simulated a log cabin, a pirate ship's cabin, and a farmhouse attic, all intended to offer city boys settings outside their realm of experience and to make historical figures like Christopher Columbus come alive.

Ironically, these two mammoth YMCA buildings, the largest ever erected in New York, opened at the very outset of the Great Depression. In this time of widespread unemployment, construction also began on two more YMCAs, one in Harlem and the other in east Midtown, at

Two massive YMCAs opened within a month of each other, the William Sloane Memorial and West Side Branches.

Association President Cleveland E. Dodge, right, laid the cornerstone of the new West Side building with Hon. Charles Tuttle, attorney for the State of New York.

A ship's cabin at the West Side Y offered city boys an educational experience outside of their usual realm.

The 500-bed West Side YMCA, said to be the largest in the world, featured Spanish-style interiors and a pool with Spanish tiles.

a total cost to the Association of more than $8 million. The newly named Grand Central Railroad Branch, after departing from its "Old 390" building on Park Avenue and a brief stint in the former Harlem Branch building on 125th Street, settled into a new $1.5 million building on East Forty-Seventh Street in 1932. This ten-story YMCA expanded to serve other members as well as railway workers. The YMCA building projects provided work for nearly 6,000 men and brought income to parched communities.

After two decades, the formerly cutting-edge Young Men's Institute had seen membership drop by one-third in its outmoded building at 222 Bowery. Despite a 1915 renovation that added a new pool and larger gym, the high-minded Institute in a dissipated district closed as a YMCA in 1932, as the survey recommended. (The historic building, still standing, was designated a New York City landmark in 1999.)

In 1927–28, also at the suggestion of John D. Rockefeller Jr., the Brooklyn and Queens Association had surveyed its newly consolidated organization and clarified its plans for growth and expansion. In this instance, Rockefeller financed the $25,000 survey, which was also conducted by Professor Swift. The committee included Fisher, who participated in the New York survey; F. Ernest Johnson of the Federal Council of the Churches of Christ in America; and Eduard C. Lindeman of the New York School of Social Work. Frank C. Munson, president of the Brooklyn and Queens Board, and J. C. Armstrong, general secretary, were ex-officio members.

The typical adult member, the survey found, was 25 years old, a clerical worker or laborer, an unmarried American-born Protestant who lived at home, and a "privilege buyer" chiefly in the Physical Department. Half the men worked in Manhattan, primarily in Wall Street. Boys who were members represented the same general social class, while other boys served were considerably younger, less likely to be American citizens and more likely to be Roman Catholics.

The survey called for "considerable improvement" at the Carlton, Eastern District and Seamen's Branches. The Association, which included the city's largest borough, Brooklyn, with more than 2.5 million inhabitants, developed plans for a $400,000 building for Prospect Park; a $40,000 gym and dormitory annex for New Utrecht; and the new Branch building in Flushing, Queens. The Bedford YMCA, having discontinued work at 420 Gates Avenue, planned a new building for boys. A

The Railroad Branch built anew on East Forty-Seventh Street, opening a ten-story structure in 1932.

A new $400,000 Prospect Park Branch replaced the earlier, smaller building.

The heavily immigrant New Utrecht Branch added a $40,000 gym and dorm annex.

Branch organized in Flatbush in 1924 for men and boys was also seeking space. In 1936 that Branch acquired a Union League property for $80,000, but fire consumed the building in 1942.

John D. Rockefeller St. had strong ties to the Brooklyn and Queens YMCA through the influential Pratt family. His former Standard Oil colleague, the late Charles Pratt, had served on the Association Board, and Charles' son Herbert L. Pratt was a vice president of Standard Oil Company of New York. Herbert's brother Frederic B. Pratt had secured an unconditional Rockefeller gift of $100,000 for the Association's 1902–1905 Jubilee Fund. Richardson Pratt, of the Standard Oil Company of New Jersey, was a member of the Swift survey committee. Now, as the Association launched its 75th anniversary campaign in 1929, Rockefeller Junior offered $1 for every $3.50 the YMCA raised, up to $725,000. The Association reached its minimum goal with pledges of $2.4 million in September that year, but collected only $947,000 in cash. When the stock market crashed in November, many pledges were rendered worthless. On the strength of the Rockefeller pledge, the Association labored mightily until 1931 and was finally able to close the campaign with $2 million in cash gifts.

Staten Island, the smallest borough, also conducted a pre-Depression survey to study the needs of youth, at the request of the local Citizens Committee. The joint YMCA-YWCA survey of 1929–30 recommended organizing services for young people of both sexes in a centrally located activity center near Silver Lake and Clove Lake Parks, either jointly or separately administered by the two organizations. The constraints of the Depression prevented the YMCA and YWCA from implementing the recommendations in full, but nevertheless, fundraising for a YMCA initiative began slowly in 1929. By 1941, local citizens accumulated a nest egg of $3,237, which they turned over to the New York Association as the initial capital funds for a future Staten Island YMCA.

Struggling With Segregation in the YMCA

THE ASSIGNMENT OF blacks and whites to separate facilities was a consuming issue in the YMCA, as it was in society at large. By 1926, the African-American membership at 135th Street had risen above 1,000 and Harlem's black population to 200,000, quadrupling in less than a decade. The 1919 building was already inadequate, overcrowded and worn, and needed program space for boys, a

The Harlem community turned out for a parade to mark the cornerstone-laying at the new YMCA on 135th Street.

Railroad YMCAs, also needed accommodations. A $750,000 Building Fund Campaign was launched in the following year to build on a site on West 135th Street directly across from the existing Branch facility.

The new 135th Street building opened on January 1, 1933 as the world's largest YMCA serving African-American men and boys. Its total cost of $1 million was financed in part with $75,000 from the Phelps-Stokes Fund and $25,000 from the estate of Julius Rosenwald. In 1935, it would be renamed the Harlem YMCA after its world-famous community. The 1919 building was put on the market and might have sold if business conditions had been better. Instead, it was used during the Depression by the city welfare department. By 1938, the Branch re-equipped it as the "Harlem Annex" to house its boys' department. (In 1996, it was remodeled again, reopening as the Harlem YMCA Jackie Robinson Youth Center.)

supervised dormitory and counseling facilities for the thousands of youth leaving school each year to seek work in the community. Transient "Red Caps," Pullman porters and dining car men, who were not allowed to use the segregated

As the Depression devastated the African-American community, the Harlem YMCA felt a special obligation to non-members. It offered an Activities Week Celebration.

Theme *for* English B

"*The instructor said,*

    Go home and write
    a page tonight.
    And let that page come out of you—
    Then, it will be true.

I wonder if it's that simple?
I am twenty-two, colored, born in Winston-Salem,
I went to school there, then Durham, then here
to this college on the hill above Harlem.
I am the only colored student in my class.
The steps from the hill lead down into Harlem
through a park, then I cross St. Nicholas,
Eighth Avenue, Seventh, and I come to the Y,
the Harlem Branch Y, where I take the elevator
up to my room, sit down and write this page. . ."

—LANGSTON HUGHES,
excerpt from poem

A cultural center unto itself, the Branch hosted and housed renowned writers such as Claude McKay and Richard Wright. With black people banned from many public facilities, the Branch attracted theater-goers, overnight visitors, and diners to its excellent restaurant, where writer Ralph Ellison worked as a fill-in for vacationing waiters and countermen. On his second day there he was introduced to the poet Langston Hughes, who was living there and attending college; through Hughes, Ellison also met Richard Wright.

Aaron Douglas painted wall murals in the Branch during the Depression, one of which remains in place, and Jacob Lawrence held his first one-man exhibition there in 1938. Negro history was taught and discussed there. Numerous actors and playwrights graced the Harlem Y's stage in a Works Progress Administration (WPA) American Negro Theatre program initiated during the Depression, which continued into the 1970s. The Little Theater Guild hosted such leading lights as Ossie Davis, Ruby Dee, and Cicely Tyson. Columbia University law student Paul Robeson took a part there in *Simon the Cyrenian*, where his acting talent was discovered. Eventually, he performed on Broadway in Eugene O'Neill's groundbreaking *All God's Chillun Got Wings*.

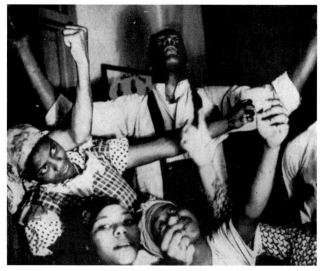

Harlem's Little Theater offered dramatic productions to community members during the Depression.

Jacob Lawrence (below) held his first one-man show at the Harlem YMCA, while Aaron Douglas painted the mural below on a wall of the Y.

While a law student, Paul Robeson was "discovered" acting at the Harlem YMCA.

In 1936, at the Harlem YMCA's Activities Week Celebration, this Branch highlighted its special role in the community, "the new capital of the Negro." Its "obligations and special purposes" required it to share with the community, "not only its religious activities, but its whole program … because of the restricted economic and social opportunities of the great masses of people in this district." The YMCA would focus not only on members, a "relatively small group of men and boys," but would endeavor "to partake of and stimulate every wholesome development in our community life." The Branch intended to work for community advancement, inspiring its youth to higher goals and creating opportunities for them, to express the people's just economic and social demands and to serve as a cultural center that would nurture local artistic talents. Despite the economic dislocations of the Depression, the Harlem Y's employment service managed to place 768 men in jobs the following year, from a field of 2,000 applicants.

The 135th Street YMCA was clearly a physical and spiritual focal point for Harlem's developing black community, but the Branch boldly declared its intent to serve members of any race, creed, or color: "Segregation, in any form along racial lines, is diametrically opposed to the teachings of Jesus Christ whose life the association seeks to instill into the lives of young men and boys so as to inspire them to become more useful men and citizens, friends, and fathers."

While the de facto segregation that prevailed for some time in the New York and

Brooklyn YMCAs may be viewed negatively today, it provided an environment free from other influences where African-American leadership developed freely and flourished. Channing Tobias, who replaced Jesse Moorland in 1923 as the national Colored Work secretary, stated his firm belief that only separate YMCAs allowed black Americans to "develop leadership in a way and to an extent that would never be possible... in branches made up largely of white people."

In the 1920s a rift was emerging in the national YMCA over segregated memberships, which increasing numbers of leaders felt to be in conflict with the Association's Christian purpose. But in the YMCA's characteristically gradual fashion, many "hoped to improve segregation by making 'separate but equal' truly equal," observed Nina Mjagkij, author of *Light in the Darkness: African Americans and the YMCA 1852–1946.*

The national organization took a major step in 1923 when a new YMCA constitution abolished the ruling International Committee, which had been composed entirely of professional YMCA secretaries, and replaced it with a National Council of secretaries and Association laymen. The new Council could make policy but could not impose "legislative authority" on local Associations.

Despite his conviction that separate Branches promoted African-American leadership, Tobias became a vocal internal critic of the YMCA's racial stance. At the World's Conference of YMCAs in Helsinki, Finland, in 1926, he condemned racism in the American YMCA and criticized the U.S. Associations for failing "to live up to the brotherhood ideas of Christ." Black Americans, Tobias told the gathering, were "puzzled about a Christian leadership that has for more than fifty years without serious protest witnessed flagrant violations of the Fourteenth and

The old 1919 Branch building was used by government agencies during the Depression, and later reopened as the Harlem Branch Annex for boys.

Harlem residents could learn to paint or gather to sing at their YMCA.

Fifteenth Amendments to the constitution." His criticism continued to be heard at subsequent World Conferences.

Young people in the Intercollegiate YMCAs also took up the cause. A 1926 editorial in *The Nation* about the struggle over segregation within the YMCA movement noted that most college campus Branches "call race discrimination un-Christian."

At the end of the 1920s, the discussion changed as America was hit by the stock market crash of 1929 and the subsequent financial calamity. The Great Depression had a devastating effect on both African Americans and the YMCA. Black people, already concentrated at the bottom of the economic ladder, tumbled further and harder. Their unemployment rate rose to 50 percent, twice that of whites. The YMCA, traditionally dependent on revenue earned from memberships and programs, and local community support, found itself in a classic bind: As support in poorer communities—from locals and from philanthropists—diminished, community needs increased, and YMCA work became more essential than ever. As the Depression deepened, the Colored Work Department staff was cut deeply, and black YMCAs fought for their lives. Staffs, budgets and salaries were reduced even as they struggled to provide essential services: food and clothing distribution to needy local families and morale-building entertainment programs.

The first World Conference of YMCAs held in the United States (in Cleveland, Ohio) in 1931 was a watershed. When dark-skinned delegates were refused equal treatment at hotels, the U.S. YMCA threatened to withdraw from the conference unless hotel managers reversed their stance. At the Conference, 765 of the 1,028 delegates endorsed a resolution condemning racial discrimination and calling for an end to segregation in the YMCA. Acknowledging that change might take time, the delegates nevertheless declared "that patience without effort toward improvement is unchristian" and recommended that all Associations offer educational programs aimed at eliminating racial prejudices. At the YMCA's national conference later that year, delegates generally concurred by urging all U.S. Associations to "move forward in remedying this condition of inter-racial inequality and injustice as quickly as possible." Since Associations were governed locally, however, the resolution was not binding and little progress was made.

However, *The Nation*, in its article "The Y.M.C.A. Moves Forward" in September 1931, reported on the seismic shift that had occurred at both meetings: "That the Y.M.C.A., in the past usually ultraconservative and unwilling even to discuss 'dangerous' issues, is becoming liberalized appears clearly from the resolutions passed concerning race relations, especially if one recalls its Jim Crow policy in the United States.... Even more encouraging is the fact that... it urged these next steps in order that 'the ultimate goal of the institution may speedily be reached, namely, the enlistment and full participation of all classes of young men and boys in the community without distinction of race, culture, or nationality.'"

In an editorial, *The Nation* cheered that the national YMCA "now stands for absolute social and communal equality, without which surely no religious association has the right to carry on in the name of Christ." However, progress was halting in the Associations. A 1936 National Council study found that American YMCAs "are very far from living up to Christian ideals of racial relations." Tobias kept up the pressure at national conferences, while the rise of totalitarianism in Germany, Italy, and the Soviet Union also served to prod the American movement to re-think its record on civil rights. Denial of equal treatment, it was clear, could drive people to embrace violent ideologies.

World War II brought the issue to a head within the YMCA. Accommodationism had failed and African Americans were running out of patience, as a Harlem Y newsletter made clear: "Even in times of national stress... the Negro remains loyal and keeps faith with his country. But we might inquire, how long!!!"

Black Association leaders around the nation announced that they had "arrived at a state of mind which no longer permits them to accept the inferior and discriminatory status assigned them within the framework of American society in general, and in the Young Men's Christian Association in particular." They demanded that YMCAs remove all bars to membership based upon race and color alone.

New York City's most prominent "white" YMCAs, despite a number of efforts toward greater tolerance, had also engaged in discriminatory practices. In one instance, a self-described "group of Negroes and Whites, some of them religious and social workers" wrote to the YMCA board of directors in 1941 that they had surveyed downtown YMCAs and found them "excluding Negroes from their dormitories and facilities in general." Homer Nichols, past president of the Harlem Christian Youth Conference and a member of this group, had been refused a room in Sloane House, where he was told "we send *you fellows* up to the Harlem Y." The indignant group declared that "here is a *Christian* association violating the basic tenet of Christian brotherhood."

Some YMCA Board members voiced dismay over that and other incidents. One director, Hubert T. Delany, wrote to Raymond L. Dickinson, New York Association executive vice president, in 1943: "I, of course, received the camp folder announcing the opening of the Huguenot Camps. . . I must state quite frankly that I am not satisfied that the New York Association continues a policy in denying admission to its camps of Negro boys, while even Brooklyn does not deny this opportunity to its fellow-constituents."

After 20 years of dissent and struggle within the ranks, the National Council finally ruled in 1943 that YMCAs had to open their membership to people of all races. The trend in the movement, Tobias could finally declare, "is now in the direction of integration . . . rather than toward the strengthening and multiplication of separate racial branches."

Nevertheless, in November that same year the New York Association Board reviewed its membership policy with respect to race and failed to impose a binding policy. It fell back on Branch local autonomy with this recommendation: "that the Board of Directors refer the matter [inter-racial policy] to the individual branches for further serious consideration and continued study; that the branches be urged to continue to make advances and progress in racial understanding and cooperation." Like

many mostly white Associations, the New York YMCA may have hesitated to desegregate during World War II, just as it had worried about fracturing the antebellum Association over the slavery issue. After the War, buttressed by an internal survey, the New York board adopted a policy that all new Branches (but not existing ones) be completely interracial, essentially "grandfathering" the exclusionary practices of existing Branches.

The Carlton YMCA for Colored Men and Boys in Brooklyn sought to expand after it conducted the most successful membership and fund-raising campaign in its history. In 1944 the Branch raised nearly $8,000 in two weeks and enrolled 2,313 new members, bringing its total membership to 5,000, the *Brooklyn Eagle* reported. At the conclusion of the successful drive, Norman B. Johnson, vice chairman of the Brooklyn and Queens Board of Directors, called for a new building for this Branch in the still predominantly white Bedford-Stuyvesant section: "The present building, for all its virtues and facilities, is totally inadequate in view of the leaping membership and increasing population," Johnson said. "At the moment there are 150,000 Negroes in Brooklyn as against 50,000 less than 15 years ago."

The overcrowding of the Carlton Y's small building, with its long-inadequate facilities, would soon lead to discontent and eventually to its closing, in 1954. No longer would one Brooklyn and Queens YMCA for African Americans suffice for the changing population of Queens, which needed more convenient facilities. The closing of Carlton effectively opened all Branches in the Brooklyn and Queens Association to people of every race. Many Carlton Y boys chose to go to the Bedford YMCA.

Former chairmen of the Harlem Board of Managers included (from bottom left) John S. Brown (1901), Dr. E. P. Roberts (1907–21); Henry C. Parker (1921–1930); Judge Hubert T. Delany (1947–48); and Dr. Peyton F. Anderson (1930–46) (above left).

Ending the Male Monopoly

IN THIS SAME period, the YMCA brought to an end another kind of separation it had long practiced. Certainly its name, the Young Men's Christian Association, unequivocally defined the individuals the organization intended to serve. But by the early twentieth century, major changes were under way in American society, which was basking in a new spirit of freedom. Women had played significant roles in World War I and after decades of struggle, female suffragists finally gained the right to vote in 1919. They were associating more casually now with the opposite sex, and were eager to assert their influence in public life.

This new freedom caused concern among those who feared a potentially negative effect on family life if women diluted their roles as wives and mothers. As industrial

society was believed to be contributing to a weakening of the family unit, marriage partnerships were seen as the force that would stabilize society. Many YMCAs began working to fortify the family by promoting more social interaction between the sexes, dating, and marriage, thereby providing greater entrée to women in the Association.

Beyond their ornamental and help-mate functions in the early auxiliaries, women had been powerful fund-raisers for the YMCA. Two New Yorkers in particular, Helen Miller Gould, daughter of Jay Gould, and Margaret Olivia Sage, widow of Gould's right-hand man Russell Sage, gave and raised significant sums especially for Army, Navy and Railroad YMCA buildings. Through her gifts, Mrs. William E. Dodge kept her eminent husband's legacy alive in the YMCA.

Women, of course, could join an organization all their own, the YWCA, which was founded in 1858 in New York City. But YWCA purposes and activities differed from the YMCA's, while the latter also offered women a desirable proximity to husbands, sons and the opposite sex in general. The YWCA occasionally intersected over the years with the YMCA, notably in joint fund-raising drives before World War I for the Harlem and Bronx Union YMCAs, but steadfastly remained separate despite off-and-on merger discussions promoted by supporters of both organizations.

Their differences were not solely gender-related. The Swift survey had found that some people considered the YMCA "conservative" because of its reluctance to take

Some 2,600 women YMCA secretaries served as volunteers in France during World War I.

stands on controversial issues. A respondent who headed a large Protestant organization and lectured frequently at the YMCA observed: "I find the YMCA isn't as brave in facing social and economic questions as the YWCA. It stands back while the women take hold of these questions in good Christian fashion."

Any talk of merger raised a red-flag issue for the YWCA: the possible sacrifice of autonomy and equality of its members, who could exercise full leadership in their own association and liked it that way. They risked being relegated to secondary roles in the YMCA and also feared the powerful men's organization would claim a greater share of funds for its interests and facilities for young men. On the other hand, if YMCAs moved to admit women, the YWCA risked losing members to them. A 1926 article in *Men of New York* rejected the idea that the YMCA and YWCA should consolidate but suggested "that these two organizations join in a carefully-planned program of experimentation in social and other events. . . unless [they] fearlessly face these larger needs and opportunities they will fall short of their possible serviceability to the youth of the nation."

The YMCA recognized that all-male bastions risked becoming an anachronism. The 1926 New York Association report revealed its understanding of the need to change: "Modern young people are in the habit of facing the same problems and working them out *together*, and other young people's societies, notably the Y.M.H.A. and the Y.W.H.A., no longer segregate the sexes in separate buildings. . . In this field, far from being a leader, the Y.M.C.A. is actually behind the times." Swift strongly urged an experiment in cooperation between the YMCA and the YWCA, pointing out that "sex attitudes are strongly determinative of character and of the quality of the home. The Association must in some way bring about the supervised mingling of young men and young women in all the varied interests of their common life."

A number of YMCAs were already including women and girls in their programs and activities, as participants or even as members. The West Side YMCA, for one, sponsored mixed socials before the War and decided in 1918 to admit women to all classes of its education department, and to admit those who volunteered for the Red Cross Motor Corps to its Auto School "even though we break even or lose money."

Public perception was also turning negative toward the self-indulgence of single men and those who abetted it. In 1918 the *New Republic* had faulted the YMCA: "The Association has not been a home builder. It has been charged with being a home-destroyer. It has always ren-dered at least lip-homage to the home. But it has built [sic] magnificent club-houses for the accommodation of bachelor young men, and has often been censured for having delayed the setting up of the necessarily humbler home by the luxurious beguilements of bachelorhood."

YMCA leaders were eager to show more support for marriage and family values. In 1927, the West Side Y promulgated a new rule that stipulated that men could no longer live in its dormitory for more than a year. The *New York Times*, in an article entitled "YMCA to Evict 2,000 Bachelors," noted that "The YMCA quarters have been so comfortable and inexpensive that they are practi-cally all occupied by permanent residents." The YMCA suggested that the long-timers were keeping other men from finding short-term lodgings, but the *Times*, noting that 42 percent of New York men ages 24 to 34 were bach-elors, reported that "the YMCA hopes the new rule will result in an increase of city marriages."

Society's new distaste for the self-centered bachelor was exacerbated by growing suspicions of homosexuality in all-male clubs, as the rising influence of psychology cast intense same-sex relationships as "perversion." The YMCA, whose very foundation was Christian fellowship among like-minded single men, was in a bind. The early YMCA had provided a place where spiritual and emo-tional friendships could flourish among men. Based on shared Christian beliefs, their companionship often grew into lifelong bonds with each other, and the YMCA. For McBurney, Sumner Dudley, and Robert Weidensall, a revered national leader in the nineteenth century, their abiding love was their work among young men. They remained lifelong bachelors as did nearly one in three early YMCA leaders, according to John D. Gustav-Wrathall, author of *Take the Young Stranger by the Hand*.

The male-bonding model had worked very well in the previous century, when enduring male-male friend-ships were the social norm, but in the twentieth century manhood was increasingly measured by the responsibilities men took as husbands and fathers. In this climate, a pro-gram orientation that could strengthen marriage and the family seemed ideally suited to the YMCA's purposes. Amid the now inevitable social changes the YMCA, in seeking to build families and communities, could remain a civic and religious force above suspicions of homosexuality.

By now, the YMCA had decades of experience in and commitment to sex education programs. Initially the subject was offered solely for young men, focusing on the importance of chastity and avoidance of homosexuality. By the 1920s YMCAs began offering sex education for both genders as preparation for marriage. In "A Boy and

His Girl Friends," a 1927 lecture by C. C. Robinson, an "employed boy authority," the YMCA's prevailing philosophy is clear.

Robinson, addressing 500 older working boys at a noon-time meeting of the Wall Street Boys YMCA, asserted that a constructive social life would help young men in their business careers just as "loose social living" would harm them. Moreover, they would be helping to stabilize society. "The young men and women of this generation are the only ones who can turn the tide in saving America from the divorce evil and broken homes. . . ." Divorce, which he blamed on "the growing independence of woman," would be inevitable unless young people carefully considered the importance of marriage. "The stabilizing of the homes of the future will depend on the attitudes which young men and women take towards each other in the late teens and early twenties," Robinson declared.

When it came to "the excesses in social life—drinking, smoking, petting, and things much worse, both the boys and girls are inclined to blame upon each other," Robinson told his audience. "The fellow who is clean, courteous, and fine in his manners has a good chance of winning out in the long run." But, he cautioned: "Like the boys in the coeducational colleges, young men in big business houses must learn to keep their minds on their business during business hours."

As co-mingling of the sexes became commonplace, the Association also began to question the prevalence of bachelor secretaries, traditionally the staff in its all-male culture. Internal reports declared that too much same-sex activity was "quite abnormal (and) may lead to homosexual tendencies," Gustav-Wrathall noted. The YMCA sought to provide men with more "normal" experience, something the integration of women could accomplish. Quite rapidly married men replaced bachelors as the prototypical secretary, and new organizations cropped up for "Y wives." In great contrast to leaders' close, warm relationships with members in the nineteenth century, a 1927 operations manual described the ideal secretary as one who would be "friendly but not familiar" with young men. Although most secretaries were married men by the 1920s, the YMCA would continue to promote male bonding and devoted friendships among its leaders.

The inclusion of women within the YMCA did not proceed quickly or smoothly. There was no unanimity on this subject. Some YMCA men felt strongly that admitting women was nothing short of an abandonment of the Christian men's movement in favor of providing social services. They feared a "feminization" of their Association.

Some of those in favor of joint YMCA-YWCA endeavors saw in them a way for the YMCA to avoid fully integrating women as members. Men and women could interact socially, and both organizations could keep their autonomy.

The matter would resolve itself naturally as new YMCAs were created. In newly established Branches, there was less resistance to women's memberships. The new Flushing Branch, for example, admitted women and girls as members from the outset, and turned over its facilities to them one day a week. By 1927 its membership totaled 2,408 men and boys and 893 women and girls. The 1927–28 survey of the Brooklyn and Queens Association noted flaws in the YMCA's limited program for women: it was carried on by men, and made no provision for women's participation in planning and administration. A female secretary was in charge of women's activities, but the women's committee was not represented on the Branch Board of Managers.

As new YMCAs were created, female participation grew naturally. Young women competed as swimmers at Prospect Park in the 1920s and participated in McBurney's 1937 May Festival.

Finally, in 1933, the national YMCA constitution was amended to allow women to full membership but local autonomy was allowed to prevail, with individual Ys deciding whether to admit them. Programs for women and girls would be introduced in many YMCAs and expand noticeably during the Depression. In 1934, the West Side YMCA enrolled its first woman member.

By 1940 the Brooklyn and Queens Association reported that among its 55,000 members were 5,000 women and girls "who add interest and reality to programs of social nature and discussions of marriage, home making, civic problems, and international affairs." But hesitations still surfaced: a 1953 Association trends study suggested that a "discreet balance" be maintained in adding women and girl members, and that it was "thinking of including women as representatives on committees and boards." The New York Association's 1951 report revealed that a few women were serving as assistant program secretaries; by 1953 "new men and women" had been added to the professional staff. But women apparently advanced little; the 1958 report stated that the Association hired "the best men for the job."

Association buildings, constructed on the assumption of male-only programs and activities, would eventually be modified to accommodate women. New ones would be built on the assumption of participation by both sexes. The most impressive membership leaps began after

After World War II it was Association policy to admit women to all recreational activities and encourage intermingling of the sexes. Left, an informal gathering at Harlem; right, swimmers at West Side.

World War II; women's and girls' memberships in the New York Association increased to 2,828 in 1946, up from just 1,612 in 1944. In 1946, the New York Board agreed "to encourage the various Branches to extend their full recreational membership and work in all fields of activity where youth and young adults of both sexes can effectively be dealt with together." In 1948, the New York YMCA took the unusual step of appointing a woman as a Branch executive director, for the Fort Slocum Army Branch. Throughout the 1950s, the city's YMCAs would provide a popular site for young adults to socialize and a welcoming place for those with growing families.

By 1940, girls' programs were common in Brooklyn and Queens, like this girls' club at Highland Park.

Religious Barriers Tumble

BY THE MID-1920s, life in New York City was brimming with interesting activities and a heady sense of freedom, making the YMCA's religious lectures much less of a draw than they once were. Overall, religion no longer occupied the central place in the culture it had in the nineteenth century. Although some YMCA street-corner preachers persevered in garnering recruits for the Association, large-scale religious revivals were a thing of the past. Evangelism in the YMCA had disappeared almost completely by this time, the Swift New York survey noted, and the influence of Protestantism in city life was steadily declining as that of Catholicism and Judaism was rising.

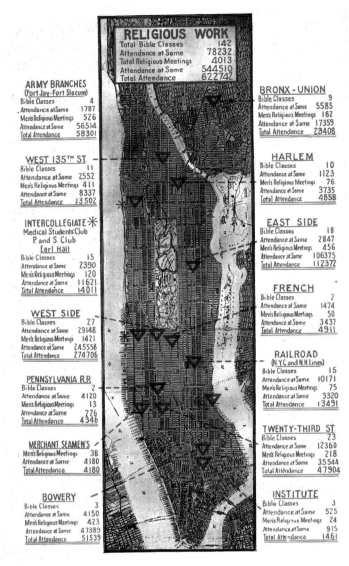

RELIGIOUS WORK

Total Bible Classes	142
Attendance at Same	78232
Total Religious Meetings	4013
Attendance at Same	544510
Total Attendance	622742

ARMY BRANCHES
(Fort Jay-Fort Slocum)

Bible Classes	4
Attendance at Same	1787
Men's Religious Meetings	526
Attendance at Same	56514
Total Attendance	58301

WEST 135TH ST.

Bible Classes	11
Attendance at Same	2552
Men's Religious Meetings	411
Attendance at Same	8337
Total Attendance	13502

INTERCOLLEGIATE
Medical Students'Club
P. and S. Club
Earl Hall

Bible Classes	15
Attendance at Same	2390
Men's Religious Meetings	120
Attendance at Same	11621
Total Attendance	14011

WEST SIDE

Bible Classes	27
Attendance at Same	29148
Men's Religious Meetings	1421
Attendance at Same	245558
Total Attendance	274706

PENNSYLVANIA R.R.

Bible Classes	2
Attendance at Same	4120
Men's Religious Meetings	13
Attendance at Same	226
Total Attendance	4346

MERCHANT SEAMEN'S

Men's Religious Meetings	38
Attendance at Same	4180
Total Attendance	4180

BOWERY

Bible Classes	3
Attendance at Same	4150
Men's Religious Meetings	423
Attendance at Same	47389
Total Attendance	51539

BRONX - UNION

Bible Classes	9
Attendance at Same	5585
Men's Religious Meetings	162
Attendance at Same	17359
Total Attendance	23408

HARLEM

Bible Classes	10
Attendance at Same	1123
Men's Religious Meetings	76
Attendance at Same	3735
Total Attendance	4858

EAST SIDE

Bible Classes	18
Attendance at Same	2847
Men's Religious Meetings	456
Attendance at Same	106375
Total Attendance	112372

FRENCH

Bible Classes	2
Attendance at Same	1474
Men's Religious Meetings	50
Attendance at Same	3437
Total Attendance	4911

RAILROAD
(N.Y.C. and N.H. Lines)

Bible Classes	15
Attendance at Same	10171
Men's Religious Meetings	75
Attendance at Same	3320
Total Attendance	13491

TWENTY-THIRD ST.

Bible Classes	23
Attendance at Same	12360
Men's Religious Meetings	218
Attendance at Same	35544
Total Attendance	47904

INSTITUTE

Bible Classes	3
Attendance at Same	525
Men's Religious Meetings	24
Attendance at Same	915
Total Attendance	1461

Religious work was still strong in New York Branches in 1927.

the New York Association's physical work, 1,126,000 strong in 1927, and those who stayed in its 2,100 clean, inexpensive dorm rooms, no matter what their persuasion, would sometimes encounter a heavy-handed religious emphasis. One such incident was described by the late Massachusetts Congressman Tip O'Neill in his 1987 memoir, *Man of the House.*

O'Neill recalled a trip to Washington from Boston at age 21 when he and a friend, Lenny Lamkin, stopped over in New York and stayed at a YMCA. "We had to keep quiet about that because Monsignor Blunt, our local pastor, wouldn't allow us to go to the Y, which was run by Protestants—not even during the Depression, when the Y gave out free memberships to the unemployed," O'Neill wrote. "Blunt spoke from the altar and proclaimed that anyone who went to the Y had to tell about it in confession because it was a sin.

"So there we were, Lenny and I, a Jew and a Catholic, staying at the Sloane House, which was run by the Y. A night's lodging was sixty-five cents, which was a lot of money. But if you signed up for the Episcopal service, it was only thirty-five cents, with breakfast included. We were nobody's fools, so we signed up for the thirty-five-cent deal and figured to duck out after breakfast and before the service. But apparently we weren't the first to think of this brilliant plan, because they locked the doors during breakfast, which meant that we were stuck. Although I was in my twenties, it was the first time in my life that I had ever listened to a Protestant minister."

Bible breakfasts continued for many years at Sloane House.

In 1927, the citywide YMCA membership was 62 percent Protestant, 29 percent Roman Catholic, and 7 percent Jewish. Swift neatly summed up the New York Association's religious quandary: "There is still a great deal of confusion in the minds of its friends and officers as to its true relation to the church and to the community. Everybody has his own 'interpretation.'" The Brooklyn Association survey noted that "the organization is thought of as a place where certain chiefly physical and economic wants may be taken care of rather than as a source of very thoroughgoing spiritual leadership." By 1946, the equilibrium had altered remarkably in Brooklyn, reflecting a dramatic shift in population. Membership at the representative Central Branch was only 27.5 percent Protestant; Catholics predominated at 55 percent and Jewish members accounted for 14 percent.

However, Protestant religious activity had hardly disappeared from either YMCA's program. Participants in

The YMCA was not about to change because of growing secularism in society or the shrinking Protestant sect in the city. At times the YMCA placed limits on the number of Jewish members. By 1936, when Jews comprised more than half of members of religious bodies in Brooklyn, Catholics nearly one-third, and Protestants just over 10 percent, Rabbi Alexander Lyons defended this Association policy: "The YMCA is a Christian organization for the promotion of Christianity. The Jewish young man who seeks affiliation has absolutely no Christian inclination or interest. He desires principally the magnificent gymnasium facilities… In spite of this attitude of his, the Association admits him through what appears to me to be its concessive Christian spirit. If it removed all restrictions from Jewish affiliation it would in time undoubtedly become proportionally more Jewish than Christian. Only an unfair Jew would want this or an unthinking Christian consent to it."

A Christian program emphasis, in liberal doses, still had strong proponents in New York. Eugene Field Scott, head of the suburban White Plains Association who later led the Brooklyn and Queens YMCA, explained the societal shifts at the 1926 state convention. He exhorted his colleagues to resist secularization and keep the YMCA a vital force in the lives of men and youth because of "its religious foundation and its genius at adaptability—ever changing to meet changing needs, conditions, opportunities and all within the framework of a Christian religious emphasis."

World War I, Scott said, had lessened the emphasis on creeds, theology and denominations, and contributed to "a breakdown of morals, a disintegration of spiritual standards." Larger social, political, international and economic issues directly impacted individuals and families, bringing about a shift in traditional attitudes and a willingness to change. "The YMCA" he declared, "has been living on its inherited religious capital, and as it grew flabbier spiritually it developed very few new techniques to meet the changes of the day."

Losing its distinctly religious and Christian appeal was threatening the YMCA's base of financial support as well, Scott said. The Community Chest, he noted, was "shifting almost entirely to certain aspects of character education.… If the Young Men's Christian Association is to continue as a potent, vital factor in our communities and in the nation, it must cease trying to be all things to all men [and]… be a spiritual factor, a religious force, a Christian character-building agency for youth." The necessity for religion in society would increase, he asserted, and the YMCA had a great opportunity to differentiate itself by holding firm to its "Christian character moulding [sic] motives" and emphasizing its religious message through Christian personnel and leaders in programs and activities.

Between 1926 and 1946, the different faiths of the YMCA's constituency would provoke long internal debates, with action deferred or referred to various committees, as the Brooklyn and Queens Association did. Its gradual fashion of adapting to change was once again in evidence, and conservatism still dominated the Board. Only in 1949 did the Association revise its Charter and constitution, deleting clauses that included the evangelical requirement for membership but sustaining the Protestant prerequisite.

> ## The YMCA Purpose,
> # 1947
>
> ❧
>
> "The purpose of the Young Men's Christian Association of the City of New York is to help young people develop Christian character and to aid them in building a Christian society, by the maintenance of such activities and services as contribute to their physical, social, mental, and spiritual growth, and by such other means as may conduce to the accomplishment of this Purpose."

Norman Vincent Peale
was the featured speaker at a 1938 Easter breakfast at the Twenty-Third Street Branch.

Easter Breakfast Speaker

Dr. Norman Vincent Peale

Prayer services continued at camps for many years; here, Camp Brooklyn in 1957.

contributors as well as members, and observed that "in light of our constituency, there may be situations where we can not teach Christianity, but it is essential that we continue to teach and exemplify the Christian way of life." The New York Association stated forthrightly that it did not try to teach "any one creed or doctrine," and that it was "inaccurate to single out any particular part of the YMCA's program as being religious." Rather, its purpose was "developing Christian character in a Christian society." By 1955, that Association noted that its membership cut across all religious lines, but that its programs were "permeated with Christian principles in the broadest sense." However, it graciously encouraged all members to join a church or synagogue and sharpen their religious beliefs.

Purposes and *Objects* of the YMCA of Greater New York

"**T**he improvement of the moral, spiritual, mental, physical, and social condition of young people, primarily men and boys, by the support and maintenance of lectures, sermons, libraries, reading rooms, social meetings and such other means and services as may conduce to the accomplishment of these objects, always appropriate to and in unison with the spirit of the Gospel."

—From the Certificate of Consolidation, January 10, 1957

The Associations realized that with the city becoming more diverse by the day, they were toeing a fine line. They were reluctant to relegate their Christian orientation to the shadows yet were eager to appear inclusive. The 1953 trends study in the Brooklyn and Queens YMCA noted the large number of Catholics and Jewish

Adjusting to War, and a Post-War World

IN 1939, WITH the Depression on the wane and war imminent in Europe, the New York Association took an audacious step in erecting a handsome building at the New York World's Fair in Flushing Meadow, Queens. The fairgrounds, on the site of a former refuse dump, welcomed 100 million visitors in 1939 and 1940. In 1937 and 1938, the New York Association had invited the Brooklyn YMCA and the YWCA of the City of New York to share in this building project, but the proposal was turned down. The national YMCA agreed only to handle exhibits at the pavilion.

Undeterred, the New York Association assumed full responsibility for the project's development and operation—the first time any YMCA had mounted a structure at a world fair or exposition. Architect Dwight James Baum, who had designed the imposing West Side YMCA, created a handsome pavilion-style structure, with two columns supporting a central portal bearing the motto "Dedicated to the Honor of God and the Service of Youth." Inside were large social rooms, a cafeteria and coffee shop that served 1.5 million meals indoors or on an outside terrace. The building enjoyed a prominent location close to the Fair's central sphere, and the risky move paid off. The New York Association attracted positive worldwide attention to the YMCA, recouped its investment of $175,000 and spread its message to more than 6 million visitors.

The New York YMCA's international aspirations would be diverted by the Second World War. The national Association's historic involvement in war work was again solicited by the United States government in 1940, when it asked the YMCA to join in a newly created entity, a broad coalition called the United Service Organizations for National Defense (USO). Five other national voluntary organizations would participate, bringing other major faiths into the effort: the YWCA, National Catholic Community Service, Salvation Army, National Jewish Welfare Board and National Travelers Aid. The USO mandate was to serve "the religious, spiritual, welfare and educational needs of the men and women in the armed forces and defense industries of the United States, and in general, to contribute to the maintenance of morale in American communities."

The national YMCA gladly complied and operated 646, or 25 percent, of USO units in World War II. The YMCA now worked with personnel from enlistment to demobilization. Its service, newly limited to the continental United States, took place outside training camps and Navy yards, away from field armies or battleships, and excluded Army canteens. Yet the YMCA served many more soldiers since the magnitude of this War was far

The New York Association boldly erected a YMCA Pavilion for the 1939 World's Fair.

greater than previous wars, with 12.1 million men—and women—in uniform, triple the participation of 4.3 million in World War I. The addition of service to workers in war industries meant stepped-up activity in New York's defense plants. The Brooklyn Navy Yard alone employed 70,000 workers during World War II.

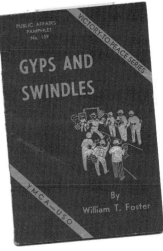

A YMCA-USO pamphlet warned returning soldiers about people who would help them "invest" their G.I. loans and war bonds.

The national Association also served 6 million soldiers who were prisoners of war in thirty-six foreign nations, as well as thousands of German and Italian POWs held in the United States. At home, volunteers and local churches were widely recruited to assist the YMCA effort. Displaced persons were a particular concern after the war's end, and the YMCA provided recreation, repatriation and resettlement services and camps for thousands of boys and girls, until all refugees had been placed.

Presenting the
New York YMCA
to the *World*

T*he visitors' brochure to the 1939–40 World's Fair declared that the YMCA was an "international, inter-racial and interdenominational movement" in 59 countries with a program "intended to help youth to meet the complex problems of present-day living . . . in the realm of employment, leisure time, health, education, social adjustment, spiritual growth, citizenship training or vocational guidance." Its purpose was firmly stated: "To help young people develop Christian character, and to aid them in building a Christian society."*

New Yorker Dr. John R. Mott (second from left), leader of the World Alliance of YMCAs, received the Nobel Peace Prize in 1946.

For these outstanding war relief efforts, national and international YMCA leader John R. Mott was awarded the Nobel Peace Prize in 1946.

Local Branches were hubs of activity during World War II. In 1943, the New York Association tallied more than 3,235,000 uses of its facilities by enlisted personnel. Sunday morning breakfasts for service men were staples at McBurney, as were religious meetings at the Harlem,

Sloane House and West Side Branches, which drew large crowds. A soldier's uniform was accepted as a pass to any YMCA. At the four active military Branches around the city—Governors Island and Forts Totten, Hamilton and Slocum—the two Associations provided recreation for service personnel, and the Navy YMCA stepped up its efforts to serve increased numbers.

Sloane House and other YMCA Branches with residences had few vacancies, with their clean, reasonably priced rooms in great demand by the uniformed forces. Off-duty soldiers and sailors could swim, use Branch libraries, tour the city and socialize with young women who volunteered to provide hospitality. The West Side Y housed, fed, or provided recreation to more than a million servicemen from 1941 to 1945, including a specialized physical fitness program for the Army Air Corps. The Branch's physical department was used two hours per day by a Military Police Unit, and twice weekly by an aviation mechanic unit. The Coast Guard trained in rescue operations in West Side's pool and took over several residence floors for use by 400 men. Seamen's House housed another 600 Coast Guardsmen. As well, every New York Branch organized for air raids.

The Uptown Branch maintained a tent chapel.

Sailors staying at Sloane House enjoyed an escorted bike tour on the West Side.

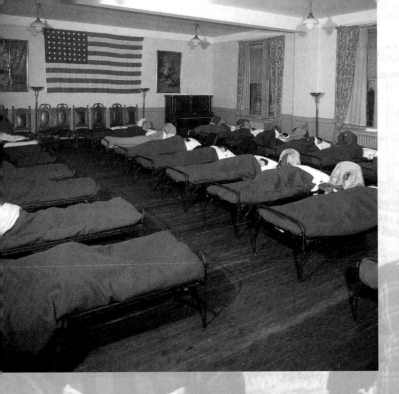

In great demand by servicemen during the War, there were few vacant beds at Sloane House, West Side, and McBurney Branches.

Volunteers at Branches helped the war effort, through paper drives.

Anticipating the war's end, the New York Association conducted a major survey in 1944. Led by Dr. George Strayer, who had chaired the Swift survey committee, the survey sought to help the YMCA plan for the future. The results would shape Association work for the rest of the century, especially in its renewed resolve to emphasize programs for youth. Even as services like lodging and food had expanded since the 1926 Swift survey—certainly boosted by legions of military personnel—program growth had been static, the Strayer survey found. As a result the YMCA would accelerate its work with boys as well as young men and women, and would reach out to underserved neighborhoods in the city. The survey also advised increasing efforts for returning servicemen.

The Association offered three months' free use of all facilities to recently discharged men. However, education was perhaps the finest service the YMCA rendered to World War II veterans. As men arrived home by the thousands, they were clamoring for knowledge, skills and degrees that would allow them, aided by the GI Bill of Rights, to find good situations and earn healthy wages. The New York and Brooklyn YMCAs were well suited to this mission, having honed their educational programs for half a century.

USO activities, such as this wedding at the Harlem Branch chapel, continued after the War at New York YMCAs.

Women, who had enrolled in West Side classes since 1918, took a course during the war to qualify as ambulance drivers.

In Brooklyn, Bedford's Trade School by now had nearly a half century of experience in offering courses needed for jobs in the city's factories and industries. It was up on the latest technologies, including aviation. Foreign servicemen streaming into New York sought out the YMCA's long experience in teaching English.

In 1930, all educational work of the New York Association was consolidated at the new West Side Branch under a single director. At the time 4,600 students—men

Bedford's Trade School offered courses in the latest technologies, including propeller repair.

and women—were enrolled in 102 courses at all Branches. Lynn A. Emerson assumed the position in 1931, the year same that work began on the five-story Trade and Technical School building adjacent and connected to the main West Side building. The School's broad offerings, which included the oldest automobile course in the Eastern states, kept pace with the newest technologies, helping men qualify for jobs as demand for them grew. In 1931, it added a course in operating television equipment.

"Radio, the talkies, refrigeration and other recent developments have found the Y alert to offer courses to assist young men to find employment in these fields," noted a 1934 review of West Side's educational work in *Men of New York*. The article highlighted the Branch's "marvelous" McBurney prep school, and the admission of "young ladies" to its Evening High School. Under the direction of William A. Lotz in 1942, Association educational work expanded to encompass a Technical, or Junior, Institute and a new Civil Service Institute.

French sailors could study English at the Navy YMCA in Brooklyn.

In 1945, formal educational work was transferred from the West Side YMCA and reorganized in a Schools Branch, with Lotz as executive director and Dr. N. L. Engelhardt of Teachers College as chairman. The Branch brought under one umbrella the Trade and Technical School, started in 1903; the McBurney School for Boys; the Walter Hervey Junior College, established in 1946, incorporating the New York Business Institute; the YMCA Evening High School, begun in 1869 at the Twenty-Third Street Branch where it continued until 1927; and the new Civil Service Institute. The Branch boasted a full-time faculty of 100 plus 80 part-time instructors.

Fully 60 percent of students in the YMCA Schools Branch were veterans, eager for a fresh start upon return home. The Branch would see enrollment leap to 6,200 in 1947–48, up from 2,556 in the Depression years of

1930–31 and a low of 1,688 during 1940–41. The Schools Branch offered 100 courses, from the sixth grade through high school and the first two years of college.

The YMCA was not content just to offer classes, but served them up with a generous helping of spiritual mission and character building. "The Schools, while adhering to sound educational practice, seek to create in students a spiritual understanding of human nature, and the ability to get along with people, both prerequisites for sound citizenship," observed the 1948 annual report. As well, the Schools sought to help students develop "a mature religious philosophy."

Walter Hervey Junior College had its beginnings in the New York Institute of Accountancy, formed in 1907 at the Twenty-Third Street Branch. A curriculum in business administration was added in 1908 to train young men for executive and administrative positions. In 1937, the renamed New York Institute of Accountancy and Commerce, by then at the West Side YMCA, was accredited by the State Board of Regents and renamed again, as the New York Business Institute.

In 1942, plans were made for a junior college offering business and technical courses on a cooperative plan for practical training to assist young men and women who might otherwise be unable to attend. It would offer two-year college diplomas in eight fields, and would continue the evening work of the Business Institute. The college would also "provide, in a Christian environment, opportunities for ethical and cultural development."

In June 1946, Walter Hervey Junior College received its charter from the New York State Regents. Named for Dr. Hervey, who had shaped the West Side Education Department in 1908, the college had a separate board of directors, who were also members of the New York YMCA Board. Its campus was a refurbished building at 15 West Sixty-Third Street, adjoining the West Side Branch, and a 10,000-square-foot space on Eleventh Avenue for laboratories. The College closed in 1957, having fulfilled its purpose of educating World War II veterans. The building it vacated was occupied by the McBurney School, which the Association touted as "one of the finest college prep schools in New York."

The YMCA stepped up to help educate thousands of returning veterans, like these men who stayed at the McBurney YMCA.

By 1940 the New York YMCA had employment centers at five Branches, which made 5,500 placements that year in a field dominated by 1,000 private employment agencies. The Association had wanted to unite its placement and counseling services under one umbrella since 1931, but the Depression and war years had stalled its progress. In January 1944, it was able to open the Vocational Service Center (VSC) at 40 East Fortieth Street. The VSC not only consolidated the work of five Branches but also assumed the work of the old Bowery Branch in 1946 as the latter closed operations on East Third Street. The Bowery YMCA's employment services and credit plan merged with the VSC's counseling, testing and placement functions.

The West Side YMCA Trade and Technical School offered one of the oldest auto repair courses.

The YMCA Vocational Center offered a major benefit for returning service personnel, serving many of them under contract with the Veterans Administration (VA). It was so much in demand that appointments were scheduled a month or two in advance. The VSC maintained an auxiliary at the McBurney Branch for interviewing and testing vets, across the street from VA headquarters. While two-thirds of those using its services were veterans or about to be, the VSC also served the "occupationally maladjusted, those not progressing in their work, those who need to know how to find work, youngsters just out of school, young men needing temporary assistance in seeking work." As well, it offered an occupational library and credit to needy young men. Businesses found the YMCA Branch a good source of employees and a testing center for workers whom they were considering for promotion.

By 1948, with the intense needs of returning servicemen diminishing, the VSC could give more attention to youth and young adults in the community, reaching them through YMCA Branches. To help high school students find not just a job but the right job, the Center offered them industrial testing, counseling and occupational information. Of the 21,000 total interviews it conducted that year, 10,600 were for employment, 6,600 for counseling, 3,500 for recruitment for YMCA jobs and 400 for credit aid. Some 22,000 aptitude tests were given and 1,230 job placements made. The Branch moved to larger quarters at 11 East Thirty-Sixth Street in 1955.

In one sense, the work of the Vocational Service Center harked back to the 1926 Swift survey, which had recommended that personal guidance be the controlling principle of future Association programs. While that survey no doubt also intended more spiritual or moral guidance, the Center's intense focus on individual needs came close to fulfilling its advice. In the twenty-first century New York YMCA, the personal guidance principle guides intensive programs such as *Teen Action NYC* and FutureWorks.

A 1944 planning survey urged expansion of boys' work at the Harlem, West Side and Uptown Branches.

Sharpening the Focus on Youth

AMERICAN SOCIETY CHANGED swiftly and dramatically after World War II. Returning vets were eager to establish homes and form families. The proliferation of cars and federal highway projects made suburban communities more attractive and accessible than before, and the GI Bill made owning a single-family home a possibility for many who had only known life in rented apartments. Many women who had held paying jobs in record numbers during wartime returned to being full-time homemakers. After all, jobs were plentiful for their husbands. Families grew in record numbers from 1946 to 1964, producing so many offspring—76 million—that these children collectively came to be known as the Baby Boom.

The New York Association's 1944 planning survey seems prescient in pinpointing the needs of those babies, children and adolescents. Programs and services tailored to them and their parents—in fact, to entire families— would be the order of the new day. Guided by the survey's recommendations, the New York YMCA began to lay groundwork for those programs, based on its traditional character-education and group work.

The Strayer survey urged expansion of boys' work at three Branches: Harlem, West Side and the Uptown Y, created in 1933, as well as in new centers, preferably in communities with a substantial Protestant population. First came an aggressive expansion of programs for boys

ages 9 to 18, tailored after the national Hi-Y program. Created early in the century when public high schools first proliferated, Hi-Y programs were clubs open to all high school boys, although their Christian purpose was strong. Conducted after school, Hi-Y clubs emphasized "clean speech, clean athletics, clean living and service to the community." Their principles were carried forward in Leaders' Clubs, first organized for boys in 1957 at YMCA Branches and still a linchpin of the contemporary YMCA youth program.

Young men and women, the survey recommended, should be integrated in programs particularly at the four general YMCAs: West Side, Harlem, McBurney and Bronx Union. Sloane House services and camps should also begin to include women and girls. Community outreach should become a priority in residential neighborhoods like the Bronx, and increased membership sought in Manhattan, the Bronx and Staten Island. The New York Association should serve national or racial groups such as Chinese and Spanish-speaking people, "but not as an exclusive group," the survey stressed. In anticipation that the YWCA would open memberships to young men, joint conferences were advised with that organization.

Several Branches urgently required expansion or remodeling to serve new populations in new ways. But a

The 1904 Twenty-Third Street Branch, later renamed for McBurney, needed renovations.

The new Westchester-Bronx Branch included both boys and girls; here, a teen dance in the 1940s.

1939–40 capital campaign had not met its goal, and building needs had only grown since then. Renovations of Harlem and Seamen's Branch annexes, extensions for West Side, a more suitable building for Bronx Union and a renovation study at McBurney were called for, as was a major new YMCA in the Grand Central Terminal area with a residence that would accommodate both men and women.

By 1946, efforts were underway. A full-time Boys' Work Secretary had joined the headquarters staff, Branches had doubled staff for boys' work and an aggressive program was in progress to increase Hi-Y involvement. Association-wide, boys' memberships were up by 25 percent. The Bronx Union YMCA began work for boys and girls in 1946 with summer extension programs, expanding to six days a week at the request of parents. Two-thirds of boys served by this

---

A YMCA SWIMMER'S
Innovation

Henry Myers, *a young swimmer competing in a meet at the Central Brooklyn YMCA in December 1933, introduced the exciting new butterfly stroke. It was the first time this modification of the breast stroke was seen.*

YMCA came from "low-rent" areas, a survey found. Two new Branches—Staten Island and Westchester-Bronx, in the eastern part of that borough—also put major emphasis on work with boys and girls.

The Brooklyn and Queens Association had also considerably stepped up its work for boys, sponsoring 60 Hi-Y chapters in 1944. Two years later, with Brooklyn's port activity starting to decline, the Association studied the feasibility of boys' work at its Seamen's Branch. This YMCA was located in an entirely Catholic neighborhood, however, where a Catholic seamen's organization also rendered service to boys. The Y's Sullivan Street location was fairly inaccessible, and posed another problem. In the early 1950s, white seamen in Brooklyn were still resisting integration, so the idea was dropped. In New York, an outmoded Seamen's Annex at 507 West Street was briefly considered for use as an activity center for boys and young people, but the property was sold in 1946.

As youth work topped the YMCA agenda, the aging of long-serving Board members and long-staying dormitory residents presented a stark contrast. The New York Association approved recruitment of younger men—in their 40s—as directors, but failed to approve a retirement age for them of 68 or 70. It did vow, however, to widen the religious denominations and vocations represented on the Board, and to hire younger staff secretaries. Branches with dormitories asked residents over age 25 to secure other quarters and make room for younger men.

On Staten Island, where youth programs had been attempted without result around 1930, citizens set up a summer day camp and four Hi-Y clubs in 1946. Serving both boys and girls, these programs were so effective that a Staten Island Branch was organized anew in January 1947. From modest rented quarters near the St. George ferry terminal, YMCA work was initiated in small communities such as New Dorp, Mariners Harbor, and Tottenville, with Hi-Y, youth clubs, and an extensive day camp program. By summer 1953, with a permanent staff of four, the Branch accommodated 600 day campers in twenty-nine camps in local communities. The first Board of Managers was twenty-four strong, and included three single women and two rabbis as well as Protestant ministers.

In the YMCA Centennial year of 1952, the Staten Island Branch acquired a 2.5-acre parcel at 651 Broadway, felicitously located across from the Staten Island Zoo. A century-old stone homestead on the property served as temporary headquarters until 1957, when a modern YMCA building was opened. Post-War Staten Island was the fastest-growing borough, composed of mostly middle-class families, and Branch programs were designed for the entire family. The low-rise facility, quite different in appearance from Ys built in the 1920s and 1930s, included a gym, pool and excellent outdoor playgrounds. It cost more than $500,000, with 80 percent allocated from a Centennial Fund Campaign, which had aimed to raise $20 million for expansion in new areas of Manhattan, the Bronx and Staten Island.

In contrast, Branches in Manhattan and the Bronx served youth who came primarily from poor areas and families. Of 3,322 boys served in their programs in 1944, 2,500 were underprivileged, from low-income homes or families living near poverty in economically depressed areas. Four Branches (West Side, Bronx Union, Harlem, and Uptown) operated 14 separate centers that provided extensions into needy neighborhoods. The New York YMCA had long offered its programs at low rates for boys who needed help. By 1944, most boys' work was subsidized, with only 12.4 percent derived from dues and fees. Boys in those four Branches and the McBurney Y, many of them from broken homes and on scholarships, participated in camps such as Camp Custer, a new YMCA facility in New York's Bear Mountain area.

Camping had been the New York Association's strongest boys' program for decades. This work was formalized in 1945 as the Camp and Outing Branch, comprised of Camps Greenkill and Talcott, Custer and Oscawana. By 1955, Camp Custer had become inadequate; the Association gave up that site and acquired a third resident camp, McAlister, adjacent to Greenkill and

Camps Oscawana and Talcott were popular with YMCA campers.

Talcott in Huguenot, New York. McAlister, designed as a low-cost interracial camp, accommodated 192 city boys ages 9 to 15. A lake was created on its forested lands and twenty-two pre-fabricated lean-tos served as bunks. Oscawana, in Putnam County, had been used by the French Branch and then by young adults from the Grand Central Branch. The Association acquired it from the New York Central Railroad in 1957 for $1, but the camp ran a deficit and was later closed. At this time, the Brooklyn YMCA was operating Camp Brooklyn in Paupack, Pennsylvania, and Camp Pratt in Palisades Interstate Park.

The interracial Camp McAlister opened in 1955.

The New York Association added a major resource in 1947 with the purchase of Holiday Hills in Pawling, New York. Acquired from the Consolidated Edison Company, which had made it an employee retreat, Holiday Hills fulfilled the YMCA's goal of offering more outdoor activities to groups. The facility, which had earlier lives as a race-horse training farm, sanitarium, and Air Force convalescent center, occupied 535 acres of rolling Dutchess County land. Holiday Hills became a conference and vacation center within easy reach of the city for young adults who came to enjoy its lake, bridle and hiking paths, trout streams and tennis courts.

At the Harlem Y, 600 boys and girls participated in an extension program in summer 1946 at the Walker Memorial Baptist Church. The Association-wide survey revealed that all boys who participated in Harlem Branch activities lived in overcrowded, depressed Central Harlem. Six out of 10 were from families in trouble, on relief or in need of charitable assistance.

Boys at the Harlem YMCA gained a great mentor after Jackie Robinson made history in 1947, breaking the

Jackie Robinson, right, and Roy Campanella worked with Harlem YMCA boys for a decade.

participants and, not infrequently, are elected to statewide leadership positions. Hundreds of bills first drafted and introduced by teens, such as the mandatory seat belt legislation of the 1980s, have become law.

During the Depression the West Side YMCA had instituted clubs for boys to engage them in productive activities such as arts, chemistry, electricity, woodworking, and metal crafts. Boys from Fifty-Sixth to Eighty-Sixth Streets could also take educational, swimming and gym classes at the Branch. More than 80 percent of club members came from less privileged neighborhoods near Columbus Circle (by contrast, just 45 percent of total Branch membership lived in low-income areas). Their neighborhoods incubated gangs, as immortalized in Leonard Bernstein's *West Side Story*, particularly at a time when few boys could find work. One-third of the city's unemployed in 1940 were between ages 15 and 24.

color barrier in major league baseball as the first African-American player. Executive Director Rudolph J. Thomas invited his close friend to work off-season as a coach and counselor to boys at the YMCA, where Robinson had frequently worked out. Joined by Roy Campanella, his black teammate on the Brooklyn Dodgers, Robinson acted as a youth director with the Branch Boys' Division for a decade. Although the pay was insignificant, the payoff was great: "We are both crazy about children," Robinson told the press. Youth membership doubled as the legendary ballplayer inspired legions of local boys through his coaching as well as his accomplishments. Robinson and Campanella also served on Harlem's Board of Managers, with Robinson raising $50,000 in 1958 for a complete rehab of the Youth Division building. (In 1996, when the 77-year-old Branch building on West 135th Street was renovated, it was renamed the Harlem YMCA Jackie Robinson Youth Center.)

Youth and Government, a program created in the New York State YMCA in 1936, had become a firmly established endeavor in New York City Branches. This model government program was an outgrowth of the Older Boys' Conference held in Albany, and had its roots in the Hi-Y. During the New York State Constitutional Convention in 1935, 300 youth participants from across the state met to discuss implications of the new constitution. A Boys' Work secretary, Clement A. Duran of the Albany YMCA who was later employed by the New York City Association, was one of two founding fathers of the program. Youth and Government took hold in YMCAs nationwide and has since grown to involve thousands of teens in state model government programs. Teens from the YMCA of Greater New York continue to be enthusiastic

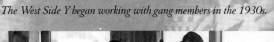

The West Side Y began working with gang members in the 1930s.

Boxer Rocky Graziano spars with members of a West Side boys' club.

Alarmed by the rapid rise in juvenile delinquency west of its building, the West Side Y had obtained funds from the Civil Works Administration in 1934 and pinpointed all community recreational resources and gangs operating in the area. The Branch began a comprehensive program, working with twelve groups of gangs and more than 200 boys unable to pay program fees. When federal funds dried up in 1937, the Y formed the Park West Boys' Club with two other neighborhood organizations, enrolling 450 boys by the next year. With funding from the National Youth Administration, the Branch employed 400 young people in 1939, and incorporated the Park West Boys' Club in its boys' program in 1941. By 1942, the number of gangs in the area had declined.

In 1944 a new strategy was proposed to strengthen YMCA physical education programs to appeal to both sexes. Its emphases included developing health education and more competitive sports activities; providing a physical fitness program and more outdoor programs for groups; making full use of aquatic facilities; and adding handball, squash and individual exercise areas. In 1958, the Association would offer its first full-fledged Learn-to-Swim campaign, and introduce scuba lessons. The Flushing Y would boast the largest Judo Club in the eastern United States, and West Side a national title in boys' gymnastics.

In the post-war years the Uptown Branch, formed after the first Harlem Branch closed on 125th Street, operated five community centers, four of them in very depressed or low-income neighborhoods in East Harlem and the Upper West Side. Its work also extended north to Washington Heights. Based on Amsterdam Avenue near 126th Street, the Branch focused primarily on needy boys, many of them poor whites, and gang members in need of sympathetic leadership and wholesome recreational activities at minimal rates.

By 1953, youth dynamics had changed radically in the city. The New York Association annual report noted an "explosive increase" in the younger population, as the post-war Baby Boom was inflated by a new wave of immigrant children; One-third of the Association's Centennial Fund proceeds was designated for Boys' Work, in particular at extension sites. Membership in Boys' Work programs, which by now included girls, leaped 25 percent in a year. The Uptown Branch was the largest contributor to this daunting growth. The youth it served in 1953 nearly doubled, to 1,443 participants, from 780 the previous year. Moreover, that same year monolingual Spanish-speaking children jumped from 20 percent to 80 percent of participants. The upsurge in immigration, fueled by air travel, was coming largely from the island of Puerto

Rico, and these young newcomers nearly overwhelmed the Branch's primarily English-speaking staff, causing the Association to arrange for its existing employees to study Spanish. By 1954, 95 percent of Uptown's members were Puerto Rican, posing a large and unanticipated challenge to the Association.

By then, the Association was using the term "juvenile delinquency" to express one of its major concerns. Boys who were juvenile delinquents participated in gangs, committed criminal offenses and/or dropped out of school. Their numbers were increasing, causing great apprehension in adults, and the Uptown Branch area had one of the highest delinquency rates. The Association mobilized quickly, stepping up its extension work for youth. By 1956, it had staffed extension projects in three new sections of the city and two housing projects, and employed nine City Youth Board workers. Only four Branches—Seamen's, the two Railroad Ys, and Sloane House—did not do youth work, although they contributed funds to the program.

The following year a Neighborhood Youth Branch was organized as an outgrowth of the Westchester-Bronx Branch, which had acquired property in 1951. Utilizing available space in churches, schools, vacant stores and lofts, YMCA extension work now reached youth in Washington Heights, Yorkville and the Kingsbridge-Inwood neighborhoods, where extensive tenant relocations due to Robert Moses' "renewal" projects in the Bronx had swollen the population. Staten Island recorded a fivefold increase in youth group enrollment in 1957, and West Side offered a storefront extension for youth at 15 West Sixty-Third Street, near its main Branch. In 1958,

Male and female students at five colleges who joined the Intercollegiate YMCA Branch took part in public service projects.

the annual report referred to increased delinquency among "teens," a term that had gained popularity for boys and girls ages 13 to 18. By then the YMCA was serving all but two of 14 areas of high delinquency in the city, with programs that emphasized prevention.

YMCA day camps gained popularity in the city as families grew in the post-war years. By 1958, 17 Branches of the YMCA of Greater New York enrolled 3,610 children, 844 of them girls. In 1959, it enrolled 5,000 boys and girls in 55 day camps. For older teens, a Counselor-In-Training (CIT) program offered a meaningful camp experience and prepared a cadre of future day camp counselors. By that year, there was no doubt about whom this YMCA intended to serve: "our major concern is with youth," declared the annual report.

College student programs came under scrutiny too in the post-war period. In 1946, the Board of Protestant Student Work was established, led by the Intercollegiate Branch. Intended for Protestant students but open to others, the Board advocated admitting women to its programs in co-educational institutions, serving foreign students better by working with the YMCA's Committee for Friendly Relations and giving "special attention to Negro students." At this time, the Branch operated five main centers, at City College of New York's uptown and Twenty-Third Street campuses; New York University in the Bronx and Washington Square; and Columbia University.

The Civil Rights Era

THE 1944 NEW YORK Association survey urged Branches to "continue to provide opportunities for inter-racial aspects of the program and provide facilities and services for groups of Negroes living outside the Harlem area with provisions for interracial participation." But since this remained only a suggestion, it is hardly surprising that desegregation in the New York YMCAs proceeded at a sluggish pace. Full compliance would take decades.

However, in a 1946 New York Association report, "real progress" was cited: eleven New York Branches were completely interracial, four accepted "Negroes" under certain conditions and only two had taken no definite steps. The YMCA Camp Branch told an even better story. In 1944, Camp Custer had begun operations as a fully interracial camp, and by the next year the two resident camps at Huguenot were opened to all races.

Black Enterprise founder and publisher Earl G. Graves Jr. recalled, in an address to the YMCA in 2000,

Eleven New York Branches, including West Side, were completely interracial well before 1946.

his childhood experience with the Brooklyn Association. An eager swimmer who had acquired the skill at the Carlton Y, Graves went on a field trip to the Brooklyn Central Branch and was impressed by its much better pool. When he returned to swim there, he was called out of the water. A director told him it was for the "white kids," and that he must swim at the Colored Y. At his mother's insistence, the two returned to Central where, after her discussion with the director, the pool was effectively integrated.

In 1944, a flyer, probably distributed by the New York–based Congress of Racial Equality (CORE), cited dissatisfactions with segregated YMCA programs and facilities. It detailed specific abuses: the Railroad Branches "maintain a lily-white policy" by excluding African-American railway employees; the William Sloane House, "the largest Y Hotel, sends all black people, including servicemen, to the Harlem Y," located five miles away; the McBurney Branch "serves Negro servicemen but not Negro civilians"; the Bronx Union Y "allows Negro boys to participate in Boys' Clubs, but not to become members" despite their need for neighborhood services; the West Side Branch "has admitted a few 'token members' during the past year, but still gives Negro applicants 'special handling.'" By contrast, the flyer pointed out that "In the Harlem Branch, the Intercollegiate Branch, and the Seamen's Branch, Negroes and Whites are given equal service, and they like it." It concluded by demanding that all racial discrimination be eliminated at the YMCA.

LET'S THROW JIM CROW OUT OF THE "Y"

HE ISN'T ALLOWED:

(1) In the McBurney Branch. During the past two years there has been no discrimination. All the facilities of this Y. are fully used by the young men of the community and those from outside.

(2) In the Seaman's House there is no Crow's Nest. This Y. serves seamen of all races and national backgrounds.

(3) In the Harlem Branch, white young men have been welcomed as residents and members throughout the years. Every courtesy has been extended to visitors of other racial backgrounds.

HE ISN'T NEEDED:

(1) In the West Side Branch. During the past year a few Negro men and boys have been admitted as members enjoying full privileges. Applications of Negroes are still specially handled, rather than being treated the same as those of whites. All discrimination should be eliminated from this branch.

(2) In the Bronx Union Branch. Negro boys are allowed to work with boys' clubs, but membership has never been granted. Negroes live near this Y. and would use the full privileges if they were made welcome.

(3) In the William Sloane House, largest Y. hotel, which now serves mostly service men, and still sends Negro applicants, including service men, to the Harlem Branch.

(4) In the Railroad Branches, which serve railroad workers while they are in the city, but maintain a lily-white policy, Negro railway employees being excluded.

(5) Any Y.M.C.A. in the City of New York. If Negroes and whites get along together in some of these Y's, why not in others? Can we allow unscientific, undemocratic, and un-Christian prejudices to violate the principles on which the Y's are founded? Let us demand that the Y.M.C.A. Board put an end to all discrimination in the Y.M.C.A.'s of this city.

A 1944 flyer, "Let's Throw Jim Crow Out of the 'Y,'" detailed discrimination at some Branches.

The flyer spelled out the challenges ahead of the YMCA in the next three decades. CORE picketed the Bedford Branch in 1951 over claims of racial discrimination. In the increasingly black Bedford-Stuyvesant area, African Americans had been denied membership privileges except for athletics and a few civic programs. Following the CORE action, Eugene Field Scott, by then general secretary of the Brooklyn and Queens Association and Howard Anderson, executive director of Bedford, announced that the Branch would accept all Negro applicants for membership. In 1959 Anderson retired and Russell N. Service, from the Buffalo, New York YMCA, became the first African-American director in Brooklyn, at the Bedford Branch. His challenge was to revitalize the Branch, which by then was in a "crucial area of need."

In 1953, the New York Board of Directors reviewed its past decade and policies with regard to race. It noted advances made by every Branch except the Pennsylvania Railroad Y, which had refused membership to a group of Negro Redcaps in 1943, a move that generated bad publicity for the Association. The Board put forth this resolution: "It is the policy of the YMCA of the City of New York to have no qualifications for membership covering race, creed, or color. All branches are urged to conform to this policy at the earliest possible time."

Despite that and other resolutions, a 1958 survey of Branches revealed significant patterns of segregation by race. Branch memberships tended to mirror the ethnic composition of surrounding neighborhoods: in particular,

the Harlem and Bedford YMCAs, both in predominantly black neighborhoods had, respectively, 98.5 percent and 80.5 percent non-white memberships. The West Side Branch, located near a heavily Puerto Rican community and drawing its membership from a wide area, had a 27 percent Puerto Rican youth membership and a non-white youth membership of 34 percent. By contrast its adult fee-paying members were less than 2 percent Puerto Rican and less than 1 percent non-white.

In Brooklyn, the Central Branch had a non-white youth membership of 9 percent and only 3 percent adult non-whites. Eight New York City Branches—Flatbush, Flushing, Pennsylvania Railroad, Greenpoint, Holiday Hills, Intercollegiate, Prospect Park, and Westchester-Bronx—grouped together in the survey, had a combined membership of 0.6 percent non-white youth and 0.2 percent of adults.

In 1956, the New York annual report revealed a diversification of the New York professional staff, which by then included blacks and whites, men and women. Yet as the civil rights movement was gathering force, ignited by the 1954 Supreme Court decision *Brown v. Board of Education* that effectively desegregated public schools and facilities, the New York City YMCAs' responses, in spite of national and local policies promoting integration, had been tepid at best.

"Bigger, Better and More Needs Than Ever"

IN 1957, AFTER nearly three decades of discussion, the New York and Brooklyn and Queens Associations merged, forming the YMCA of Greater New York. Immediately, it became the largest YMCA in the United States with members spread among thirty-six Branches in all five boroughs. So joined, this YMCA would again lead the national movement in several important areas in the latter part of the century.

John W. Cook, then general secretary of the Brooklyn and Queens Association, had first proposed the idea in 1931 to leaders of both YMCAs. Cook noted the trend of like organizations in New York—relief agencies, "Hebrew" agencies, the Boy Scouts and Federation of Churches—to consolidate their multi-borough operations. The municipal consolidation in 1898, giving New York City one government, and transport lines that linked both Brooklyn and Queens directly to Manhattan, made a YMCA merger—and a 50,000-strong membership—both feasible and desirable.

Cook's major motivation was financial: residents were moving among boroughs, costing his Branches support. With Manhattan the dominant financial center and headquarters for industries based in Brooklyn and Queens, a merger would encourage Manhattan-based companies to donate to one YMCA for all New Yorkers. Consolidation would also offer economies and efficiencies in administration, and make possible stronger leadership. Acknowledging the New York Association's strength and success in programs—especially physical, educational and boys' work—Cook advocated the merger as a way to improve programs in Brooklyn and Queens, and to solve problems through joint efforts. He conferred with Herbert and Richardson Pratt, A. H. Greeley, Edwin P. Maynard and his counterpart in the New York Association, Walter Diack. Adding punch to his proposal, he told them that a powerful supporter, the office of John D. Rockefeller Jr., had given assurance that it would approve of such a merger.

However, the New York Association had balked at this entreaty from its weaker and poorer sister, and the plan was quashed. Diack and the Board's executive committee, chaired by Cleveland H. Dodge, noted the "great difficulty in preserving the local Branch interest in the community and community interests in the respective Branches" which it deemed "absolutely essential to a successful YMCA." The merged Association's potential unwieldiness and possible loss of local interest and identity proved to be deal-breakers, although the group agreed to a joint committee for "intensive study."

The Depression's length and severity, followed by extraordinary demands on the Branches during wartime, apparently tabled the matter, which did not surface again until 1944. This time Brooklyn and Queens YMCA representatives, saddled with $2.3 million in debt, went directly to Cleveland H. Dodge with their appeal. They were dipping into capital reserves for operations and their buildings, heavily used by servicemen without compensation, desperately needed rehabilitation. They couldn't make debt and interest payments and their local fund-raising was altogether inadequate in a changing population of nearly 4 million residents, many of whom had fewer financial resources than their prosperous predecessors. Many local industries in these two boroughs were based in Manhattan, making them inaccessible to the Association's fund-raisers. Two of the Brooklyn men flatly stated that merger was "the only solution to the Brooklyn problem."

Other priorities dominated the post-war years, however, and the matter was shelved. Finally, in 1954 an Inter-Association Conference Committee was formed to study a merger, chaired by Presidents Robert S. Curtiss (New York) and Rodney C. Ward (Brooklyn and Queens). The National Council of YMCAs may have provided some impetus, since it had considered Brooklyn and Queens a hardship case for some years. In 1956 both YMCA Boards voted unanimously to bond in a new corporation as of January 1, 1957. The newly named "metropolitan office" set up headquarters at 422 Ninth Avenue, adjoining Sloane House. Despite concerns about a Manhattan "takeover" and retention of individual Branch management practices, the newly consolidated YMCA would emerge stronger through this, "the only sound solution," in the words of R. L. Dickinson, New York Association executive vice president. The YMCA of Greater New York embarked on a self-described "shakedown cruise," promoting itself in citywide television, radio, newspaper, and car-card advertising as "bigger and better" with "more needs than ever."

One unstated issue that the stronger Association could now confront was the continuing reluctance of certain Branches to integrate their memberships. Consolidation would call for some compression of staff, and a committee took the opportunity to recommend the retirement of four long-time employees, two of them at Bedford, and a new mandatory retirement age of 65.

Gayle J. Lathrop, the executive vice president to whom all Branch executive directors now reported, set forth firm expectations of the twenty-six YMCAs and their thirty-six sub-Branches in the new Association's first year. The YMCA would be reaching out to people where they lived, not just waiting for them to come to Branches. Furthermore, he emphasized, "In each Branch, in all its programs and activities, its business dealings, and personnel relationships we expect a climate and practice in harmony with our Christian aims and purposes. The needs of a boy or young man or woman for our services and our ability to help them regardless of race, religion, color or economic status are the determining factors. Within each Branch and between Branches we expect that there will be a spirit of mutual concern, helpfulness and cooperation." Lathrop's unequivocal mandate foreshadowed a decade of profound changes in the YMCA of Greater New York.

5

1960-1980

An Era of Upheaval

THE 1960 NATIONAL election, resulting in John F. Kennedy's becoming the thirty-fifth President of the United States, marked a turning point in American society and within the YMCA. The nation had chosen a young Harvard-educated Catholic to lead the fifty states at a critical moment in history: the Cold War was freezing international relations, the Vietnam conflict

was heating up and the domestic civil rights movement was about to reach a boiling point. Kennedy's idealistic leadership in everything from racial equality to physical fitness would have profound reverberations within the YMCA. His assassination in 1963 ushered in an era of disillusionment with people and institutions that had once been respected. Harmony and unity were its victims in the city and the nation, and the turmoil was felt deeply in the YMCA.

In the early 1960s the national Civil Rights Movement was also reaching a climax. Sit-ins and student-led protests in the South culminated in a march of 250,000 people on Washington, D.C., in 1963, where the Rev. Dr. Martin Luther King Jr. articulated the aspirations of black Americans in his momentous speech, "I Have a Dream." At least three New York Y Branches participated

in the march. Bedford's Business and Professional Club chartered a bus, with Executive Director Russell Service as captain of the group of thirty-eight. Many Harlem YMCA members attended with their church and civic groups, and the Intercollegiate Branch sponsored two bus-loads of marchers.

Landmark legislation followed, in the Civil Rights Act of 1964 and the Voting Rights Act of 1965. Simultaneously, President Lyndon B. Johnson introduced his twin domestic initiatives, the War on Poverty and the Great Society, which would lead to vast federally funded programs in the vital areas of housing and health care,

The Rev. Dr. Martin Luther King was a guest speaker at the Holiday Hills YMCA during an annual Christian Women's Retreat in 1966.

education and economic opportunity. But the 1968 assassination of King, followed closely by that of New York Senator and Presidential candidate Robert Kennedy, ushered in a devastating era for both the city and the nearly 200-year-old nation, which was already reeling from the escalating war in Vietnam.

The 1960s became an extraordinary period of introspection and self-scrutiny for the Association. Unexpected changes in society and family structure—mounting desertions and divorce rates, mothers joining the full-time workforce—led to a strong focus on early childhood and family programs. Grave urban problems of racism, poverty and criminal activity in youth motivated the YMCA to take rare public stands on pressing issues of the day. The city's fiscal crisis, a national recession coupled with rampant inflation and a new wave of immigration in the 1970s brought further changes to New York's communities and to the Association.

In a 1959 speech to fellow urban YMCA leaders, Gayle J. Lathrop, who became chief executive of the YMCA of Greater New York in 1957, foresaw that the 1960s and 1970s would be decades of profound change, and articulated a vision of the YMCA's role in the "inner city." A graduate of Yale Divinity School, Lathrop was a religious man and an idealist, one who believed that the perplexing manifestations of urban distress were a God-given challenge to the YMCA. He felt an urban Association could no longer survive by focusing solely on the easier-to-reach and -serve middle class. New York had essentially lost its long-established white majority, he pointed out. Every week 1,500

residents fled the city for the suburbs, replaced by "Puerto Ricans, Negroes from the South, and White young people from the hinterland." New York City was now 48 percent Catholic, 26 percent Jewish, and only 23 percent Protestant. Lathrop expected that by 1970, 40 percent of New York City children would be Puerto Rican and non-white. Moreover, the inner city, where most of them lived, was deteriorating rapidly. A considerable number of boys and girls ages 9 to 18, the YMCA's core service group, was in trouble with the law and in need of intervention.

"If we ignore the challenge of serving problem kids because these are not 'our type,'" Lathrop asserted, "we raise a serious moral dilemma and lay ourselves open to public censure of avoiding our fair share of the tough jobs the community-serving agencies of our city have to tackle." The age and deterioration of urban YMCA buildings would make a tough job tougher, he added, but the alternative to modernization was "slow death." Lathrop pointed out that slums had grown up around New York City Branches—"our problem children"—in older neighborhoods, and noted that Branch staff did not reflect the bilingual, multi-racial communities they served. Many Branch Board members had joined the march to the suburbs and were no longer representative of their YMCA's neighborhood constituents, as had once been typical.

The latter half of the twentieth century, Lathrop accurately predicted, would be a historic time of rebuilding the cities, and he was convinced that it presented the YMCA with unprecedented opportunity: to upgrade its properties, cooperate in urban renewal efforts and reach out to help people in need in their own communities. The Association could not turn its back on the city as a wicked place, he said, as rural Protestants historically had done.

Gayle D. Lathrop (right), chief executive of the New York Association who set the course for the urban YMCA of the 1960s, congratulates Bedford Board of Managers Chairman Oliver D. Williams (accompanied by his wife), on his appointment as the first African-American State Supreme Court judge in 1962. At this time, problems were emerging in the inner city.

Lathrop's vision of the city had nothing to do with Sodom, Gomorrah or Babylon and everything to do with Zion, the new Jerusalem—in his words, "the city of our God."

Lathrop urged his YMCA colleagues to use long-range master planning to project their work to 1975, as the New York Association was doing, by taking the initiative and involving the residents of Branch service areas. Invoking YMCA founder Sir George Williams, Lathrop asserted that the urban Y must minister to the city's needy individuals by being thoroughly immersed in their environments, gearing programs to their needs and not to the structure of YMCA buildings or traditional patterns. "What we do must be relevant," he stated. "This is God's will for us."

The New York leader's vision pointed the way to an unprecedented extension of YMCA work beyond its buildings to reach New Yorkers in need, wherever they lived. As the Association put into practice what Lathrop had preached, it would evolve into a more human-needs oriented and less facility-centered multi-service agency. This would not be an easy road. "Our strength, courage and sincerity would be tested," Lathrop and Board Chairman Robert S. Curtiss noted in the 1959 annual report. Their successors concurred with that assessment in 1973, noting that "New York City is a continuing challenge. The YMCA must change as new needs arise, and it must undertake new activities, develop additional resources and recruit new leadership, if we are to cope with the problems and continue to be a vital force toward a better way of life."

Cries for relevancy echoed throughout the 1960s and 1970s, as American society and its burgeoning youth population called into question nearly every tradition and authority they had once revered. The YMCA of Greater New York heard from its share of doubters— especially its own staff and young people—and worked diligently to bring about significant changes in its methods of operation. Just as the YMCA historically served men in special groups, from students and shop workers to railway employees and merchant seamen, it now turned its attention to other unique populations. Vocal groups with particular needs were asserting themselves all at once, and the YMCA made every effort to accommodate them even when it was stretched thin. Disadvantaged New Yorkers, women, youth of all ages, senior citizens and disabled populations would find Y programs designed especially for them. In turn, they would fuel unprecedented growth in the New York YMCA.

But before it could address these challenges the Association, still coping with the after-effects of its far-reaching consolidation in 1957, had to put its own house in order. Topping the list of Board Chairman Alfred H. Howell's priorities and concerns in 1964 was that of achieving one Association rather than twenty-eight separate YMCAs.

The Association would add a director of citywide planning the next year, and the new Board committee on planning attested to its importance. The Y's major challenge, noted the 1965–66 annual report, was to "overcome resistance to change and static apathy generated by years of having 'always done it this way.'" By 1968–69 the citywide director was helping Branches formulate their own planning processes. Four Manhattan YMCAs—Grand Central, McBurney, Sloane House, and West Side—were also conducting, for the first time, a joint marketing study.

Howell emphasized the necessity of uniformly high standards in buildings and equipment and strong, qualified staff to bolster the YMCA's programs and citywide image. New management, "promising young men and women," should be recruited from outside the YMCA, Howell said, not just those with "previous indoctrination" as Y professionals. He stressed that integrity and a youthful outlook, regardless of chronological age, were essential to relate to the growing cadre of youth served by the YMCA.

Speaking to a YMCA laymen's conference in November 1964 on "Relevant Leadership for a Time of Dynamic Change," Lathrop echoed Howell's theme. He emphasized the importance of helping young people take responsibility for themselves, and feel they were needed and useful, in order to counter the prevailing disaffection of youth in society. He noted the current breakdown of morality, the racial revolution, the school dropout phenomenon, and worrisome unemployment among young people, and urged the assembled laymen to be full partners in providing meaningful programs. (Lathrop would die in office the following September.)

The growing ranks of disaffected youth, coupled with the confrontations and sporadic violence characteristic of the era, dismayed the genteel laymen who were devoted to the elevation and education of young men and more recently, young women. They were unfamiliar with—and not at ease with—the urban areas most in need of service in the mid-1960s. Yet the YMCA's top leadership understood that the problems they were confronting were those facing the entire city. The Association resolved to join with other voluntary organizations, government agencies, educational institutions, and others working for equality for disadvantaged groups in order to be more effective and make a real difference in New Yorkers' lives. Sensitive to accusations of "white racism" and of maintaining the "white power structure," which were thought to be the cause of many problems in society, the overwhelmingly white-led YMCA determined to focus on "social action" and become more relevant to the city's most critical needs.

A Wake-Up Call from Within

THE 1960 ANNUAL report, "Developing Character and Leadership," graphically depicted the YMCA's aspirations toward more diversity, at least in the people it served. The cover illustration portrayed three young men with arms linked, striding forward; the man in the middle was black. The report's message was idealistic in tone: "Our members are moving more closely together in a fellowship which knows no barriers among men and which, we hope, eventually will prevail not just within the YMCA but throughout the world." But the YMCA realized it first had to look within, and formed a "racial consultation" group to study its own patterns. "If at this moment of history we can do what God wants us to do," said Lathrop, "we can make one of the major contributions which the YMCA has made since its founding."

When the Uptown Branch's constituency changed in one year from predominantly white to predominantly Puerto Rican children, the YMCA realized the inadequacy of having only English-speaking staff. Its immediate solution was to provide Spanish lessons for employees, but by the 1960s it was apparent that staff was culturally unprepared as well. In 1960, only thirteen of the twenty-eight Branches had an interracial staff, and only ten interracial Boards of Managers. Having predominantly white leaders serving increasingly minority communities signaled an "us-them" philosophy that ran counter to the spirit of the times. Nor was the YMCA leadership adept at designing programs for a growing underprivileged class.

The New York Association's determination to change, and to diversify its management, was sincere but typically slow. In 1963, a staff committee presented a ten-point program to "amplify and implement" the Association's interracial policy, "to assure continued progress in this critical area." The Board's Executive Committee passed a resolution taking note of the "revolution in the area of civil rights and human rights in the USA" and calling on YMCA Branches and members "to share in Christian conscience in the struggle for full equality of opportunity for all persons." The resolution stated that this might mean "a change in personal conduct

The Uptown Branch's constituency had changed in one year from primarily white to predominantly Puerto Rican children.

for some of us." To be sure, only four Branches at that time had commendable diversity of staff: Bedford, Central Queens, Sloane House, and West Side.

In 1966, an Ad Hoc Committee on the YMCA and Racial Tension gathered at the Hotel New Yorker. Rhetoric was heated, with equal participation by black and white YMCA staff. Black employees asserted that the Y was "all talk, no action" and unwilling to recognize the racial issue as a major problem. Later that year the national YMCA, which had been pressing local Ys for maximum diversity and affirmative action in hiring, held an emergency conference in Newark. It was chaired by New York executive Russell Service, who told the national YMCA that as black and non-white staff had struggled in the climate of 1960s urban despair, "It became abundantly clear that the YMCA, of which they were a part, was itself a major part of the problem." Service had left the Bedford Y during this time to join the metropolitan staff as head of urban affairs.

In 1968 the New York YMCA named its first Asian executive director, John Lee, at the Prospect Park–Bay Ridge Branch, and hired a Hispanic man, Abraham Reyes, as executive director of the Uptown YMCA. But the pace of change was slow, and the Association got a jolt from its staff in 1970 at the annual All-Staff Meeting when a group of staffers interrupted the agenda and came forward with a "manifesto." The Association had not acted on the changes it promised, they declared. It was time for more non-white staff and new, more relevant programs to address the needs of the city's disadvantaged groups. Calling themselves BAN-WYS (Black and Non-White YMCA Secretaries), this group had been meeting for two years to examine the YMCA's role in minority communities and to figure out how to eliminate white racism from within. The New York Y and a key African-American staffer, Jesse N. Alexander Jr., youth extension director at Highland Park and later assistant executive director of Bedford, would emerge as leaders in a national BAN-WYS movement.

Speaking at the first BAN-WYS conference, Alexander indicated a new preference for indigenous leadership at Ys in minority neighborhoods rather than integrated staffs. Existing black Branches, he said, were meeting important psychological needs and were in close contact with their people." Noting the deterioration of YMCA buildings in poor areas, Alexander called for "spiritual renovation," with blacks running programs in their own communities and whites helping to fund them. In 1969, as the group's focus changed from solely black leadership to embrace all non-white groups, Alexander became head of the Black and Non-White Concerns Division of the National Board of YMCAs.

At the 1970 All-Staff Meeting, employees accused the YMCA of Greater New York of avoiding discussion of

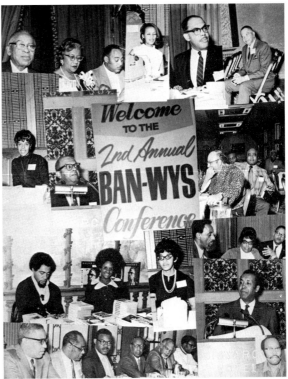

Some twenty New York BAN-WYS members accused the Association of being unresponsive in a manifesto read at the 1969 All-Staff Meeting.

the problems and being self-congratulatory. There was a lack of meaningful jobs for non-whites in the YMCA, they said, and the Association was unresponsive to them and the people it served. By their very nature, YMCA programs and services failed to meet needs of urban residents—drug abuse prevention, community control, education, job training to meet local economic needs, a shortage of low-income housing, and an end to alienation.

William Howes, chief executive since 1966, responded extemporaneously to the manifesto, citing financial pressures the Association was facing and the large sum it expended on personnel. "I have…no quarrel with the need to be more relevant," he said. "The task I have is how to manage…these resources in a way that *enables* us to become more relevant." As an example of his worries, he noted that "a drop of one percent in residence occupancy would mean a drop of more than $80,000 in income."

Howes, who is remembered as an urban missionary, was not unsympathetic to his staff and their issues. Just as Lathrop had been a spiritual leader, Howes had the heart of a social worker, eager to tackle and solve the complex problems of contemporary society. However, he was alluding to a mounting concern about YMCA Branches now situated in non-white, relatively poor neighborhoods where community members could not be self-sufficient in financing their YMCA and its programs, as was the custom. The increasingly poor Branches depended on

A national conference of Black and Non-White YMCA Secretaries (BAN-WYS) met in 1968 to discuss racial problems within the YMCA.

their richer siblings to share revenues from residence programs; if the latter did not thrive, neither would they.

Following this wake-up call, a citywide task force was formed, including Howes, Service and an outside consultant, Dr. Harvey Hornstein. Non-white staffers stated their priorities: more "power" positions, programs to meet the needs of inner-city communities, drug abuse programs, and observation of the new national holiday honoring Dr. King. Later they would add their desire to see more non-whites on boards, committees, and staff. The group's lowest priorities were building new facilities downtown and organizing new YMCAs, World Service programs and international management services, which they believed detracted from fundamental community needs.

The YMCA moved quickly to adopt task force recommendations that were based on those priorities. It moved to fortify existing inner-city programs by going aggressively after government funds. In 1971 it won a 10-year contract for an alcohol treatment program financed by the city's Health and Hospitals Corporation and Model Cities. The Association observed its first annual Martin Luther King holiday on January 15, 1973 and began work on an Affirmative Action Program.

Dr. Leo B. Marsh of the Harlem Branch (below) conceived the Salute to Black Achievers in Industry in 1971, and took the successful program nationwide (left, the 1985 awards program cover by artist Jacob Lawrence).

Black Achievers act as mentors to Harlem youth.

That same year the Board agreed to strengthen Boards, committees and staffs by increasing the number of female, black, Spanish-speaking, and other underrepresented minority groups "who, bringing their unique insights, understanding, and leadership... will help the YMCA serve the needs of the total population in the service areas." By 1975, the Association implemented its new Affirmative Action Plan with aggressive recruitment goals for minorities and women at all levels. In just two years the goals were met. Out of 65 new professionals hired in 1977, 38 percent represented minority groups and 38 percent were women.

In this time of sweeping change, the Harlem YMCA initiated one of the most dynamic and enduring programs. The 1971 "Salute to Black Achievers in Industry," brainchild of YMCA volunteer Dr. Leo B. Marsh, honored 188 black men and women in positions of influence and executive leadership nominated by their corporations, highlighting those that were offering positions to African Americans. By 1973, Black Achievers was an annual event whose striking success had gained nationwide attention (and Dr. Marsh had moved to the National Council of YMCAs). The next year, 50 corporations involved in the Black Achievers program hosted 125 Harlem Y youth in an effort to raise their career sights. The program expanded its goal of showcasing African-American men and women business leaders with a mentoring program added in 1979. Honorees developed one-on-one relationships with young people and sponsored activities such as a spring tour of historically black colleges and universities. The program, in all its facets, continues to thrive; through 2001 some 4,000 Achievers have been honored, 150 corporations have taken part and significant sums have been raised for youth.

Programs for the Inner City

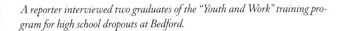
A reporter interviewed two graduates of the "Youth and Work" training program for high school dropouts at Bedford.

DESPITE COMPLAINTS FROM staff, the YMCA had hardly been ignoring the needs of the inner city. By not following its core membership to the suburbs, it had manifested its commitment and its intentions. Since 1958, both Board and staff had worked intensively to assess the YMCA's role in a changing New York. In 1962, the Board hired an educator, Dr. Robert King Hall, to guide its Program Evaluation Committee in designing a long-range strategy. That year-long effort resulted in *A Strategy for the Inner City,* a volume of more than 400 pages. Its assessment was hard-hitting: the New York City YMCA had to become more relevant. Although it presented an amazing diversity of programs, with hundreds of offerings at its Branches, the overall Association program had "failed to inspire" since World War II, and only big changes would win back the loyalty of young people. "If the leadership will identify one critical, obvious, overriding need of the 'inner city' and meet that need with spectacular success, the whole image of the Association will change," Hall concluded.

Like its predecessors—the Swift surveys of 1926 and 1927, and the 1944 Strayer survey of the New York Association—the Hall study appraised current programs in relation to Association goals, community needs and problems in order to develop priorities for the future. The assessment measured whether YMCA programs, then primarily for boys and young men, were contributing to affirmative changes in social behavior and attitudes and strengthening moral and ethical values.

The report included hundreds of specific recommendations, many of which were adopted. Hall found that the YMCA was a venerable, highly respected institution in the city, having weathered some very difficult years, but it was slow to act. The report urged the YMCA to be both *in* and *of* the inner city, finding ways to be effective under changed conditions. The Y must create solutions and not just correct inadequacies, Hall advised,

through involvement in programs of vital concern to New Yorkers and vigorous cooperation with community and government projects, specifically housing and urban renewal, training and youth programs.

Moreover, Hall urged the YMCA to take courageous leadership in projects—likely to be controversial—which addressed the burning issues in society. As he pointed out, those difficult and divisive problems were of great interest to young people: "The YMCA must provide them a forum." By the Y's reluctance to take clear-cut stands on social issues, "it has abdicated the very arenas where effective leadership is being developed," Hall noted. It had failed to attack social ills, particularly those which beset youth, its stated priority. The YMCA's historic leadership in social action, so prominent with soldiers, immigrants, refugees and underprivileged boys, was now limited to "modest work" with "atypical" youth in gangs and unemployed school dropouts. "Swimming, fitness and ping pong," said Hall, "are not enough."

In 1926, Swift had observed that the YMCA program consisted mainly of physical and educational work and provision of living accommodations; by 1963 it was only slightly different. Once prominent Association programs, from Bible classes and credit facilities to settlement house services on the Bowery, had disappeared, Hall pointed out. Industrial training, which had enrolled 174,000 men in sixty-six shops in 1920, now enrolled only two dozen at two Branches. Informal education, characteristic of the movement for a century, was now minor in importance. Counseling programs, which served more than 17,000 in 1935, had dwindled to less than 400 served in 1963. Hall exhorted the Y to step up participation in community and government projects: "Once the YMCA was the acknowledged leader," he observed, "but today it leads in few things."

Reacting to that stinging assessment, the YMCA leadership mobilized to build on its existing expertise and put its assets to use for disadvantaged communities, creating a Department of Urban Affairs in 1966 for cooperative action and collaboration with other agencies and resources. Some 7,000 of the city's 12,500 school dropouts were unemployed, constituting the city's most critical sociological problem. In Harlem, juvenile delinquency rose 56 percent in the 1960s, and in 1964 30 percent of Bedford-Stuyvesant teens did not finish high school. By 1966, the Association had implemented Training Resources for Youth, Inc. (TRY) at its Bedford Branch, patterned after the

Training Resources for Youth (TRY) offered male dropouts instruction in occupational skills such as refrigeration, welding, culinary arts, and auto repair at the Bedford Trade School.

existing Youth and Work project, a 16-week training program for school dropouts run jointly by the Vocational Service Center (VSC) and Bedford Trade School with funds from the city's Youth Board and private grants. TRY offered male dropouts, largely from the neighborhood, a curriculum in occupational skills, such as refrigeration and air-conditioning appliance repairs, and "coping" skills designed to engender a positive outlook and a sense of self-worth. Later it would add advanced secretarial training. Its slogan, "Learn Baby Learn, Earn Baby Earn, TRY is where it's at!" was a twist on the threatening slogan "burn baby, burn" that was used by protesters.

Not coincidentally, TRY also rescued the Branch financially, whose previously middle-class white members had been replaced by a primarily poor black constituency. TRY was a federally financed corporation with a $4.3 million budget for fifteen months led by "indigenous personnel" and supported by YMCA administrators, board and committee members. The Bedford building enjoyed a top-to-bottom $1 million renovation to accommodate TRY, moved its Trade School to new quarters in downtown Brooklyn and converted its youth building into space for youth, adults, and community programs.

Following a $1 million renovation, the Bedford building became closely associated with TRY.

The program, directed by Russell Service, was a success. In its first year TRY provided 600 young men, many of them married with families, with vocational training and job placement, counseling, and technical instruction, and follow-up counseling on the job. A government official commented that "the YMCA, dollar for dollar, had done far more with the appropriation to finance its TRY project than the government would have obtained for the same amount of money." In 1973, the TRY Board merged with Bedford's Board of Managers, giving the Branch complete program accountability. The program, which secured jobs for 88 percent of its graduate trainees, expanded the next year as an Employment Service Training Project for trainees in all five boroughs. That year the Branch joined with the city's Health and Hospitals Corporation and Youth and Action Inc. to establish an alcoholic rehabilitation center and expand community services. Bedford's Technical School Program underwent major curriculum redesign, firmly establishing the Branch as a provider of critical and comprehensive social-educational and rehabilitative services for the community.

In 1969, the Association introduced CHOICE, another inner-city program, in partnership with the Private Vocational Schools Association of New York City. Its goal was to provide unemployed or underemployed men and women over age 18 with better opportunities for successful job training. Administered by the Counseling and Testing Services Branch, CHOICE was based at the Harlem YMCA and the Bedford Trade School. The training program, funded by the state Departments of Education and Labor, was the most comprehensive of its kind in the city, offering 12 weeks at the YMCA of pre-vocational training in basic skills and exploration of 65 possible occupations, and up to 52 weeks of vocational training in one of 28 accredited private trade schools. By 1973, CHOICE had a 68-percent job placement record. From 1970–1977 it trained more than 1,000 youth and adults ages 18 to 55.

Other Branches had their own programs. In 1964, Prospect Park–Bay Ridge participated in the Operation Bootstrap Program to raise the educational level of disadvantaged adults in the area. Harlem sponsored Storefront Outreach Programs and Back-A-Block, which provided saturation services to residents of a single block. And Bedford participated in the Model Cities Program with an experiment in machine shop job training for young deaf men. By 1972, government-funded programs accounted for $3,429,000 in income for the YMCA of Greater New York out of $14 million total.

At this time, the YMCA began taking public stands, a practice it had once scrupulously avoided. In 1969, the Board endorsed in principle the Kerner Commission Report on Civil Disorders and the objectives of the Poor People's Campaign. In 1971, the Association declared its intention to take positions on public issues which related to its role and objectives. That year the Board adopted a resolution following the Attica prison uprising that resulted in death for a number of prisoners. In a press release, it noted the need for "basic changes" at Attica and other institutions that housed large numbers of New York City residents, and offered the YMCA as a resource to correction officials. This use of Association muscle caused consternation among a large number of Directors who viewed public position statements with alarm, while others applauded the Y's attempts to "change the system."

Two years later the YMCA publicly expressed its concern about Governor Nelson Rockefeller's drug program, which mandated stiff prison sentences for those caught with drugs. The Board's Urban Affairs Committee issued a position statement expressing support for the Governor's program to punish drug sellers, but expressed "deep concern" about its intent to punish all convicted with the "extreme penalty of 'life.'" It also spoke out against "senseless ambushes" of police officers, and reductions in Federal funding for social services, noting that the Association had thirteen such projects serving 5,000 people at nine Branches.

The New York YMCA seriously considered becoming a sole or joint sponsor of low-cost housing or pairing with the Model Cities program as a housing provider. The Association investigated non-profit housing in the St. Nicholas and Brooklyn Atlantic Terminal Urban Renewal Districts, and also contemplated establishing a YMCA program in the new World Trade Center in lower Manhattan, for workers and residents of Battery Park City. Instead it tempered those ambitions by choosing a less risky commitment, operating YMCA programs and social services in neighborhood facilities, particularly in housing projects. By 1974, the Association had programs up and running in Baisley Park, Borinquen Plaza, Jonathan Williams Houses, Markham Houses, Glebe Avenue, and Bailey Avenue projects. Grosvenor House on West 105th Street in Manhattan was also under Association management.

The YMCA's greatest efforts for the inner city focused on its traditional strength, youth work. While continuing to offer programs for a more affluent, dues-paying membership, the YMCA trained its expertise on young people in the "ghettoes," the city's most destitute neighborhoods. To keep its membership base—the source of 92 percent of its revenues—viable, it determined to serve both the "haves" and "have nots." The 1965–66 annual report noted that "poor children plus millionaire businessmen in athletic or businessmen's clubs" met in Ys throughout the city. "Stripped to a pair of gym trunks and sneakers, the Madison Avenue executive drawing $60,000 a year may be difficult to distinguish from the stockroom clerk making $6,000 a year, and the latter may be able to lick the daylights out of the former on the handball court."

Branches began to fan out of their facilities, establishing YMCA programs in public housing projects such as Borinquen Plaza.

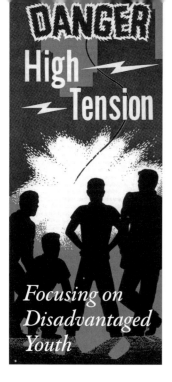

DANGER High Tension

Focusing on Disadvantaged Youth

IN 1959, LATHROP and Board Chairman Curtiss had asserted that "Based on experience, our best constituency seems to be among the lower middle class of people— youngsters of good potential... whose self-assurance and emotional security are threatened by the uncertainties of the social climate in which they live." The development of character and leadership, they pointed out, was the basic purpose underlying YMCA programs. Several pioneer projects had been initiated for teenagers and young adults that emphasized leadership training, such as a weekend seminar for 65 Hi-Y officers. At the 1963 Metropolitan Youth Conference, held at Camp Greenkill, co-ed workshops addressed serious issues of concern proposed by the teens, among them drugs, venereal disease, and capital punishment.

Throughout the country, the leaders noted, cities were confronted daily with the "pressing problems of youth and often shocking delinquencies," and New York City was especially vulnerable. "The YMCA aims to prevent [delinquency] by opening doors of opportunity for youth and young adults in their formative years, encouraging them to develop discipline, purpose and a sense of responsibility," the annual report stated in 1961. The high percentage of school dropouts without jobs—"social dynamite"—topped the Association's list of concerns. Thousands of youth it served, of course, were not in that dire situation but nevertheless looked to the YMCA for recreation, guidance, physical fitness, fellowship and fun. Many couldn't pay the full cost, and were subsidized in Y programs through annual Branch fund-raising campaigns for youth.

Juggling a number of balls in the air, the Association conducted youth work for relatively untroubled young people with leadership potential and the underprivileged, who were exposed to a plethora of bad environmental influences. The YMCA had correctly ascertained that it must reach disadvantaged youth where they lived, and had developed numerous program extensions. By 1963 the Y had a presence in six of the seven areas with the highest rate of ethnic change since 1950, and six of the seven with highest socio-economic need, including

Harlem, Williamsburg, the Bronx, and Jamaica. The Neighborhood Youth Branch was reorganized as a city-wide operation, and Brooklyn Central and Bronx Union sold their old buildings to apply funds once destined for maintenance to outreach programs in schools, churches, and other institutions. YMCA youth programs were now receiving substantial government subsidy.

In 1967 the YMCA put its extension effort on wheels, creating "Instant YMCAs." The Vocational Service Center acquired and staffed six vans as Jobmobiles to reach teens in their neighborhoods, on streets and in housing projects. Counselors set up folding tables and chairs on sidewalks and offered on-the-spot counseling, information and assistance in job placement, plus educational and career guidance counseling, to anyone who happened by.

A fleet of Youthmobiles, vans staffed by youth directors, allowed the Association to fan out far and wide. After selling its building, Brooklyn Central used one to reach boys and girls in Fort Greene and Gowanus. The northwest Bronx program had its own Youthmobile, and the Highland Park Branch utilized two of them to reach more youth in East New York where a sizeable majority of permanent residents existed on welfare or Social Security. Greenpoint's vehicle focused on hard-to-reach youngsters, and Prospect Park–Bay Ridge used its Youthmobiles to provide trips for summer day camp participants and outings during the school year for teens.

More than 70 percent of Eastern District youth were Spanish-speaking by the 1970s, and bilingual YMCA staff deployed Youthmobiles to reach them with crime and drug prevention programs, counseling and referrals, and recreation. The Branch's mobile units, funded by Pfizer Inc., were used to create instant play-streets in recreationless Williamsburg: volleyball nets were attached to facing tenement buildings on a street closed

The Vocational Service Center deployed its Jobmobiles in city neighborhoods, where counselors met with teens on sidewalks.

off by police. By 1976, after the Branch building was sold, Eastern District's Youthmobile program was serving 2,000 youth at ten locations.

Staten Island purchased its own vehicles to provide summer programs on the streets. In 1968, eight Youthmobiles served 30,000 young people; the next summer, ten vans served 48,500. The Branch also used two Jobmobiles to serve more than 1,500 adults by operating six days a week, thirteen hours a day with a staff of more than 100 college students and teachers.

Hot summers, racial tensions and unemployment made a volatile brew for New York City youth in the 1960s, and the YMCA sought means to alleviate tensions and provide positive alternatives to acting out. As one of five organizations in JOIN (Job Orientation in Neighborhoods), the YMCA offered vocational counseling and guidance to more than 5,000 youth in 1963. In 1964, Bedford participated in an "Emergency Youth Project," employing forty-seven teens in various departments with government funds. The following year the Association, under contract with the New York City Youth Board, employed sixteen full-time group workers who provided program and social services for disadvantaged youth in the city's highest delinquency areas. Workers made home and school visits, consulted with other community agencies about the needs of the total child and made referrals for specialized services such as health and remedial education.

The YMCA conducted Anti-Poverty Council programs for youth in Harlem and South Jamaica, including educational, cultural and recreational activities.

Another 150 Neighborhood Youth Corps trainees worked for the YMCA in 1965, providing on-the-job training for dropouts; nearly 100 social science students worked with the Association in needy areas in the summer of 1967 through the federal Work Study Program. City Anti-Poverty Council programs were based at the Harlem Y, offering boys and girls remedial classes and day camp recreation, and at the Central Queens South Jamaica Extension, where youth participated in athletic, cultural and educational activities. In 1968, Harlem created a new department to meet youth employment needs. Some 3,000 young men completed Harlem's TRY program, which the Y estimated would get at least 10,000 people off relief. By 1969 more than 1,100 college students had summer jobs at the YMCA, many in its camp programs; City College of New York (CCNY) students were tutoring Harlem youth and counseling teens at the Branch. In 1974, federal and city funding of nearly $600,000 allowed more than 1,400 youth to work in YMCA programs.

In his study, Hall had remarked on the success of YMCA Youth Clubs. At Harlem a group of young men who called themselves the "Social Play-Boys" had entered the Branch as a youth gang. Just two and a half years later, they had formed a chartered Hi-Y Club and were acting as leaders in citywide and state YMCA youth meetings.

As drug use escalated among youth, prevention became a major concern. In one three-month period, teenagers accounted for one in four deaths from drug overdose. In 1971, the Harlem Branch launched its Youth Enrichment Program (YEP), a social group work effort for drug use prevention, funded by the city's Addiction

Youthmobiles allowed the YMCA to reach youth in disadvantaged communities citywide, delivering on-the-spot recreation with police cooperation.

The college Work-Study program enabled this student to work as a summer counselor with day campers on Staten Island.

Service Agency with a matching grant from the New York City Criminal Justice Coordinating Council. By 1974, thirty-five students from CCNY were tutoring more than 125 of the 1,000 boys and girls in the YEP program. In turn, the Y's Operation Pipeline at CCNY tutored high school graduates to help them perform well in college and take advantage of the City University's new open admissions policy.

At eight Branches, drug-free Young People's Centers were funded by a contract with the city's Youth Services Administration; fifteen workers walked the streets to find kids and take them to one of eight Ys for counseling on problems and coping strategies. Some centers, like the Bronx "Apothecary," were run as coffeehouses, which at the time were hangouts favored by young people. In Brooklyn the YMCA Coffee House was a lively, noisy, drug-free place where students congregated.

Harlem initiated a Youth Enrichment Program (YEP) for drug-abuse prevention in 1971.

Some Branches sponsored coffeehouses, a preferred youth hangout in the 1960s and 1970s.

In 1974 Central Queens offered an unusual delinquency and drug prevention program, the National Youth Program Using Mini-Bikes (NYPUM), in partnership with the Honda Corporation, which provided the two-wheelers. Nearly forty-nine boys, most of them referred from the Family Court Office of Probation and local junior high schools, participated and the successful program was expanded to include girls. A Branch program with the State Parole Board helped early parolees adjust to residential and community living and deter their return to crime.

Starting in the early 1960s, the Association had been enrolling some twenty-five to thirty young parolees in its programs. A decade later, juvenile justice was a major focus. In conjunction with the city's Criminal Justice Coordinating Council and the Youth Services Administration, the Association sponsored and operated Independence House at 503 West Twenty-Seventh Street as a short-term voluntary residential and self-help program for young men ages 17 to 21 released from local prisons like Rikers Island who would otherwise be homeless. The program aimed to prevent recidivism through 24-hour counseling, guidance, job placement and other activities. By 1974, it claimed that 85 percent of men served were employed, more than 95 percent were drug-free and more than 80 percent had not been rearrested. The Harlem Y staffed a Parolee Center for ex-offenders, emphasizing reintegration into society through education and therapy, and assisting participants in getting jobs and adjusting to the world of work. The Grand Central and Sloane House Ys ran Work Release programs, providing housing, guidance and other assistance to mostly young first-time offenders. By 1974 the Association worked city-wide with 150 young ex-offenders annually.

The Association ran programs to help young ex-offenders reintegrate into society and prevent recidivism.

added a preventive Narcotics Control Program with group therapy for addicts or those vulnerable to drugs. In keeping with the YMCA's philosophy of self-help and leadership development, the Center was directed by a voluntary committee including community representatives. In 1967 it became a full-fledged Branch, and the YMCA was credited as a major influence in improving the area. In 1974, the Center added an experimental junior high school with 168 students, and enrollment soon grew to 270.

The West Side Y had operated an extension since the early 1960s in the rundown neighborhood known as Hell's Kitchen, where recreational and social facilities were lacking and drug pushers and users roamed the streets. (Sloane House ran a Pied Piper program for 11- to 13-year-olds in that neighborhood, who met with college counselors.) West Side obtained an unused Magistrate Court building at 315 West Fifty-Fourth Street for $1 a month rent after kids had picketed to be able to use the quarters, stimulating public interest. CBS and the Rotary Club partnered with the YMCA in this effort, and the Astor Foundation provided funds for the $996,000 renovation of the Clinton Youth Center as a multi-service facility for children ages 3 to 20 and their families. It later

During this period of extensive outreach, the McBurney YMCA was focusing on another underserved community, Chinatown. It instituted a Chinatown Youth Resources Program in 1972, and expanded it in 1974 to involve leaders from the Chinese community. By 1976 this outreach program served 640 youth at two centers, the Mariners Temple and the McBurney Branch, with athletic, recreational and social activities, including a teen center, camping, trips, crisis intervention and counseling. The program aimed to lessen truancy, delinquency and the school dropout trend that plagued the community. Its first day camp, in 1978, began by enrolling twelve youngsters, and its first Summer Street Fair attracted 400 youths to a local park. Two years later an after-school program was added.

The West Side Y worked for years with youth in "Hell's Kitchen"; here, the San Juan Hill Boys Club. Its Clinton Youth Center for children and families focused on drug prevention and treatment. Youth picketed to locate the Center in an unused Magistrate Court building, which the city leased for $1 a month.

Homeless youngsters in Brooklyn took part in educational community programs in 1971.

McBurney also aided nearby Spanish-speaking families through its Chelsea Committee for Child and Family Development, funded by the Youth Services Administration. It offered diversified services and activities for kids from 3 to 19 and their families, including tutoring, homework assistance, nutrition, trips and camping. When it lost agency funding in 1977, the McBurney Y arranged to continue the program for this disadvantaged community with private donations. Homeless families staying in Brooklyn hotels participated in YMCA educational and recreational programs in summer 1971.

The YMCA's decentralized program centers included a facility at Fort Totten, formerly used by the Armed Services Y and acquired by the Association in 1971 for community youth-police dialogues. Those took the form of weekend-long discussions and recreational activities. Another project reached into Manhattan's East Village, a magnet for young runaways drawn to alternative life styles and experimentation with drugs in the late 1960s. Sloane House put its City College Unit to work in "Hippyville" near Tompkins Square where many of them congregated. Four workers offered overnight accommodations and food to rootless young people, assisting them as well in getting jobs, permanent living quarters, counseling and referrals to medical treatment.

The Association was concerned with and sympathetic to the youth revolution, which was marked by inter-generational conflict, anti-war and anti-poverty activities and a search for relevance. YMCA Young Adult Programs for ages 18 to 30 sought to help participants act on personal and societal dilemmas. In 1969–70 a YMCA Human Relations Laboratory involved 200 youth in acquiring communication skills, trust in relationships, and insight leading to self-development.

The YMCA was mindful of Hall's 1963 assessment that its programs were not vital, exciting or particularly relevant to young adults. In this era, fewer of them were interested in traditional YMCA activities; contemporary young people preferred informal groups and drop-in activities, like Bedford's Teen-Age Canteens, to group work like Hi-Y that the YMCA treasured. Hall recommended setting up coffeehouses near campuses and seeking young people's opinions, and the Association took heed. Sloane House offered an "Imago" coffeehouse program for up to 1,800 men and women in residence, as well as jazz concerts, modern dance exhibitions and films. Folk music and musicales attracted enthusiasts who brought their own instruments. West Side's Playwrights Place, a showcase for dramatists and actors intended for adults under age 30, offered original plays between disco dance sessions in an espresso house atmosphere.

Four full-time Y professionals worked on campuses, including New York University, Long Island University in Brooklyn, Pratt Institute and three City University colleges. The YMCA operated a coffeehouse called "The Basement," at 155 East Twenty-Second Street, for Baruch College and NYU students, and a storefront student center at 133rd Street and Convent Avenue to accommodate CCNY students.

To give youth a stronger voice in Association programs and affairs, one Branch set up a junior board of managers and others moved in that direction. Young men and women were encouraged to speak their minds at directors' and staff meetings. Prospect Park–Bay Ridge started a Teen Council for improved program planning and a teenage "Encounter" group to get teens to look at themselves in a group situation and set personal objectives. By 1974, the Association offered Junior Leaders programs, built on the Hi-Y model, that encouraged initiative, achievement

The former Army YMCA facility at Fort Totten was used for weekend police-community encounters, which included dialogues and recreation.

Early Leaders' Clubs were composed of volunteers who instructed others in physical classes; by the 1970s the clubs fostered values like initiative, achievement and personal responsibility.

of goals and acceptance of responsibility. Universally called Leaders Clubs by 1979, the programs challenged and helped teens mature through work as camp counselors and directing children's activities at Branches.

Youth and Government, by 1962 a nationwide YMCA program, provided a stellar platform for youth to practice specific skills in effective democratic action. Participants tackled tough subjects of concern to them and introduced bills at their annual model session in Albany such as laws legalizing abortion, which caused "grave concern" among some YMCA lay leaders. Some bills they crafted and forwarded to legislators later became law: requirements for turn signals on cars and pre-marital blood tests originated in Youth and Government assemblies.

Camping offered a natural base to extend YMCA activities to more youth. The resident camps at Huguenot—Greenkill, Talcott, and McAlister—were still boys-only in 1961, although Camp Brooklyn was co-ed. The mix changed rapidly. Greenkill became co-ed in 1965 and by 1969, Talcott hosted all resident camping for girls. In 1969 the Camping Services Department (formerly a Branch) of the Metro YMCA joined with the New York City School Board to offer Black Awareness and

The Youth and Government program gave YMCA teens an opportunity to lean how to confront issues of concern to them in a political forum.

In 1969, Camp McAlister was still for boys only.

By 1969, with concern growing about the environment, the YMCA fielded interest from schools in using its camps year-round as environmental education centers. In the early 1970s, Holiday Hills began hosting both public and private school classes throughout the school year for hands-on environmental instruction. After several years on a trial basis, a full-scale year-round program was introduced with a director of education and an added program goal of improving reading skills. YMCA day camps made trips to parks with instruction focused on nature and ecology. When Greenkill was winterized for year-round use in 1973, it too offered environmental education. Each week eighty fifth and sixth graders, accompanied by teachers, participated in a weeklong program of colonial living there. By 1977, the program enrolled 2,000 students.

remedial reading at its 42 day camps and summer fun clubs. The Uptown Branch added two- to three-day summer camping trips in 1969, offering boys and girls primarily from Puerto Rican, African-American, Dominican and Haitian families an opportunity to experience the out-of-doors and gain a greater sense of self-worth. In 1973, a YMCA-YWCA Camping Services Council was formed to expand the use of five camps for young people from diverse backgrounds and interests. The following year it offered Canadian Wilderness Canoe Trips in Ontario and Quebec for teen campers.

A two-week camp at Greenkill served an additional 150 disadvantaged city youth, while remedial reading and math programs became a standard feature at day camps. By 1975, YMCA camps were placing special emphasis on developing skills, fitness, interpersonal relations and education. Some 35 to 40 summer day camps, sponsored by most Branches, welcomed thousands of co-ed campers ages 6 to 15. One quarter of them received scholarship funds.

Sports Camps in judo, gymnastics and volleyball began in the 1970s.

The Uptown Branch added overnight summer camping trips for boys and girls in 1969. That year the YMCA joined the New York City School Board in offering Black Awareness and remedial reading in day camps and summer fun clubs.

Along with traditional camp activities, remedial reading and math programs became a standard feature at day camps.

The YMCA also introduced Sports Camps in this period, which specialized in gymnastics, judo and volleyball. A new pavilion at the Huguenot site hosted nearly 1,000 youth and young adults who worked with top coaches from Japan, Canada, Poland, Belgium, Russia and the United States. Holiday Hills also offered a sports camp. West Side hosted a special gymnastics camp, and Staten Island added a performing arts day camp. In addition that Branch devised an Education-through-Travel program in which 120 boys and girls visited historic sites in five states and Canada, including a 40-day camping caravan to California.

anti-war, feminist and gay liberation movements, others were highly focused on career achievement. As they gained college degrees, many young adults flocked to the cities in the 1970s for promising positions. These so-called "yuppies" (young urban professionals) also redefined family structure when both husband and wife worked, as became commonplace, creating an unprecedented demand for care of their young children. If parents were single, their needs for support escalated tremendously.

Inner-city working parents desperately needed help in this area but affordable child care was sadly lacking, especially after the city's fiscal crisis caused publicly funded programs to shrivel and the recession made low-skilled

Caring for the Youngest Children

IN THE 1960S and 1970s, the first wave of Baby Boomers was reaching maturity. The dominant youth culture they had created was wielding significant influence in American society. While some participated in communal living, college takeovers and civil rights demonstrations,

The YMCA was already providing child care in its summer day camps.

The Uptown Y offered a summer program for kindergartners in 1967.

jobs at livable wages more difficult to find and keep. In an environment where socio-economic divisions had grown so pronounced, the YMCA would come to serve people at both ends of the economic spectrum with wide-ranging child care programs, including its thriving summer day camps.

One of the first child-care programs in a YMCA began in the 1960s when a parent, Barbara Wilson, volunteered to start a nursery program for 14 children from ages two to five at the West Side YMCA. The Y contributed space for a Co-Op Nursery School, which became one of the first early childhood programs in the United States. In 1968, Central Queens established a preschool nursery program in its Baisley Park extension for disadvantaged youngsters in the housing project.

The biggest push came in 1969 when the YMCA joined forces with the YWCA to plan for jointly run day

Officers and staff of YMCA-YWCA Day Care Inc. "helped" with construction of a new center in Jamaica for 150 children.

care centers; the first to open was in the YMCA's Clinton Youth and Family Center, with funding from the city's Department of Social Services. These centers, staffed by graduate teachers and paraprofessionals, were designed to meet community needs. They were open from 8 A.M. to 6 P.M. five days a week for up to 55 children of ages three to six. YMCA-YWCA Day Care Inc. constructed and opened a new center in Jamaica in 1972 to serve 150 children in that area. In a program called Y-PEP, the partnership also trained workers for the day care sites. The YM-YW network was designed for low-income young mothers, often single parents in need of after-school "latch key" programs for their elementary school children. Parents' fees covered only 6 percent of costs.

YMCA swimming pools were a bonus for tiny tots in child-care programs.

By 1975, the joint venture was serving 230 children ages 3 to 12 in the Clinton and Merrick Centers. A third, the Polly Dodge Day Care Center, named after Pauline Dodge, wife of Cleveland E. Dodge, opened in 1976 at 538 West Fifty-Fifth Street with $700,000 in federal, state and city funds, plus $37,000 each from the YMCA and YWCA. The Brownsville Child Care Center followed in 1977 for fifty-five pre-school and forty-two school-age children. Merrick, in Jamaica, Queens, also added an after-school program for eighty-five kids from ages 6 to 12. The Richmond Early Learning Center on Staten Island and the Grosvenor Neighborhood House Day Care Center in Manhattan were added, bringing the total of YMCA-YWCA Centers to five.

Thus the YMCA assumed leadership in the critical field of early childhood education by providing expert care and stimulating learning experiences for children in safe, healthy environments, inspiring its Branches to do likewise. In 1974, the Highland Park Branch started its own nursery school, as did the new Eastern Queens Branch. The Ridgewood (Queens) YMCA offered a Serendipity Club for pre-school children to broaden their horizons and learn to grasp concepts, and the Westchester-Bronx Branch added a Tiny Tots program for ages 3 to 5. By 1979, many Branches were operating licensed nursery schools. The swimming pools and gym equipment in most Ys made them unique in recreational opportunities.

Making Way for Women

Women, such as these teammates at the Harlem Branch, were increasingly joining the YMCA for fitness and sports opportunities.

CHILD CARE WAS undoubtedly the YMCA's major contribution to the lives of many women. But both mothers and other women increasingly wanted to join the YMCA for various reasons, including its fitness options and family programs. The Association had been somewhat slow to welcome women as members, partly because of facility inadequacies. It was also hesitant to put female employees and volunteers in leadership positions. Women were initially involved in YMCA boys' work, a natural in their role as nurturers, and in war work. But YMCA leaders—still overwhelmingly male in the 1960s—found it difficult to

make the transition from viewing women as auxiliary members or "helpmates" to welcoming them as equals. The 1961 annual report noted that the YMCA helped young people move from adolescence to maturity: "A young *man* on his way up in the world needs a job and a future," it stated, even as the accompanying photo showed a young woman taking a test.

Until the late 1960s the Association was still honoring its "Men of the Year," a practice begun in 1958 to recognize outstanding volunteer service at each Branch. In 1967, there was a breakthrough: Mrs. Julius Leicher from the Uptown Branch was honored as a Man of the Year, as was Mrs. Fred Daniels of Holiday Hills in 1968. Finally, in 1969, the award was renamed "Men and Women of the Year" and included Myrtle Whitmore of the Bedford Branch and Mary Stewart of Long Island City. In 1970, three women awardees were joined by three non-white men, apparently a first.

The year 1970 was a watershed, with a first mention and recognition of "women's liberation" in the annual report, and which acknowledged women as "another new emerging group of young and old concerned with everything from women's liberation to pollution." The first women were named to the citywide Board of Directors, including Mrs. Frederick W. Appell, President of the YWCA of the City of New York; Mrs. Edwin N. Beery, President of the YWCA of Brooklyn; Dr. Adolfina Montes of Teachers College, Columbia University; and Mrs. Whitmore, Manager of Brooklyn's Carver Houses. In 1972, Mrs. Whitmore was appointed to the Board's Executive Committee; by that time she was Housing Manager at the city's Housing Authority. The *New York Times* also noted as a "first" that four women were appointed that year as unit directors.

A student was also named to the Board for the first time in 1970, Christine Epifania of York College. By 1972 there were four student members, three of whom were girls. Younger women may have made inroads at the YMCA more easily than their elders. In 1963, Adrienne Belzel of the Bronx Union Y became president of the citywide Inter-Branch Teen Council. Four years later Elizabeth Noel, also of Bronx Union and an African American, was the first girl elected as youth governor in the state Youth and Government program. Later she would enroll in Fordham Law School, uncommon at the time for young women. In 1973 the McBurney Preparatory School became co-ed, after 50 years as a boys' school. Its enrollment immediately jumped by 15 percent.

The Hall report had observed that New York lagged behind the national YMCA system in admitting women

Elizabeth (Betty) Noel of Bronx Union was the first girl to be elected YMCA Youth Governor in New York State (left, City Council President Frank O'Connor; right, Majority Leader David Ross).

Nevertheless, Branches were busily adapting old buildings and planning programs to accommodate more women and girls. In 1968, Central Queens included women in its physical fitness program, and Prospect Park added a program just for them. In 1964, Harlem became the first to open a residence floor to accommodate women. Sloane House and Prospect Park–Bay Ridge also made their dorm facilities co-ed, helping to alleviate a critical shortage of low-cost housing for both sexes. By 1973 a full physical education program was in progress at West Side, Vanderbilt (the former Grand Central Y, renamed in 1972), McBurney and Flushing. The latter two featured newly expanded women's locker rooms. Weight-training programs at McBurney and West Side were designed for women to "become better at their sport," and new aerobic fitness classes were added. By 1977 McBurney claimed 1,000 women as members, up from just 123 nine years earlier. Greenpoint performed major renovations to accommodate female members, and the fledgling Flatbush Y completed its co-ed gym, locker rooms, and weight-lifting room.

Thirty women joined the West Side Y as full members in 1974, and their numbers doubled by the next year. The Branch also opened its residence to them for first time that year, allowing female students from the nearby Juilliard School of Music to occupy one floor. By 1977 West Side had 1,000 women members and 1,300 on

and girls, who accounted for only 17 percent of members in 1962. He recommended shifting the priority from traditional programs for men and boys to emphasize co-ed and family memberships. BAN-WYS too had taken up the cause of women in the YMCA. In 1970, the group accused the YMCA of practicing "male supremacy" as much as "white racism" by putting women in second-class roles as employees and members.

Women, at first slowly, joined exercise classes at McBurney but numbered 1,000 members by 1977.

THE YMCA AT 150

More Than
SWIM-and-GYM

The YMCA's fitness facilities were a big draw for women members. But that wasn't all the Y offered them. In 1977 the McBurney Branch featured these special programs: "The Working Woman's Selling Game," "Working and Mothering," "Yourself and Your Child" and "Self-Defense for Women." The West Side Y provided "Assertiveness Training" for use on the job, dealing with bosses and "other out-of-family figures," including other women. Overall this YMCA offered more than 200 programs with a traditional focus such as dressmaking, cooking for women and girls and needlecrafts.

The YMCA annual report in 1961 declared that finding the "right girl" and establishing a home were high priorities for young men. That image sometimes contrasted with the reality of Branches that were especially popular with gay men.

a waiting list. Vanderbilt more than doubled its female memberships that year, from 350 to 800. Locker facilities were the key: By the time a locker room was added at West Side in the 1980s, women accounted for half of its membership.

The Association boldly proclaimed in its 1976 annual report that "the time has long past since the YMCA was a 'men only' organization. Today, women make up more than 33 percent of YMCA membership, and virtually all programs are co-ed." By then the YMCA was also using the honorific "Ms." for female directors on the Board. By its 125th anniversary in 1977, the Association was celebrating its diversity and position "as a bridge between diverse elements of community."

A Changing Constituency

THE ASSOCIATION HAD another reason to embrace a growing female membership. Homosexuality had become a concern in the New York YMCA residences, which the 1963 Hall survey deemed a congregating point

for "undesirables." Certainly the population of residents had grown older and attracted many men who did not especially want to move on. The Association was founded on the principle of strong male friendships, but since the war years its residences had become not only "flophouses" but popular with gay men as a covert meeting place, where rooms could be shared without suspicion. This reality contrasted greatly with the YMCA's preferred image of the transient men it housed: "Whether dancing with a pretty hostess or getting help from a 'Y' Secretary regarding a personal problem—the 'G.I.' at the YMCA is always in an atmosphere which makes him feel like an individual," stated the 1961 annual report.

Forming somewhat of an insiders' club, more than half of Sloane House occupants were referred by friends, and enough were homosexual to pose a concern to the Association at a time when society was less accepting of them. Hall recommended that the New York YMCA adopt a "firm and prudent policy" on gay men, and concentrate its efforts on "removing the social problem" from Y premises. One way was to emphasize a "normal Christian family atmosphere in Y residence halls," converting them rapidly to co-ed use. The thirteen general and three special residences, old and outmoded as many were, overwhelmingly comprised the largest program activity in the Association. In 1961, some 100,000 men per year used Y dorm facilities, making residence a significant revenue source. But Hall advised redirecting energies to other parts of the city with family-type program facilities that would not contain residence halls.

YMCA Board Chairman Howell pointedly stated in 1964 that Branches must tactfully or forcefully separate "undesirables," especially from their dorms. In typically non-confrontational YMCA fashion the New York residences made no full-scale moves to eject gay men, which would conflict with long-cherished Y values of welcoming all people, tolerance and concern for newcomers to the city. The Association did, however, become more vigilant to quell obvious homosexual activity in its residences. It also took heed of a national YMCA study of this issue, known as "Code H," by moving quickly to make its dorms co-ed.

The national Association, based in New York City, had grown concerned by the persistent image of homosexual men frequenting YMCAs. The Code H report, while urging more co-ed use of residences, affirmed the YMCA's philosophy of treating all people with dignity and by doing so actually led to a greater acceptance. As well, the liberation movement beginning in the late 1960s gave gay men much more leeway to meet others openly and comfortably. The issue surfaced again, briefly, in 1978 when the Village People released their disco song "YMCA," with lyrics widely interpreted as a message about homosexuality in the Association. (The McBurney YMCA may have been the song's inspiration, according to popular legend.) Now the enduring popularity of the song has come to be welcomed widely by YMCAs.

At this time, the New York City YMCA was continuing its transition from a Protestant organization to an ecumenical acceptance of all people, and progressing toward a more secular than a religious orientation. During Gayle Lathrop's term as CEO, he frequently emphasized the YMCA's traditional passage from Scripture, John 17:21, "That they all may be one." Despite the pronounced Christian beliefs of many in leadership positions, the YMCA knew it was living in a changed world, one where organized religion was questioned and the trend toward secularism seemed inevitable. The Association had struggled over the years with how Christian its emphasis should be,

even as its wide scope of programs revealed a shift away from that focus. The last reporting of enrollment in YMCA Bible and religious discussion classes appeared in the 1970 yearbook, when some 15,000 enrolled in New York and less than 10,000 in Brooklyn. Both figures represented a fraction of total enrollment in physical classes. Furthermore, YMCA staff rated religious observance last in importance to them, with character development the overriding objective in all youth programs.

Supplemental Statement of Purpose, 1960

"Generally and broadly stated, the YMCA of Greater New York is a fellowship of members, primarily young people, whose purpose is to develop character and leadership in accordance with Christian principles."

Religious programs had begun disappearing in the New York YMCA by the 1960s.

The YMCA had evolved from an organization for Protestants to an ecumenical embrace of all people and a more secular orientation.

The largely Protestant middle-class exodus to the suburbs, and its effect on the YMCA had been noted in the 1953 Brooklyn and Queens Association trend survey: "In light of our constituency, there may be situations where we can not teach Christianity, but it is essential that we continue to teach and exemplify the Christian way of life." This was partly a pragmatic decision. The report remarked on the YMCA's large numbers of Catholic and Jewish contributors as well as members.

Nevertheless, the YMCA of Greater New York still adhered to Christianity in its mission. Its 1957 Certificate of Consolidation mandated that at least three-fourths of members of the Board of Directors and Trustees be members of churches affiliated with the National Council of Churches of Christ in the USA, which represented Protestant denominations, but specified that not more than a third should belong to any one sect. In 1962 a four-year Planning Committee study culminated in a recommendation that leadership, program and facilities contain the "essential Christian purpose of the YMCA."

The 1963 Hall report noted that with progressive secularization in an increasingly multi-faith and often religiously indifferent constituency, the YMCA's formal religious work and emphasis had almost ceased. The last vestiges were token expressions of piety such as required attendance at religious services for young campers and a few Bible breakfasts which, the survey found, "could be quietly discarded with hardly a ripple of protest." The YMCA, Hall asserted, had ceased to be Protestant and had changed its character in an attempt to avoid offending other religious groups, specifically Roman Catholics and Jews. Some Protestant leaders praised the YMCA for its "inclusiveness" and "ecumenicity," while others derided it for "watering down" or "eroding" its Christian emphasis.

Significantly, in 1960, Pope John XXIII had removed the Vatican's longstanding objection to the YMCA. During the Rome Olympics the Pope summoned Joel Nystrom, a former director at the West Side YMCA and then an executive of the International YMCA, to his residence. He "confessed" to Nystrom and asked the YMCA's forgiveness for telling Catholics to have nothing to do with the YMCA, which the Vatican had long held "made Christianity too easy."

Hall emphasized character development as an important hallmark of YMCA programs. The Association considered its ethics essentially Christian, but this presented a dilemma. Many New Yorkers would question the presumption that Christians had an exclusive right to the ethics and motives underlying sound character development. Hall advised keeping the YMCA Christian in

Pope John XXIII told International YMCA executive Joel Nystrom (right) that the Catholic Church had been wrong in warning its members away from the Association.

motive, leadership, and service but open to all by emphasizing the ecumenical movement, avoiding secularism and guarding against indifference. He felt strongly that the YMCA of Greater New York must reverse the slow drift toward indifferentism and secularism. The Association would grapple with this over the ensuing decades while struggling to find the right definition.

Annual reports in years just following the Hall report noted that the Association "took more steps to fulfill the important role we perform in critical areas of... religious ecumenism." All YMCA programs, they stressed, related to the development of the "whole man, in Mind, Body, and Spirit," but averred that "the YMCA is [not] becoming less concerned with the spiritual purpose that brought it into being and gave it meaning. Quite the contrary is true. The development of character and leadership in accordance with Christian principles—the official purpose of the Association—is at the heart of all we do and provides the motivation for our work." One particularly striking passage pointed out that Jesus also had to cope with extremes and resulting tensions in society in his day, along with apathy and resistance to change. He worked with all people, with one message for all. If he were here today, the report speculated, "He would observe Rosh Hashana with his family."

The 1971 Association objectives professed an intention to "develop and live by moral and ethical values consistent with the teachings of Jesus." The passage from John 17:21, the report declared, expressed the "YMCA commitment... that people of every race, every nation and every religious faith can experience brotherhood by application of the ethical principles taught by Jesus."

By 1974, references to Jesus and the Bible were decidedly toned down. Spiritual development at the YMCA was now a more general endeavor, "reaching individuals through means that enable them to determine a spiritual basis for their lives," according to that year's annual report. The Association was "interested in stimulating the process of developing... values which are in

1971
Statement of Objectives

The YMCA of Greater New York is an educational, religious, charitable Association whose role is to enable individuals, primarily the young, in our City's many and varied communities and groups to:

+ Develop confidence and self respect
+ Grow as responsible members of their families
+ Act as responsible members of their communities
+ Develop their capacities for leadership
+ Further interracial and intergroup understanding
+ Achieve and maintain health of mind and body
+ Develop and live by moral and ethical values consistent with the teaching of Jesus

—From 1971 Annual Report

harmony with high ethical and moral principles" through programs that provided "opportunities to increase spiritual development through the sharing of experiences and convictions. The Y is a bridge... in which people of many faiths are comfortable working together as individuals and families to enrich and improve the quality of their lives." The Association was giving people "the practical opportunity... to follow the basic Y principle—service to others."

This seismic shift continued in 1977, with the annual report emphasizing the YMCA's unique character in helping individuals live with stresses in highly complex communities, through its ever-expanding and changing programs. The report stressed its focus on filling gaps left by curtailment or abandonment of programs in the city's fiscal crisis such as adult language classes, job training and day care centers. The Association was reaching out to youth where they were in trouble; expanding programs for women and girls, who now comprised one-third of members; expanding its facilities; and targeting special needs, such as families headed by single-mothers and school dropouts. The YMCA of Greater New York was now a multi-service agency, serving tots to seniors. Significantly, unlike most YMCAs outside New York City, its statements of purpose and mission in 1978 and 1979 no longer included the word "Christian." The predominantly secular focus had effectively been achieved.

Supporting a Health-Conscious Culture

"WE HAVE BECOME more and more not a nation of athletes but a nation of spectators," President John F. Kennedy declared in 1961. Hoping to motivate an increasingly sedentary American public and its youth, he reinvigorated the President's Council on Physical Fitness and Sports, which had been established in the Eisenhower administration. The Council administered a series of physical fitness tests to millions of school children and those who passed received a Presidential Physical Fitness Award. In 1968, the New York YMCA introduced its new Youth Fitness Program, endorsed by President's Council on Physical Fitness and Sports, and the Association began bestowing the Presidential awards on qualifying youth members.

For New Yorkers, the new focus on youth and physical fitness proved timely and important. In the city's ensuing fiscal crisis and recession in the 1970s, school physical education programs such as the Public School Athletic Leagues were cut back or cut off. A number of YMCA Branches were able to offer alternative fitness programs for youth. By 1979, for example, the Bronx YMCA was operating gym activities in six parochial schools.

The early YMCA offered physical education to help young men with office jobs and time on their hands burn off excess energy. Now it emphasized good health and fitness, countering obesity, relaxation from urban stress and reduction of heart fatalities. Since the 1944 Strayer survey, New York YMCAs had been focusing on health education, competitive sports activities, strong physical fitness programs, more outdoor programs for groups, and

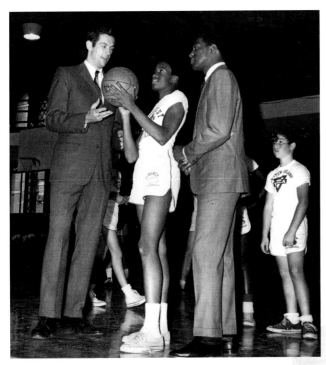

The YMCA developed youth fitness programs as schools canceled them; here, students met New York Knicks star Bill Bradley.

full use of their aquatic facilities. A number had added handball and squash courts as well as individual exercise facilities. In 1962, Leonard Covello was named the Association's first executive for health and physical education, overseeing a YMCA exhibition at the Coliseum's Outdoor Show that year which showcased fitness training, judo and fencing classes as representative of its physical programs citywide. In 1963, the Association instituted a Measured Mile walking program at all Branches. Total attendance in YMCA physical departments that year was 365,000.

The McBurney Y administered blood pressure and fitness tests to residents of the community in 1974.

As it had been since the nineteenth century, the YMCA's approach to health was holistic, emphasizing integration of spirit, mind and body, and it promoted that message creatively. The West Side Y sponsored a Smoker's Clinic in 1964 with the New York City Department of Health, removed cigarette vending machines from its premises, and mounted an anti-smoking campaign in its Physical Department. Sloane House and McBurney opened meditation rooms. The Harlem Back-a-Block program sponsored a Health Fair with the Colgate-Palmolive Company that attracted more than 500 youth in 1974. That year McBurney administered blood pressure and physical fitness testing to 265 community residents, and made its facilities available to drug rehabilitation units of the Veterans Administration, Daytop Village and Phoenix House. In 1975 the Association designed a program to help New York City firemen maintain peak physical condition by using YMCA facilities and exercises prescribed for them in "The Official YMCA Physical Fitness Handbook."

The Grand Central Branch cultivated businessmen working nearby with a "deluxe athletic club for executives."

Responding to widespread concern about heart attacks—by that time the leading cause of death in middle-aged men—the YMCA developed an innovative program in 1966. The Grand Central Railroad YMCA, which enrolled many nearby businessmen in its "deluxe athletic club for executives," instituted noon-hour "scientific physical fitness clinics," designed for prevention of heart attacks. After an initial forty-five minutes of testing, specialists reviewed the results and recommended appropriate activities. The Y's conditioning classes could help sedentary men qualify for the life insurance previously refused them due to obesity or high blood pressure. The Association was the first Y in the nation to offer this

Jogging and sprinting were basic to the YMCA's signature cardiovascular program, developed by Alexander Melleby.

in-depth program, which was endorsed by doctors, scientists and educators. Alexander Melleby, the Association's executive for health and physical education, had pioneered the Cardio-Vascular Physical Fitness Movement in New England and introduced evangelist Billy Graham to the program.

The Central Queens, West Side, Harlem, and Prospect Park Branches also adopted this cardiac fitness program, based on walking, slow jogging, sprinting, stretching and deep breathing, in their extensive fitness programs. In 1969, 1,500 men took part in the program. Two years later, participation had doubled, to 3,000 members. The program's object was to make exercise palatable and enjoyable so as to "ward off sickness, the disease of aging, and mental decay." Popular sports such as golf, bowling and tennis did not necessarily develop fitness, the YMCA warned (the Association had closed its bowling alleys by 1963), and weightlifting could do damage as well. In a 1972 report on the program, *Time* magazine stated that "few doctors—or cardiac patients—are as familiar with the physiology of exercise as the 'Y's' trained instructors... most people need constant encouragement to remain with any calisthenics program." A five-year study showed measurable improvement in fifty men who stayed with the program.

West Side and Central Queens also partnered with Montefiore and Jamaica Hospitals, respectively, to rehabilitate heart attack victims. In 1976, the YMCA's New York Cardiovascular Health Services Program was established citywide, with a goal of reducing heart disease among seemingly well males ages 35 to 55. YMCA Branches provided screening, information, counseling and supervised programs.

In the same year another novel program, "Y's Way to a Healthy Back," debuted at New York Branches. Aimed to alleviate the increased incidence of back discomfort through relaxation, flexibility, and strengthening abdominal muscle, the pioneering effort was developed by Melleby and national YMCA medical consultant Dr. Hans Kraus. Known as the father of sports medicine in the United States, Dr. Kraus, a New York–based physician, had been personal physician to President Kennedy; Melleby, director of the Healthy Back program from 1976–86, trained more than 4,000 instructors from the United States, Canada, Australia, and Japan in the innovative exercise program. A study of 12,000 participants showed that at least 80 percent who completed the program either conquered back pain completely or reduced it significantly. The study of low-back pain and its causes was the largest ever conducted in the United States. Melleby's book, *The Y's Way to a Healthy Back*, was published in four languages.

In this era a growing, youthful and energetic middle class was more exercise-oriented and fitness-conscious than ever, and community YMCAs provided them a ready resource. Running was enjoying great popularity, and indoor Y tracks filled with joggers and sprinters of both sexes. Flushing added an outdoor running track for men and women, and its 100 Mile Club honored more than 100 runners who achieved that goal. In 1968, a now world-famous event took shape at the West Side YMCA. Fred Lebow, the new president of the New York Road Runners Club, rented offices in the Sixty-Third Street Branch, adjacent to Central Park, whose roads Mayor John Lindsay had just closed to traffic for the first time. From several offices and the auditorium, which the Y provided for larger meetings and event registration, Lebow and his committee planned the first New York City Marathon, held in September 1970. Bob Glover, West Side's Athletic Director, set up late-night practice runs and directed running classes.

A YMCA team was among the 127 runners in the first Marathon. The fifty-five who finished the 26.2 miles—four circuits in Central Park, with no water stops—received recycled bowling trophies, recalled coach emeritus Joe Kleinerman, who developed the early races. By 1976, the five-borough Marathon was created to take in the city's diverse neighborhoods; the Roadrunners Club continued to use the West Side Y as its base until 1979. The annual event has become one of the world's major marathons, attracting 30,000 runners from around the world and 2 million on-site spectators. Richard Traum, a West Side Y member and an amputee, entered and completed the 26.2 mile run. In 1983 Traum and Glover, author of *The Runner's Handbook*, co-founded the Achilles Track Club at the Y to encourage other

progressive steps in the
NATIONAL YMCA AQUATIC PROGRAM
swim the Y way for fun · safety · service

disabled runners to participate. It now has 100 clubs in sixty-three countries, and members who run the Marathon are housed at West Side.

Competitive sports flourished in this era. In 1960, Bronx Union produced the National Junior Handball Champion, Louis Russo, Jr. The Grand Central Branch hosted the National Volleyball Championships in 1964, and the Staten Island Y bought land to install basketball and volleyball courts and two tennis courts. An Annual Athletic Achievement meet at Central Queens and Brooklyn Central's Boys Indoor Athletic Meet had the added benefit of bringing together boys from all socio-economic groups.

In 1960, Lynn Burke of the Flushing YMCA, where her parents taught swimming, brought home two gold medals as the Olympic Swimming Champion. Her team, the Flushing Y Flyers, is the oldest established swim team in the area and has produced more champions on all levels than any other team, including Olympian Wayne Anderson in 1968. The Branch added a new Olympic-size pool in 1968 with a gallery for 500 seated spectators.

The National YMCA introduced an eight-level Aquatics Program in 1976.

Aquatics continued to be a signature YMCA program at most Branches, reaching more children and adults in new ways, especially through annual, free Learn-to-Swim campaigns. Staten Island offered synchronized swimming for women and girls and Flushing a summer swim project for disadvantaged youth from Corona, Flushing, and East Elmhurst. In 1976, a new YMCA Aquatics Program, developed by the National Council of YMCAs, promoted swim lessons in response to increased popular interest in recreational swimming and boating. That year the Association taught 12,675 New Yorkers to swim. Using thirty backyard swimming pools, Staten Island Y's South Shore instructors taught more than 300 kids to swim in 1979.

The YMCA acquainted children with water and water safety at very young ages. Tiny Tots programs at Highland Park, Eastern Queens, and Staten Island, for mothers and children, helped pre-schoolers develop

Learn-to-Swim programs were well attended at all Branches with pools.

Lynn Burke (center), Olympic Swimming Champion in 1960, trained and taught at the Flushing YMCA.

YMCA swim programs for the youngest enthusiasts included participation by their parents.

hand-eye coordination, rhythm and body movement, as well as social relations with other children. Eastern Queens conducted developmental swimming and gymnastics for infants six months to two years of age. By 1974 some Branches were offering swim activities to infants as young as two months. Other physical programs for young children included Flushing's Moppet Gym for ages four to seven, and Brooklyn Central's new movement education program for ages five to seven, using expressly designed equipment in classes led by a specialist.

The Long Island City Branch in Queens, which called itself the "biggest little YMCA in the country," occupied a unique niche with its borough-wide athletic leagues and sports programs. Lacking its own facility, it used more than 100 community playgrounds, up to forty gyms, many public parks and open spaces. This Y consistently served more male youth (7,300, for example, in 1973) than any other Branch, coordinating some 400 teams in a cornucopia of sports, including basketball, roller-hockey, baseball, softball, bowling, and junior football.

In 1976, the YMCA launched the Youth Basketball Association as a joint, co-ed program for youth from 8 to 18 with the professional National Basketball Players Association. Its focus was on values and fair play, which is the YMCA way with sports: "everybody plays, everybody wins." The emphasis is not on being number one, but on the fun of playing, skills development and the positive aspects of team play. In its first year eighteen leagues and 110 teams involved more than 1,000 young players. By 1979, more than 20,000 boys and girls were participating in this very popular program.

Another major shift in population trends caused the YMCA to focus attention on older people. Growing up didn't necessarily mean giving up YMCA membership: Since the 1950s, Branches had seen members age into "senior citizens" who had no intention of abandoning a place that was familiar, warm and welcoming. The Branches appreciated the support, stability and community service they rendered. In some cases this caused tension between older and younger constituencies. The 1953

Since 1920, the Long Island City YMCA has sponsored league play, using community playgrounds, gyms, public parks and open spaces, serving more male youth than any other Branch. Over the years hundreds of teams played basketball, roller-hockey, baseball, softball, and junior football.

THE YMCA AT 150

trends survey of the Brooklyn and Queens Association had cautioned Ys not to serve the "aged group" to detriment of young members. But Branches realized that older people too needed their programs and services. Over the next two decades a full menu of counseling, social, recreational, cultural, health and fitness, housing and nutritional programs would be tailored to their needs, with extensive programs at the Bronx, Flushing, West Side, and Staten Island Ys.

The Westchester-Bronx Golden Age Club for men and women over 60, begun in 1955, was one of the first, but was soon duplicated in all boroughs. In 1961, McBurney formed a Senior Citizens Club providing "recreation with mental stimulation"; its attendance rose from 40 to 150 in a year. Eastern District's Senior Citizens program, initiated in 1968, was a quick success with some 400 participants. Members of the Ridgewood Y over-60 group interpreted "YMCA" to mean the "Youth-Minded Citizens Association."

In 1972, the Bronx YMCA launched a new corporation, the Burnside-Concourse Senior Citizens Center, with the Tremont Temple and Jewish Community Council as community partners, to provide day-long programs and weekday hot lunches for more than 1,000 men and women. A Senior Residence Program at Sloane House provided 50 adults over 62 with daily maid service, counseling on personal or financial problems and a twice-weekly medical clinic, all at a cost of $35 per week.

The Bronx Union Branch moved to a housing project, the new Bailey Avenue Community Center, in 1974. There it delivered health and physical education, counseling and guidance, social, recreational, and cultural arts,

and community service for all ages. Some 150 seniors living in Bailey Houses enjoyed a hot lunch five days a week for a cash "contribution" and recreation such as folk dancing, excursions and lectures on "How to Lower Your Con Ed Bill" and "How to Care for Your Plants." Twenty home-bound seniors received lunch deliveries and a wide range of services. While eight other Branches conducted senior programs at this time, more than half of YMCA members over sixty simply enrolled in regular programs.

Increasingly, YMCA Branches focused on physical programs for the disabled. The 1963 Annual Gymnastics Show at Brooklyn Central, which featured tumbling, gymnastics on parallel bars, high-bar and trampoline, among others, included the physically impaired. In 1968, the Bronx YMCA instituted a year long social and recreational program for brain-damaged children and also ran a special day camp for them. In 1973, Staten Island taught swimming three times a week to as many as seventy mentally disabled children, and West Side conducted a physical and social program for youth in collaboration with the Association for Brain-Injured Children. Eastern Queens offered a special Asthmatic Child program. By 1979, special programs for mentally and physically handicapped children were found throughout the Association.

For the New York City YMCA, the new cadres of health-conscious members were a welcome source of support in a difficult time financially. Operations could be maintained with revenues from membership dues and dorm residents, freeing funds raised from the public for youth programs and subsidies for those who could not afford full membership or program fees.

The Westchester-Bronx Golden Age Club was one of the first YMCA programs for seniors, in 1960, but they quickly cropped up in all five boroughs.

Extending Educational Opportunities

EDUCATION, WHICH HAD long been an Association mainstay, was changing but retained its strong service orientation for lower-income aspirants. The Hall study noted that the YMCA had "largely divorced itself from formal education" and thus lost an important contact point with youth and young adults. But several educators appointed to the Board of Directors in 1970—Dr. Winthrop Adkins, Associate Professor of Psychology at Teachers College; Dr. Aaron Brown, Special Assistant to the President, Long Island University; and Dr. James A. Colston, President of Bronx Community College—attested to the importance the YMCA still attached to education.

The McBurney School, long a preparatory institution for boys, finally opened enrollment to girls in the 1970s.

The Schools Branch undertook a $200,000 modernization of its top three floors. The Evening High School, enrolling only 200 adults by the mid-1960s, now had to compete with public-funded secondary school options. The McBurney School continued to enroll 450 high-potential students in grades 5 to 12, many of whom received need-based scholarships and went on to top colleges and universities.

Informal education enrolled nearly 3,400 in 1963 at various Branches. Most offered a wide range of classes catering to specific interests or skills, such as fine arts, dancing, discussion groups, languages, music, practical homemaker skills, do-it-yourself courses, and management of personal affairs. "A woman can learn how to repair a car; a man can learn to bake a cake," the 1965–66 annual report related. "They both can learn how to Cha-cha-cha, make the correct lead in bridge, invest their money, file their income tax return, budget whatever income is left, so that two can live as cheaply as one and have fun doing it."

Brooklyn Central offered a noteworthy photography course, and horseback riding was available at Grand Central. Central Queens provided informal courses for Queens residents in cooperation with nearby York College by 1974, while Highland Park collaborated with Pace College to offer accredited courses in accounting, English, and history.

The Association initiated a new YMCA Image Program in the 1970s to teach adults time management, reading, writing, and memory skills. "Readfast" and "Writefast" were offered at the Penn Station Branch and in adult self-improvement courses at the Vanderbilt Branch. Based at metropolitan headquarters, the Image Center became an educational division of the YMCA and extended its offerings to include communication skills, business management, career development, and human relations programs at Branches and at client locations. Its speed reading and management courses were in demand by sponsoring organizations such as McKinsey and Company, Oppenheimer Company, Bowery Savings Bank, Chase Manhattan Bank, and Queens and Brooklyn Colleges.

The need for remedial education was growing, however, as public school students in particular fell behind and needed tutoring. In 1964, the Westchester-Bronx Y began offering homework help classes for school children using Queens College students as tutors. Central Queens also offered a summer remedial reading and math program. A 1976 YMCA mini-academy at CCNY provided 650 children and young adults remedial tutoring or instruction in many subjects as well as guidance counseling. These needs would only grow as more non–English-speaking immigrants, unable to help their children with homework assignments, settled in New York.

The Bedford Trade School, the state's second oldest, enrolled 200 students in six trades in the mid-1960s, including refrigeration and air conditioner servicing. The first school to offer formal training in auto mechanics, it was still meeting a great demand in that area despite the

A young woman progressed beyond hunt-and-peck at the Uptown Branch.

growth of private trade schools. Many students at Bedford were war veterans, covered under the GI Bill. From 1966–1979 the School trained more than 18,000 economically disadvantaged students, placing at least 75 percent in unsubsidized jobs.

High school equivalency exam preparation opened another growth area for the YMCA. The Counseling and Testing Services Branch offered a federally funded preparatory course with Upward Bound to help veterans get a high school equivalency diploma. By 1978, more than 3,000 adults had completed the six-week preparatory course at eight Branches. Many passed and applied to colleges, especially those with open admissions. The Counseling and Testing Y, staffed by experienced psychologists and counselors, offered educational, career, personal, marriage, family and group counseling as well as psychological testing of aptitudes and interests.

The increasing numbers of immigrants making New York their home, including an influx of Southeast Asian "boat people," caused the YMCA to revive another of its historic programs. In 1977, the beleaguered city Board of Education cancelled its evening classes in English for the foreign born. Responding to the vacuum that was created, the Flushing Branch took over local courses, employing the same two teachers. Its surrounding community now comprised the nation's largest concentration of Asians outside San Francisco. That first year Flushing enrolled 200 "Orientals" and a few Hispanics in English classes, and also offered comprehensive courses in Chinese culture and language. By the late 1970s, English as a Second Language courses could be found at many Branches.

Building and Expanding for Families

THE HALL REPORT'S recommendations led the Association to conduct a $15 million capital campaign, to address the perennial problem of aging and inadequate buildings. By 1971, Association objectives also stressed supporting and enriching family life, and diversifying the membership base. In the 1974 annual report the YMCA asserted that "through character-building programs we build resourceful individuals and stronger communities and strengthen family life." Those needs, taken together, led the Association to remodel and add a number of facilities.

The Association mounted a $15-million capital campaign in the early 1960s to restore aging, inadequate buildings. From left, Robert S. Curtiss, president; John Ellis, campaign chairman; and Cleveland E. Dodge, executive committee chairman, set their sights on a first-phase target.

The Grand Central Branch was refurbished as a general YMCA to serve more United Nations personnel, nearby office workers and youth from East Forty-Second to Ninety-Sixth Streets. In 1963 new property adjacent to the East Forty-Seventh Street building was secured for $3.5 million for additional program and residence facilities for men and women. By 1972, the Branch ceased its focus on railroad men but perpetuated the legacy of Cornelius Vanderbilt II by renaming the Branch in his honor. The Railroad Y program in the New York Central yards on West Seventy-First Street was also discontinued.

After the new Pennsylvania Station opened, a renamed Penn Station YMCA followed in 1968. The Branch was open for membership to all railroad and station workers as well as people working in the area who were not transport employees. However, its tenure would be brief. The Public Law Board ruled that the Penn Station Y was not a suitable residence. Railroad unions rejected a personnel transfer to Sloane House, and the Penn Station Branch closed in 1979.

Post-war population growth led the Association to erect its first new facility in a decade, the Eastern Queens YMCA. This extension of Central Queens, formerly operating from program centers in Glendale and Middle Village, opened its new building in 1967 in Bellerose, near the border of suburban Nassau County. Eastern Queens was a "family" Y from the outset, the first in New York State to be planned exclusively as a family-center YMCA. Membership soon topped 3,000 and Eastern Queens, "splitting at the seams," officially became a Branch and planned a major expansion. Just nine years after opening

The new Eastern Queens building was the first "family YMCA" center.

it added an outdoor track, handball court and four tennis courts on adjacent land, and saw a 20-percent increase in membership. The Branch also enjoyed extraordinary participation by volunteers.

The Central Queens Branch purchased an old courthouse building on Catalpa Avenue in Ridgewood as an extension for communities not served by other agencies—Ridgewood, Glendale, Middle Village, and Maspeth. This extension unit initially focused on Hi-Y and young adult programs. Supervision of the Catalpa unit passed to the Highland Park Y in 1978, when that Branch was renamed Twelve Towns in a nod to its surrounding communities.

Flushing added a new wing with an Olympic-size pool and a businessmen's athletic club in 1967. In 1978 it purchased, for $1, a new center for programs in Bayside from the Boys Club. Other old Branches with comprehensive buildings—Highland Park, McBurney, Vanderbilt, and West Side—adapted their facilities further to serve both sexes. Numerous men, who could no longer swim in the nude—a grand old YMCA tradition—were quite put out.

Branches such as West Side and Grand Central had businessmen's health clubs that provided valet services, tailors, barbers and their own quarters. These amenities would gradually disappear. By contrast, the Bedford Branch in 1976 discontinued all adult programs because

of a continuing membership decline, but undertook a major renovation to house an alcoholic treatment center funded by the city's Health and Hospitals Corporation and Model Cities. By 1979, the Branch's Technical School was based solely at 1119 Bedford Avenue, no longer at the downtown address.

The Ridgewood YMCA opened in a former Queens courthouse in 1965.

The Hall report had questioned whether major programs for other specialized groups—students, seamen, military personnel, and youth in street gangs—should continue, and had recommended terminating the Governors Island and Pennsylvania Railroad Ys. Operations were subsequently terminated at Governors Island Branch, following a general YMCA policy of discontinuing Ys on Army posts to render more effective and essential services away from bases. Sloane House took over that program, as it did with the Navy YMCA when Secretary of Defense Robert McNamara closed the Brooklyn Navy Yard in 1964. The Navy Y was phased out, after serving some 47 million individuals since 1899. Residents were transferred to other Branches and lockers to Sloane House.

The Intercollegiate Y, with less than 1,200 members, would not be missed, according to Hall. In 1964, the Association reorganized its student work by tying it in to Branch operations. He also questioned the existence of residence halls in relation to the Association's purpose, and its counseling, guidance and vocational placement programs. The renamed Counseling and Testing Services Branch assumed all services for veterans in 1967.

Aware of the YMCA's aging physical plant and stabilized membership, Hall stressed that renovation of old buildings was only part of what was required for the Association to do the new, relevant work in communities it served, which required extensions. In 1967, the Bronx Union Branch gave up its full facility building with a residence to focus on a broad-area community service program in three centers. The Westchester-Bronx Y started a $350,000 Founders Fund campaign for a new building that opened in 1970, while launching and expanding youth programs in the northeast and southeast parts of

the borough. In 1977, the YMCA purchased six acres at Castle Hill for a Day Camp and Family Center to serve 300 youth each week and families on evenings and weekends. The beautiful site on Long Island Sound came with an outdoor pool, bath houses, picnic areas and playing fields. At that time, Bronx Union and Westchester-Bronx merged as the Bronx YMCA.

Brooklyn Central sold its building, still said to be the world's largest YMCA, in 1967 to New York State for use as a Narcotics Addiction Training and Control Center. (Bronx Union and the Seamen's House and Laundry on West Twentieth Street in Manhattan were also acquired for this purpose.) The Central Branch reorganized as a decentralized program in neighborhood centers advised by a "Committee of 115," men and women from all segments of the community. Its youth membership had fallen from 825 to 100 when it left the aged building, but soon rose to 550 in thirty active programs, including four colleges. The recently formed Flatbush Branch occupied new quarters, a converted cinema at 1401 Flatbush Avenue that it acquired for $250,000, in 1968. This Y had developed interracial and interfaith teams in softball and basketball community leagues before establishing the comprehensive program center. Soon it would boast the "largest Y gym in the city," and the largest membership among Brooklyn Branches, with a re-established student program at nearby Brooklyn College.

The former Seamen's Branch in Manhattan became a mobile YMCA based at McBurney, largely serving foreign merchant seamen on freighters as passenger traffic declined. Two Y vans regularly met incoming ships at docking areas in Brooklyn, Port Elizabeth and Newark. In 1971, the Seamen's program came to the aid of Japanese seamen stranded in New York City due to a dock strike. The YMCA was the only agency to reach them, and provided them with leisure-time trips in the mobile van to Washington, D.C., Holiday Hills, and West Point during their enforced stay.

The Eastern District Branch in Williamsburg, one of the oldest, was in a neighborhood that had changed dramatically. By 1974 it was 40 percent Hispanic and only 44 percent white, with the latter predominantly a Hasidic Jewish population that didn't participate in YMCA programs. Williamsburg had a high unemployment and welfare rate, following major shifts in local industries. The Branch residence had declining occupancy, and the neighborhood could no longer support the operation.

The new Westchester-Bronx Branch building opened in 1970.

New York State bought the Brooklyn Central Branch building on Hanson Place in 1967 for use as a Narcotics Addiction Training and Control Center.

Beginning in 1968, the Branch had rented nine classrooms to the Board of Education for the badly overcrowded Eastern District High School, whose 250 students also enjoyed swimming and exercise at the Y. But by 1976 the building, which had never been significantly remodeled, had outlived its usefulness and was sold for $400,000. Model Cities and other agencies were actively developing housing in the area, and the New York City Housing Authority (NYCHA) provided the Branch with cost-free space in the Borinquen Center, including a gym, lockers, showers, exercise rooms, an area for seniors and administrative offices. In return, the YMCA provided personnel and programs. Along with another program it ran for youth and seniors in the Jonathan Williams Houses Center, Eastern District became a leader in the development of new community housing.

On Staten Island, membership was mushrooming: from 1960 to 1970 it rose from 1,430 to 4,600. As the Island's population grew, the Y started programs for residents at New Brighton and South Shore. In 1974 the Branch began a full-service extension as a YMCA-YWCA program on the South Shore, and relocated its New Brighton program and staff to the Markham Houses in partnership with NYCHA. In 1976 it opened a $1 million expansion of its Broadway building, with a new gym, lockers, classrooms, and three tennis courts; membership doubled in a year, to 9,000. Its new Early Childhood Development Center was designed to serve the fastest growing borough. The following year it bought a two-story building for the South Shore extension and formed a Counselor Services Agency with sixty other community-based organizations to coordinate services, information and referrals.

In 1976, the McBurney Y and St. George's Church on East 16th Street created the Stuyvesant Park YMCA extension. Together they renovated three floors of the Parish House, a six-story gray stone Gothic revival structure financed by J. P. Morgan in 1885, to accommodate two gyms, a fully equipped theater and stage, a ceramic studio and large classrooms. Members included 500 individuals and families who flocked to its after-school program when the Board of Education could no longer continue those activities. The extension program also used the nearby Friends School, giving it three gyms. One hundred children ages 5 to 13 came every day after school for recreation, leisure and skills activities. A second gym was also added to McBurney's main building in 1976.

Manhattan's Uptown Branch expanded to new headquarters at 2700 Broadway, using churches, schools and other centers for its program of in-depth group activities

The Uptown Branch moved to rented quarters at 2700 Broadway; here, members cleaned the avenue's median strip.

for boys and girls ages 9 to 18. Long Island City established a new $200,000 headquarters and program center and dreamed of building an all-sports complex to include gym, pool, lighted ball field and area for ice hockey. But its dream would be deferred until financing was complete late in the century.

Holiday Hills evolved into a conference and continuing education center in 1967, when it added its new Gayle J. Lathrop Memorial Center. Fittingly, one of the first meetings it hosted was an Interfaith Conference. Its two barns had been renovated for group use in 1961, and the Donaldson Center was constructed in 1973 to add more guest rooms. Eight tennis courts were added in 1976, and a swim and boat dock were installed a year later.

The new co-ed focus was quickly and naturally accomplished with the rise of student and foreign tourists in this age of jet travel. The largest residence, the Sloane House YMCA with 1,500 rooms, diversified its program by emphasizing community involvement. It instituted an Urban Confrontation Program, a residence-seminar series for students from twenty colleges outside the city and state, to examine urban problems through firsthand observation. Sloane also became a chartered American Youth Hostel in 1972 and initiated the Pied Piper summer program for boys and girls in its Chelsea-Clinton neighborhood. Still, in 1974 Sloane House noted that more "welfare-type guests" were coming by word of mouth, poor people in desperate need of increasingly scarce single-room housing in a clean, safe and wholesome atmosphere.

Mid-Manhattan YMCAs could offer nearly 3,000 conveniently located rooms for economy-minded tourists, and Sloane, West Side and Vanderbilt all made major investments to upgrade their residence facilities, despite Hall's suggestion to decrease them. By 1979, the growth in students and young people visiting or studying in the city was a notable phenomenon of New York tourism, and YMCA lobbies had become exciting international and intercultural centers. That year 250,000 students and young travelers stayed in Y residence rooms. The Association's International Residence Program, marketed in twenty countries through a new service called "Y's Way," guaranteed travelers advance reservations.

YMCA residences in three boroughs, including Brooklyn and Queens, provided students, senior citizens, and visitors from other U.S. cities and abroad with clean, comfortable lodgings at a realistic cost. Flushing, located adjacent to LaGuardia Airport, added 48 resident rooms in a $300,000 expansion and Greenpoint, in the city's Polish-American community, mounted a $145,000 campaign to renovate 100 rooms.

New needs for supportive housing and available government funding opened other possibilities for use of YMCA residences. In 1973, in partnership with Reality House, the Harlem YMCA housed more than eighty rehabilitated drug addicts in its annex building and provided recreational services for them in a program with neighboring Harlem Hospital and the State Corrections Department. Sloane housed methadone users.

The Association, influenced by the Code H recommendations, committed itself in 1967 to develop programs to strengthen family life and improve intergenerational communication, especially between parents and children. While all YMCA work was at least indirectly related to families, now the family became a center of concern, attention and service, and family-unit memberships were promoted and encouraged. With Eastern Queens as the model for family center Ys, several Branches, including Bedford, Camps, Flushing, Greenpoint, Staten Island, and West Side, experimented with Sunday afternoon programs for families. Offering recreational games and family swims, their motto was "Families who *play* together *stay* together." By 1970, both Eastern Queens and Staten Island had 400 families in their memberships, and by 1972 most Branches had programs especially for them on Sunday afternoons or weekday evenings. In 1973, Flushing instituted a Father-Son Weekend Camping Club, and the Uptown Branch provided family counseling. Camp Brooklyn offered a 10-day Family Camp program.

Having broadened its focus explicitly to include co-ed and family participation, the Association no longer felt as vulnerable to a perception of widespread homosexual activity in its facilities. The anxieties that underlay the Code H report no longer seemed so acute. The YMCA could now at least tacitly accept its homosexual participants in context, as one part of its diverse constituency of New Yorkers.

Just two decades after the five-borough consolidation, the YMCA of Greater New York reflected an unprecedented diversity of members, programs and communities. Each Branch mirrored the interests and responded to needs of its surrounding neighborhood and constituents. The massive influx of women and children had forever changed facilities and programs while boosting membership at numerous Ys. In poorer communities, some Branches lacked income-producing features and sought outside contracts or turned to the metropolitan office for hardship grants through an internal transfer system from excess revenues generated by Branches in more affluent areas. With few exceptions, most YMCA buildings now pre-dated World War II and were situated in communities classified as poverty areas. The YMCA had chosen to stay, and would find upkeep and modifications for new needs in those properties a continuing challenge.

The International Tradition

FROM ITS EARLIEST days the YMCA had international aspirations, fanning out from England to take hold quickly in other countries. For New York members and leaders, the Spanish-American and World Wars offered opportunities for service to people beyond national borders. Following the Spanish-American conflict, the West Side YMCA played a major part in starting a Y in Havana. YMCAs nationwide joined in an International Committee, which included Canadian Ys in the early years. Regular YMCA world conferences began in the nineteenth century, as did overseas mission work. As head of the International Committee, New Yorker Richard Cary Morse initiated a Foreign Work Department in 1889. By 1905, there were 5,000 YMCAs in 24 countries, and many received support and technical assistance through the U.S. International Committee.

Nobel Prize winner John R. Mott had advanced this work tremendously. In 1911, he formed the national Committee on Friendly Relations Among Foreign Students (CFR), with assistance from New Yorkers like Cleveland H. Dodge, Andrew Carnegie, William Sloane, and a few other stalwarts of the YMCA's International Committee. William E. Dodge Jr. was the first CFR chairman and treasurer.

The West Side YMCA started an International Club in 1935.

Work for immigrants had been a longstanding commitment of the Association. Its international perspective also had deep roots in New York City's French and German Ys, which were significant Branches in the early years. When they closed, their activity was carried on by the Twenty-Third Street Branch, which started its own International Department. The new West Side YMCA contained International Rooms with a large world map and its International Club, formed in 1935, met there to discuss ideas for world peace.

After World War II, two concerns drove the YMCA's international efforts. Associations abroad had sustained great damage during the war, and needed help in rebuilding. The other concern was the fear of communism. In a tense era characterized by air-raid alerts, bomb shelters, and the McCarthy Senate hearings, the 1953 New York annual report noted that "we are living in a troubled world... beset with doubts and anxieties," attributing them to the "menacing threat of international Communism." The YMCA, as the only youth-serving agency in many countries, considered itself "one of the most powerful deterrents to the spread of communism." In 1955, the Association boasted that the "YMCA's brand of Christianity in action is one of America's best salesmen abroad."

World Service (a name that replaced YMCA Foreign Work around 1933) was responsible for raising funds for YMCAs abroad after World War II, and later focused on the rebuilding of YMCAs in Korea and working with millions of refugees there. The New York Association was a powerful contributor to restoration of the Philippines' Cebu YMCA, which had been destroyed. New York raised

$33,500 in 1953 toward the $80,000 total cost. In that decade, the New York Association also contributed generously to World Service, with annual gifts routinely running between $100,000 and $200,000. By 1963, World Service was working in 83 countries, of which forty received financial assistance.

The International Committee conducted a special Buildings for Brotherhood campaign from 1958–1962 to construct new YMCAs abroad, setting its most ambitious goal ever. John D. Rockefeller Jr. was instrumental in the kick-off. Of the $5,337,000 raised by both U.S. and Canadian Associations, donations from the YMCA of Greater New York accounted for $1 million, fully 20 percent of the U.S. quota.

Individual Branches also sponsored programs with an international focus. The West Side and Central Queens Ys conducted a "triangular" swimming contest with members of the Jerusalem YMCA by keeping records on individual swimmers and presenting awards. The two Branches also sponsored travel to Western Europe. In 1962, Sloane House entertained 22 students from the Soviet Union on a one-month tour of the United States as part of a YMCA-YWCA student exchange begun in 1960. By 1965, Sloane was billing itself as "the International YMCA." The Intercollegiate Branch published a "Handbook for International Students" in 1963; the comprehensive guide to the city was intended for its large population of foreign students. McBurney's International Department sponsored twenty-five national clubs for young men and women who were second- or third-generation Americans, to help them preserve and continue the "peculiar charms, customs, dress, dancing, singing, folklore and indigenous qualities associated with the countries of their parental or grandparental origin."

Meeting foreign arrivals at airports and helping them clear customs is a popular service of the International YMCA.

YMCA youth were enthusiastic supporters of the new United Nations in their city. The YMCA's Metropolitan Young Adult Council had staged a UN Ball, honoring UN and youth volunteers, in 1957. The Vanderbilt Branch initiated a program focus on international affairs in 1973, taking advantage of its proximity to the United Nations by offering five seminars about the UN for groups of visitors from all over the United States, the Far East and Western Europe.

In the 1960s and 1970s, New York contributions to World Service tapered off somewhat. The 1964 donation was $80,000 and the 1976 goal of $50,000 was even more modest, no doubt impacted by competition with pressing needs at home and the objection of staff to funding other countries when New York's communities were in need. But the Association continued to respond to international needs. It sought to raise another $15,000 for a concern that weighed heavily on many minds—the World Alliance of YMCAs' Indo-China Emergency Fund for work with Vietnamese refugees. In a significant event of 1979, the YMCA of Greater New York was designated as an International YMCA Program Center.

New Challenges Emerge

THE TURBULENCE OF the 1960s and 1970s had indelibly impacted the YMCA of Greater New York. The Association had returned to its earliest orientation, helping the neediest in a time of societal ferment even as it was breaking new ground in taking on non-traditional members and neighborhoods. The New York City YMCA had stepped up wholeheartedly, in the spirit of service, daring to address many needs in the new urban crisis even as it focused on world concerns. Soon its generosity would lead to trouble, as the YMCA faced a dire financial situation.

In 1963, Hall predicted that the YMCA would increasingly face a critical problem in financing its needs. The Association depended on dues for 92 percent of its income, and was more and more reliant on government funding and poverty programs for Branch and program support. Problems mounted when those external funds began to dry up. By 1972 the Association had accumulated a substantial operating deficit of more than $600,000, despite rate increases, higher fund-raising goals, and staff and expense cutbacks.

Paul Sharar, who headed the Counseling and Testing Branch used by so many job-seekers, confided to William Howes and Russell Service in 1972 that the city was planning to curtail contracts with voluntary agencies in a time of municipal fiscal woes. Sharar also warned of cash flow problems that the Y was encountering in its contracts. The State Education Department had informed him that the YMCA's total cost and cost-per-trainee-hour for CHOICE II were too high compared to similar programs operated by other agencies.

Howes and Association President John Schumann, in a message in the 1974 annual report, stated that, "It has become quite evident that our city and many voluntary institutions are in trouble." The fiscal viability of the YMCA must be maintained, they cautioned, if its programs were to remain current and relevant to community needs. The next year, at the lowest point of the city's financial setbacks and cutbacks in services, coupled with the national recession and runaway inflation, the YMCA responded with constructive actions. It instituted an energy conservation program, and undertook facility improvements that would encourage continued growth in women's memberships. "We believe fiscal management is sound," the leaders declared, although they reminded constituents that contributions generated only 8 percent of operating revenues, which was inadequate.

In the prevailing economy, raising contribution levels was a challenge indeed. "We are a community in transition—a diminishing proportion of relatively affluent people and a constantly increasing proportion of relatively poor and underprivileged people—people with seemingly overwhelming problems in education, employment, housing, health, drug addiction, and crime prevention," the 1976 annual report noted. Those needs were increasing while resources were diminishing, aggravated by the city's fiscal crisis. Corporations were leaving the city, reducing both the tax base and sources of charitable giving. The YMCA, as one of the city's largest community-based human care organizations, intended "to exercise leadership, to be a force for neighborhood development and community renewal, and to develop and initiate those programs and services which meet the needs of individuals and families." Government-funded program contracts from 15 agencies were by then accounting for $3.5 million to $4.5 million per year.

By 1978, other concerns had surfaced. The Association's liability insurance costs had escalated 400 percent in a six-month period, draining revenues from programs. Its Prisoner-Pre-Release Program with the state had been terminated because insurers refused broad coverage for programs for high-risk groups, and the Juvenile Justice Program had not received anticipated funding. Energy costs had doubled, and threats were looming to the property-tax exemption that nonprofits enjoyed. Sources of funding were uncertain in transitional neighborhoods. As always, the YMCA needed capital resources for maintenance and improvement of its aging facilities to sustain its programs, generate income from memberships and extend services for youth in disadvantaged areas. Several Branches had waiting lists for adult memberships, which could yield revenues, but capacity was inadequate. The 1978 annual report, in calling for better long- and short-range planning, spelled out what was imperative if the YMCA were to survive and thrive for the balance of the twentieth century.

In the 1970s popular YMCA programs were threatened by diminished government funding.

Refining Purpose and Mission

1978 Statement of Purpose

The YMCA of Greater New York is an educational, religious and charitable non-profit association, whose role is to improve the mental, moral and physical condition of individuals, especially the young.

1979 Mission Statement

The mission of the YMCA of Greater New York is to provide, effectively and efficiently, services and activities which help people, regardless of age, sex, race or religion, to develop in mind, body and spirit; to recognize and fulfill their responsibilities to each other and to the larger community; and to improve the quality of life in New York City and in other parts of the world.

6

1980-2002

A Time of Reckoning

THE ASSOCIATION LEADERSHIP described the year 1981 as one of extreme pressure, given the changing needs and increasing demands of so many New Yorkers. The city's population was changing socially, economically and culturally, and community needs were unabating. Groups once referred to as "minorities" were now, collectively, a majority in the city; life expectancy was increasing, and more working parents required daytime care for their children. By 1985, eighteen of thirty-two YMCA Branches and program centers were in

designed poverty centers or transitional neighborhoods, where the needs for employment and training were great. Violent crime and drug abuse was mounting among both youth and adults, AIDS was a troubling new phenomenon, and a new infusion of immigrants was again changing the face of New York City. By the late 1980s, escalating racial intolerance threatened the city's stability. Concurrently, a sharp decline in government grants for social programs had jeopardized a funding source that the YMCA of Greater New York counted on to meet mushrooming community needs, forcing it to exist, as one leader put it, "hand to mouth."

Acknowledging in 1983 that their YMCA was facing dire problems, the Board of Directors developed another strategic plan to guide the Association. Their

dilemma was large, both fiscal and property-related. Dogged by a $3.4 million operations deficit accrued over the previous decade, the Association also had a $1.3 million loan coming due. The New York City YMCA had developed an admirably diverse program in recent years, but fiscal realities indicated that those ambitious undertakings would have to be pruned back. Despite a recovering city economy, the Association was having difficulty raising money for operations and was unable to marshal the capital needed to replace outmoded structures. The YMCA owned many buildings in all boroughs and two properties upstate, making it asset-rich but cash-poor. The strategic plan focused on these financial woes and the Association's future as a new president, William A. Markell, was taking office.

William A. Markell (right), YMCA president in the 1980s, meets with Board members Myrtle G. Whitmore and Ralph B. Henderson.

The YMCA had reduced its previous reliance on income from membership and program fees from 92 percent to 82 percent of the operating budget, but had increased the portion coming from government funds. By the early 1980s, nearly 8 percent of revenues came from government sources and 8 percent from private contributions. Some Branches, notably Bedford and Harlem, were hit especially hard when federal money for social programs began to evaporate, because their reliance on it had been so great. Bedford had largely abandoned traditional YMCA programs to focus exclusively on its Technical School offerings. Harlem depended heavily on public funding for programs like Project Redirection and the Youth Enrichment Program, even though it maintained the largest black membership in a New York YMCA. Government grants had become essential for Ys in low-income communities where residents could not strongly sustain the Branch through dues-paying memberships and private fund raising.

The public's interest in physical fitness had grown steadily and new private health clubs were cropping up, offering health-conscious New Yorkers a much wider choice of places to work out. For more than a century the YMCA had dominated this field, especially for people of more modest means. Now, however, the newcomer clubs threatened to make inroads in the YMCA's membership revenues that so heavily supported Association operations. Faced with this newly competitive scenario, the YMCA was compelled, as a matter of survival, to upgrade its long-standing fitness facilities in order to compete effectively for members.

Mission Statement 1981

The mission of the YMCA of Greater New York is to provide, effectively and efficiently, services and activities that help people, regardless of age, sex, race or religion,

✣ *to develop in mind, body and spirit;*

✣ *to recognize and fulfill their responsibilities to one another, and to the larger community; and*

✣ *to improve the quality of life in New York City and in other parts of the world.*

The 1983 strategic plan, with its upbeat title "Focus on Excellence," identified the seven strategic program areas along with the revenues they generated in 1982: youth development, $1.1 million; health enhancement, $6.3 million; child care, $1 million; camping $2.1 million; employment and training, $2.4 million; international, $1 million; residence, $14.5 million; other programs accounted for $600,000. The Association also realized non-program revenues of $4.6 million from contributions and investment income. Although the YMCA's buildings were seriously outdated, residence programs were responsible for fully half the Association's program revenues. However, the strategic plan recommended selling selected underutilized assets that occupied valuable land, beginning with Sloane House, and reinvesting funds in the first four strategic program areas.

Despite the plan's resolve to make the Association solvent and run like a business, the YMCA's bills payable rose to $2.9 million in November 1985, up from $1.4 million just five months earlier. This was largely due to higher insurance charges and revenue shortfalls at the three largest Branches. The leadership noted that nothing had been harder to manage that year than income and expenses, although it was repaying loans. Annual fund raising, the purview of Branch volunteers, was also lagging well behind goals.

Although the Association strived mightily in the 1980s to institute new budgeting procedures, improve financial management, and diversify funding sources, the times had changed greatly. Like many other non-profit organizations, the Y's increased reliance on government funds since the 1960s left it unprepared for the highly competitive environment of the 1980s, an era of fundamental change in public policy and economic realities. The Association responded with significant belt- and budget-tightening, and a marked contraction in its once ambitious programs. The venerable Schools Branch, including the McBurney School, ceased operations in the early 1980s, as did the Uptown Branch and Clinton Youth Center. McBurney's Stuyvesant Park and Tribeca Centers were quietly terminated, and the Counseling and Testing Services Branch disappeared without fanfare. In the mid-1980s the West Side Y still housed one of the largest adult education centers, offering informal courses. So did other Branches, on a smaller scale, but they provided as much social fellowship as employment-focused skills.

In 1987, a capital campaign resulted in some significant new expansion, notably at the Vanderbilt and Eastern Queens Ys, but the scope was inadequate to the Association's overall needs. Donald K. Ross, chairman of the YMCA Board of Trustees and chairman of the board of New York Life Insurance Company, put a positive face on the situation, stating that he was "proud to witness the rebuilding and renewal of our YMCA." Despite avowals of "emerging strength" in financial performance, the underlying dilemma would not disappear. By 1988, the Association was showing a $1.5-million deficit in its $54-million operation.

A New Leader for a New Era

ALTHOUGH THE YMCA'S deficit was reduced the next year to $680,000, the underlying problems remained. Following a sobering stock market crash in 1987, the decade's economic boom began to subside. Shortly thereafter, the nation fell into a recession that would persist into the early 1990s, with New York City's slump lasting even longer. The Board turned to new leadership to confront the decade ahead, leadership that could build on the Association's extraordinary strengths and historic assets.

By 1990, the YMCA of Greater New York was firmly set on dual tracks, as a membership-based and a community service organization, but lacked the fiscal strength that would assure its continuation. Its focus was now as broad as it had been narrow in 1852, with thousands of staff and volunteers managing an array of educational, health and recreational programs for people of all ages in the city's

Paula L. Gavin, the first woman CEO and a recruit from the business sector, epitomized the changes in the YMCA of Greater New York.

diverse communities. But its shaky financial foundation threatened to diminish or even curtail the good work that had accrued for so many decades and was now reaching so many underserved residents of the city. With the YMCA's vital signs imperiled, it was clearly a time for rescue.

To lead this complex organization out of its impasse and assure its survival in a new century, the Board departed from more than a century of tradition in selecting a new chief executive. For the first time ever, the directors looked outside the ranks of YMCA professionals to the private sector. And the organization that was started by men, for men, selected Paula L. Gavin, its first female president. Gavin's assets included twenty-two years of business experience and acumen as a corporate officer of AT&T. As the Board had hoped, Gavin led the YMCA to a new way of thinking by instituting management by objectives. The Association's mission now became the rationale around which the organization constructed annual goals, objectives and budgets, with each unit responsible for achieving its own aims. As the YMCA "managed to the mission," individual employees also set goals and objectives and were held accountable for reaching them. Gavin saw to it that the YMCA managed the financials as well.

The new CEO and her team began by refining the organization's mission, and articulating a 10-year vision for the Association. "Vision 2000" stated that the YMCA would be a dedicated and caring leader of personal and community growth for the people of New York City, and an aggressive leader and partner in responding to the critical needs of all New Yorkers. It would seek increasing participation by members and volunteers in the YMCA, aiming to involve one in fifteen New Yorkers in the five boroughs. The Association would work with city leaders to improve the quality of life, and would strive to be a "high-quality" organization. It would expand programs for youth and put its financial house in order. A strategic plan would make the vision a reality.

For the first time, Gavin instituted a yearly planning process in the New York YMCA. Unlike her predecessors, who had contracted with outside consultants like Swift, Strayer and Hall for exhaustive studies approximately every twenty years, she involved each Branch and department in projecting revenues, membership and fund-raising numbers as the basis for their annual strategic plans. No longer would studies sit on a shelf; employees would be held responsible for achieving their unit's annual "action plan." Branches, each led by a Board of Managers and an executive director who reported to the Association's chief operating officer, retained responsibility for program development, annual and capital fund raising, community partnerships, membership and volunteer development, and their own financial stability. Branches that could not fully fund their operations, especially those in low-income communities, could apply for funds from a pool of surplus revenues from other Branches, in a process called Intra-Association Transfer.

The annual report from Gavin's first year set the tone for the future, highlighting five goals that had already been achieved: the strategic plan of action and Branch operating plans, a focus on staff development, implementation of a new governance plan to enhance the volunteer-staff partnership, significant improvement in fiscal performance and a refocusing on the needs of youth. In that first year, the Association reported a surplus of $707,000 on its operating budget of $58.7 million. Key objectives for the following year, reiterated throughout the decade, included achievement of financial stability, investment in quality of staff and facilities, and a dramatic increase in fund-raising.

Gavin made a key appointment early in her tenure by tapping John M. Preis as chief financial officer. Preis combined a strong YMCA background—he worked first as a part-time referee at his childhood YMCA, Twelve Towns, and rose to be a Branch business manager—with a masters in business administration. Together, he and Gavin undertook a restructuring of the Association's high-interest debt in 1991. They reinvested funds in the McBurney and Vanderbilt YMCA guest accommodations program, and the strategy paid off as New York City tourism rose steadily throughout the 1990s. Preis formed a Business Cabinet and worked closely with all Branches to achieve positive financial results. (He now heads the national YMCA Retirement Fund.)

Success Breeds Success

"**W**e have to stretch and reach. And once we do, we'll see that success breeds success. Success builds upon itself."

—PAULA GAVIN,
President/CEO, YMCA of Greater New York, 1990

Thus Gavin ushered in the contemporary era of stringent financial controls that shored up the Association's base, allowing it to undertake bold citywide program initiatives and to enter into municipal and corporate partnerships. Every year in the 1990s the Association generated enough income to meet expenses, and revenues grew substantially, from $54 million in 1990 to $119 million in 2000. Volunteer involvement increased significantly, a boost to community fund-raising efforts, and the Association's financial base was greatly diversified. By 2000, only 67 percent of operating revenue came from membership and program fees. Private contributions accounted for 20 percent, while government grants provided 11 percent. The balance of nearly $2 million came from endowment income.

John M. Preis, chief financial officer in the 1990s, led a critical bond financing. He is now CEO of the YMCA Retirement Fund.

A Period of Renewal

THE YMCA'S PHYSICAL plant was aging in 1983; the median age of its buildings was 53 years. Many of them, including the residences, had become obsolescent. Valiant attempts were made to rehabilitate the structures, but problems kept cropping up. Tough financial choices had caused improvements and expansions to be postponed and maintenance deferred in order to fund day-to-day operations. The building configurations of older Branches, and even their locations, were ill-suited to new needs. Some YMCAs had become underutilized as their surrounding communities changed. Even though hundreds of thousands of New Yorkers participated annually in Branch activities, a number of communities lacked access altogether to YMCA services.

The Association's old buildings posed an image problem as well, since public perception was largely shaped by superficial knowledge of Y facilities or first-hand experience with an antiquated neighborhood Branch, perhaps one that still retained a residence populated by long-term, low-income individuals. As the YMCA advertised its fitness offerings to retain and build

its share of the health enhancement market, it only reinforced a stereotype that the organization's sole activity was "swim and gym," despite the multiplicity of YMCA programs—nearly 600 offerings by 1981—for all members of the community. The complex organization was not well understood.

Clearly, Branches had to be upgraded, enhanced, restored, expanded—and promoted. Two Branches were able to undertake significant expansions in the 1980s. Eastern Queens (renamed Cross Island in 1988 to better reflect its site as a crossroads for surrounding communities) raised $2.3 million to add a new wing with more space for programs and a special access pool used by hundreds of "physically challenged" New Yorkers. Jack Kleinoder, a YMCA member since 1919 in Nuremburg, Germany, chaired the capital campaign and received the Order of the Red Triangle for his volunteer service. The Branch currently plans to expand again, adding a new pool, a family gym, a computer center and enlarging its nursery school.

As the Hall study had advised in 1963, the Vanderbilt Y sold development rights to its building and adjacent brownstones for $4 million, allowing for renovations and a major expansion that doubled its program space on East Forty-Seventh Street. Both the Vanderbilt and Cross Island Branches subsequently saw a tremendous growth in membership, and Vanderbilt proceeded to open a new early childhood center in 1990.

The West Side YMCA also attempted an air rights sale in 1986, which was initially thwarted by a difficult real estate market in the late 1980s. A sale of its old McBurney School building on West Sixty-Third Street

Jack Kleinoder chaired the campaign for Cross Island's $2.3 million expansion.

The Vanderbilt Branch added a new early childhood center in 1990.

and two adjacent brownstones was finally achieved in 1998. The subsequent development, completed in 2001, gutted the McBurney annex but preserved its historic facade, and added five new floors of contiguous space for YMCA programs, including child care, cardiovascular exercise and a teen fitness area. Topped by a residential condominium, the development also included six floors of affordable housing for 67 individuals. The units are managed by the West Side Y.

Moving quickly to reduce indebtedness, the Association closed its 1,600-room Sloane House YMCA in 1991. The day had passed when Sloane was used by legions of transient military personnel. Now, as the YMCA refocused its programs and activities on youth, it consolidated rooms for short-term tourist stays at the Vanderbilt, West Side and McBurney Branches. The 1994 sale of Sloane allowed retirement of the Association's $3.8 million mortgage. In an unusual venture for a YMCA, a 1991 sale of $21 million in tax-free municipal bonds permitted the Association to restructure debt and provide resources for renovations at Vanderbilt and West Side residences.

A capital Campaign for Youth was launched in 1992, with a $30-million goal, the largest ever set by a YMCA in the United States. Proceeds would be earmarked to expand youth programs, improve facilities and build new ones. The three-year effort raised only $23 million but allowed for expansion at six Branches—Bedford, Harlem, Long Island City, McBurney, Staten Island, and Camping Services—and a $1 million gift from the Dodge family for a Youth Trust Fund, whose income would be allocated exclusively to youth program support.

In the 1990s, the Association committed to a program of equal excellence among its Branches, urging each one to meet uniform YMCA standards in their facilities. This required careful analysis of needs, careful budgeting and creative fund raising. With Gavin's strong encouragement the Bedford YMCA, which had evolved solely into a Technical School in the 1970s and 1980s, reopened its youth building and offered a program for youngsters for the first time in more than ten years, including basketball and track. Its initial 400 participants grew to more than 1,200 by the end of 1991. The Branch subsequently remodeled its swimming pool and invested in equipment for a new adult health enhancement program.

Another YMCA in Brooklyn, Prospect Park, undertook a major remodeling of fitness facilities in the 1980s, followed by a significant renovation of its residence in the mid-1990s with $8.5 million in financing from the city's Department of Housing Preservation and Development (HPD). The 138 new units for single adults came under ownership of Community House, with the Branch retaining management responsibilities. Some older residents remained, including retired seamen who occupy their own wing called Seafarers' Safe Haven, all that remains of the once active Seamen's YMCAs. New residents come through referrals from the city. The remodeling included significant renovation of other Branch program space. Prospect Park and six other Branches with

Teen members at Prospect Park are interviewing and recording oral histories of retired seamen.

Gordon Glazer, a Community House resident, enjoys a game of bingo with a staff member at the Prospect Park Y.

residents partnered with the Visiting Nurse Service in 1997 to provide them with on-site health screenings and referrals. Now Prospect Park plans to add a new swimming pool and special needs locker room for the physically challenged.

Social dynamics changed dramatically in the Bronx in the latter part of the twentieth century. Many long-time residents moved on, and were replaced by newly arrived immigrants. The borough became the city's poorest, and claimed the highest proportion of children. The

Bronx YMCA, severely challenged to support its greatly needed programs, consolidated its operations at the Castle Hill Day Camp it had purchased on a six-acre site near the Whitestone Bridge, closed the Jacobi Center and sold its Westchester Avenue building in 1996. In 2002, the Branch, which now runs programs at 30 sites including public schools and Hostos Community College, will complete a major expansion to transform Castle Hill by adding a new 21,000-square-foot, full-facility YMCA with modern locker rooms, an indoor pool and a greatly enlarged fitness center.

In the Staten Island YMCA, membership grew continuously with the expanding population in its primarily residential borough. Retaining strong operations at the Broadway Center, the Branch also offered programs on the South Shore and set about raising $1.7 million to build a second YMCA there. In 1997, it opened a sleek modern facility, the first completely new building in the YMCA of Greater New York constellation in 30 years. The building quickly exceeded its capacity of 10,000 members, and an expansion was planned. Its substance-abuse program, renamed the YMCA Counseling Center, had also gravitated to the populous South Shore in 1980 to focus on children of substance abusers, recovering adults, and youth in the juvenile justice system. State funds were awarded for a new center on Richmond Avenue, which opened in 1999.

The Long Island City Branch, which had never occupied a full-facility building in its seventy years of existence, took a bold step in the 1990s. A significant bequest and a donation of land from Swingline Inc., the stapler manufacturer that was relocating to Mexico, allowed it to undertake construction of a modern YMCA.

Staten Island opened an all-new YMCA on the South Shore in 1997 (above), and a new Counseling Center in 1999.

The Long Island City Branch, opened in 1999, quickly outgrew the facility and began building an addition in 2002.

The new Branch facility opened on Queens Boulevard in 1999 to the delight of the nearby community, quickly surpassing its membership projections in a former industrial area now populated largely by new immigrants. In 2002, the Long Island City Branch is crafting plans to add a gym and new rooms for youth and community activities.

The Association, having achieved positive balance sheets and average annual revenue gains throughout the 1990s, embarked on an ambitious master planning process in 1998. Each Branch building was scrutinized for its capacity to meet current and future needs, and those needs were prioritized for rational planning. As a result the 1904 McBurney building on West Twenty-Third Street, frequently rehabbed over the years, revealed many more infrastructure needs than were affordable for the Branch to undertake. A careful analysis showed that this historic YMCA would survive only by building anew. In 2000, a sale of the structure was completed, allowing McBurney to purchase two floors in a new complex rising on West Fourteenth Street which will open as a 67,000-square-foot, full-facility YMCA in early 2003. The old Branch residence on Twenty-

The Long Island City Branch broke ground for a gym in 2002.

Fourth Street was purchased by a non-profit housing provider, Common Ground, which is renovating the space to house low-income individuals. The Twenty-Third Street portion was purchased by a private developer who agreed to preserve the building's historic facade.

The Bedford YMCA, which had raised half its capital campaign goal of $1.5 million by early 2002, made plans to demolish its outsized and outmoded 1906 building on Bedford Avenue in January 2003 and to construct anew on the site. The proposed single-story structure, which will link to the existing activity center on Monroe Avenue, will include new fitness studios, a computer learning center and a 300-seat performance space. In the future the Branch may build atop the new structure, which is scheduled for completion in 2004.

The building solutions of the McBurney and Bedford YMCAs in particular represent new and creative approaches to the challenges facing a non-profit organization with an aging infrastructure. Such combinations will allow the YMCA to capitalize on its assets in the future while offering the best possible facilities for the city's neighborhoods and communities.

A new McBurney YMCA will open on West Fourteenth Street in 2003.

Landmark
YMCAs

*I*n *1998 the Landmarks Preservation Commission granted landmark status to the Harlem YMCA building at 180 West 135th Street, not only for its neo-Georgian building and tower that is a major presence in Harlem, but for its role as one of the area's most important recreational and cultural centers, and the participation of many notable African Americans over the years. In the same year, the Commission also designated 222 Bowery, the former Young Men's Institute, as a city landmark.*

Emboldened by its restored financial health and a prosperous national and local economy, the YMCA of Greater New York initiated a $50 million capital campaign in 2000 to fund a $150-million facilities redevelopment plan that will allow each Branch to pursue improvements based on its own master plan. In addition several entirely new YMCAs are envisioned, in parts of Brooklyn and Manhattan's Chinatown. A $2-million gift from the Dodge Foundation will allow for a new full-facility YMCA of 40,000 square feet in downtown Brooklyn, to be named the Dodge Family YMCA in honor of its members who have so singularly supported the New York City YMCA since its inception.

The YMCA has received extraordinary support from local government for this twenty-first-century redevelopment. Twelve Branches have received allocations. Bronx Borough President Fernando Ferrer contributed $2 million for his borough's YMCA expansion and the New York City Council gave $1 million toward a new YMCA in Brooklyn, among others. Mayor Rudolph Giuliani allocated $5 million toward the citywide YMCA effort.

Accommodating Women and Children

IN LARGE MEASURE, the YMCA's new membership demographics since the 1970s prompted the profusion of building renovations and Branch expansions. Still decidedly a minority in 1970, women had been joining YMCAs in record numbers and by 1980 comprised 40 percent of the membership. By 1990 they had reached parity with men. Women, of course, required separate locker rooms and restrooms in the fitness facilities. Young children were also flocking to YMCAs in record numbers for child care. In 1981 the YMCA co-sponsored five day-care centers with the YWCA in four boroughs, but the need for day care was greater than those centers alone could handle. By 1983 the Association had doubled its commitment and was operating ten child-care centers, with new pre-school programs at the Bronx, Flatbush and McBurney Ys, serving a total of 3,000 children.

Flatbush introduced Project Giant Step, an educational orientation program for 4-year-olds, and by 1992 could claim one of the city's largest early childhood programs. Holiday Hills added a tiny tot day camp for children from ages 3 to 5. McBurney expanded its child-care program to a new on-site center at Federal Plaza in lower Manhattan. Eastern Queens, Twelve Towns (formerly Highland Park) and West Side added new pre-school classrooms. During this time, a West Side Y employee and new mother, Eileen O'Connor, started an infant care program for children ages 6 months to 2 years (the maximum age soon rose to 5). That initiative, still flourishing as Tender Care at the West Side Branch, was one of the earliest infant care programs in the nation. Staten Island led the Branches in offering pre-natal programs for mothers-to-be, and post-natal programs followed.

Staten Island offered the first YMCA pre-natal classes.

YMCA after-school programs grew in popularity as a form of child care.

Another form of child care, after-school programs, was also in great demand for 6- to 12-year-olds, to prevent a population of "latch-key" children returning to empty homes. The YMCA added five, bringing its total to twenty after-school programs and extending them to off-site locations in neighborhoods.

Contemporary parents needed extensive support in child rearing, and the YMCA responded with a parenting initiative. By 1987, after the YMCA had separated its child-care program from the YWCA, the Association was operating thirty-two pre-school and after-school centers, and had seen a 50-percent enrollment increase in just two years.

The momentum of child-care initiatives was remarkable. By 1989, the YMCA of Greater New York could claim to be the city's largest non-governmental child care provider with thirty-two after-school programs, sixteen pre-school centers and twenty-four day camps. Holiday camps, offering care for children of working parents during school breaks, were also introduced at this time. Participation in YMCA child development programs more than doubled in 1990, with the addition of nine early childhood classrooms and six after-school programs, all in public schools. This became a trend in the 1990s as the YMCA, by now a seasoned and knowledgeable provider of childhood programs, increasingly partnered with the New York City school system. In 1995, the Association introduced the School's Out Kids Club, a free after-school program in six of the city's poorest neighborhoods.

Great disparities had emerged in the public education system since the 1970s. Overcrowded classrooms, disgruntled teachers, crumbling buildings, increasing numbers of non-English speaking immigrant children and a politicized budget and Board of Education were just some of the challenges the system faced. New York City children consistently scored lower on basic tests, such as reading and math, and many dropped out before earning a diploma. By the late 1980s, the business community in particular was alarmed that the school system was producing graduates without the basic skills and attitudes necessary for the world of work. Various private and public initiatives were created to address this troubling and tenacious problem.

In the 1990s, New York City developed Beacon Schools, public elementary and intermediate schools that are given over to community-based organizations after regular school hours. As neighborhood centers, the Beacons offer a safe, structured environment for both youth and adults after school as well as in the evening and on weekends. The Chinatown YMCA received one of the early grants from the Department of Youth Services to start a Beacon Program in 1993, and moved its base of Branch operations there. The Branch now serves more than 3,700 teens and adults in that program and more than 250 children in summer day camp. Three other Branches are the

Chinatown YMCA programs take place in a Beacon School.

Flatbush child care programs are heavily enrolled, and the Branch plans to add six classrooms.

community partners in Beacon School programs—Cross Island, North Brooklyn's Eastern District and Flushing—for a total of five managed by the Association. (The Eastern District and Twelve Towns Branches merged as the North Brooklyn YMCA in the early 1990s.)

In 1998, New York State introduced its Universal Pre-K initiative, a new program to better prepare pre-kindergarten-age children for formal schooling. The YMCA of Greater New York was selected as one of the first providers. The Association offers its Universal Pre-K programs in 2002 at the Catalpa Center, Cross Island, Flatbush, Flushing, Long Island City, and Staten Island YMCAs.

The YMCA's boldest partnership with the Board of Education was the *Virtual Y* after-school program. The initiative was devised by the Schools Chancellor and Paula Gavin, who offered the Association's assistance to help children in underperforming schools to master basic skills such as reading and arithmetic. The *Virtual Y*, so named because it takes YMCA programs and staff into the schools, creating mini-YMCAs away from Branch premises, was launched as a pilot project in ten elementary schools in the spring of 1997. Free of charge to participants, the program allows students to remain in their own schools for three hours of learning enhancement after classes end. The YMCA supplies the curriculum and trained staff, the school system designates the sites and private donors fund each site's operations. Students enjoy a 10:1 ratio with counselors, a number of whom come through the AmeriCorps School Success Program. Parents and volunteers participate as well. In the school year 2001–2002, ninety-three *Virtual Y* sites were operating in all boroughs, enrolling nearly 7,000 second- through fourth-grade students in thirty-two of the city's thirty-four school districts.

The corporate and foundation communities responded enthusiastically to the *Virtual Y*. The innovative public-private partnership claims many well-known New York businesses as sponsors. Another major collaborator is The After-School Corporation (TASC), a division of philanthropist George Soros' Open Society Institute,

Children in the Virtual Y after-school program enjoy a menu of learning enhancement activities, such as art.

Like Father, Like Daughter

Arthur Taylor has served for many years as a policy volunteer in the New York YMCA, first by chairing the Vanderbilt Board of Managers, then by serving on the Greater New York Board of Directors and now by chairing the Board of the Camping Services Branch. For his outstanding years of service, Taylor was elected to the Order of the Red Triangle in 2002. Not the least of his contributions to the YMCA is his daughter Mary Taylor, an executive with Merrill Lynch who has served on the Board of Directors and its Fund Development Committee since 1999.

U.S. Senator Hillary Clinton paid a visit to the Virtual Y in 1998 during her tenure as First Lady.

Education Secretary Richard Riley and First Lady Hillary Rodham Clinton, elected in 2001 as the junior senator from New York State. In 1999, it was named a "promising practice" by the state education department. Schools Chancellor Rudolph F. Crew called it a "major enabling device" in his quest to ensure on-grade reading by the third grade.

The program seemed to fulfill Hall's prophecy in the 1962 Association survey: "If the leadership will identify one critical, obvious, overriding need of the 'inner city' and meet that need with spectacular success," he stated, "the whole image of the Association will change." More than any other YMCA program, the *Virtual Y* has demonstrated the Y's pivotal role in the city in education, its ability to reach the neediest children and its power to bring important elements of the community together for the benefit of youth.

Meeting New Needs of Youth

BY THE MID-1980S crime, drug abuse, premature sexual activity and a growing rash of teen suicides dominated the city's concerns about its youth. The Association's 1992 annual report contrasted the increasingly severe social problems confronting contemporary youngsters with those of a half century earlier. No longer were school-age lads and young ladies primarily courting trouble by talking out of turn, chewing gum, making noise, running in the hall or cutting in line, as was true in the 1940s. By 1992, the top problems facing teens were substance abuse, violence, suicide, robbery, and untimely

which funds a dozen sites. TASC modeled its own initiative on the *Virtual Y*. Other creative partnerships in this program include that of Scholastic Inc., which annually donates a lending library of books to each *Virtual Y* site.

The *Virtual Y* gained national recognition as a model public-private partnership by the U.S. Department of Education in its first year, and enjoyed visits from

pregnancy, threats that not long before were confined primarily to adults. "Today there are those in our city who think some problems facing our youth are insurmountable," the annual report noted. "The YMCA believes that it's never too late to make a difference."

In the 1980s, YMCA youth programs were focused largely on prevention of teenage delinquency, through innovative efforts like the NYPUM (National Youth Program Using Mini-Bikes) program in Chinatown and Central Queens, which was offered as a prelude to positive citizenship for pre-delinquent youth. Central Queens also offered a mentoring program for high school students, and other Branches followed suit. The Bronx YMCA devised a Grandma and Grandpa program, calling on its considerable roster of seniors to volunteer by helping children. The Eastern District YMCA began coordinating a multi-agency program in 1985 to cope with a high rate of teen pregnancy in its community, and it has shown excellent results in helping to avert pregnancies among its participants.

Greenpoint added Kids in Control (KIC), a substance-abuse service and outreach program for youth ages 9 to 18. KIC won a "New Yorkers for New York" award in 1991 as one of the four best youth-serving agencies in the city, and was honored the next year by the Citizens Committee for New York for its work with teens in Williamsburg. The North Brooklyn Branch opened a school-based community center under the Police Department's "Safe Streets, Safe City" program, in which the Prospect Park Y also participated.

In the early 1990s the YMCA renewed its focus on youth and responded to the desires of teen members for positive values and role models, self-esteem, personal health, job skills, education, leadership and service. Within just a few years, all Branches had introduced or expanded their Teen Centers, with "Light Nights" offering youth the chance to enjoy recreational, social and educational activities with their peers on Friday or Saturday evenings, when facilities are closed to adult members—a positive, enjoyable alternative to just "hanging out." Teen Centers drew 6,600 participants in 1992. The Harlem Branch reopened its remodeled Jackie Robinson Youth Center in 1996.

Sports, traditionally a magnet for youth, continued to be a strong YMCA program area, led by the Youth Basketball Association and co-sponsored by the National Basketball Association. In 1991 another popular program, Junior Knicks, was launched with the New York Knicks basketball team for 9- to 14-year-olds, followed by Junior Mets, a program sponsored by the New York Mets baseball club. In the Bronx, boys and girls participate in a Junior Yankees program with the renowned team

Mayor David Dinkins (left) celebrated the reopening of the Harlem YMCA Jackie Robinson Youth Center in 1996 with community youth, Rachel Robinson (right), and Board member Calvin O. Butts (far right).

In YMCA Junior Mets and Junior Knicks programs, girls and boys learn teamwork and the joy of participating in sports.

in their borough. In 1992, Greenpoint and Harlem introduced midnight basketball leagues. As in all YMCA sports, the emphasis is on growth and development: every participant plays, and everyone wins. When the public schools lost varsity sports citywide in a 1995 round of budget-cutting, the YMCA picked up the slack. As Bronx Borough President Fernando Ferrer noted, "It is during these tough fiscal times that we realize just how important the Y's sports leagues, after-school events and other learning-related programs are."

YMCA programs, however, aim to add more value to young lives than simply keeping teens off city streets. The Association's youth development philosophy focuses on leadership skills and a heightened awareness, through participation, of the importance and impact of community service. Its primary vehicles are the Branch-based Teen Leaders Clubs, Counselor-in-Training (CIT) programs. and the well-established Youth and Government initiative where teenagers get practical training in democratic action through participation. Service learning, in the form of an Earth Service Corps, gives teens the opportunity to improve the environment in their own communities. A Teen Council, composed of representatives from each Branch, provides leadership and service for citywide community projects, and furnishes a youth member each year to the Board of Directors.

Individual Branches also mounted programs targeted to youth, such as the Bronx Y's Computer Learning Center introduced in 1984, which became a prototype for other Branches. The Harlem Y started a youth computer literacy program in 1991, and a youth nutrition and exercise program, and Chinatown added its Computer Kids program in 1994. The West Side YMCA pioneered its Strong Women United program in 1996, an after-school program to help middle-school girls, through mentoring, coaching, and discussions, build the confidence and self-esteem, that too often wanes between ages 11 to 14 (a counterpart for teenage boys, Strong Brothers United, was added later). All Branches join in the national YMCA Healthy Kids Week each spring with events designed to raise health awareness. In 1998, the New York Ys began to promote Child Health Plus, a state-funded free or low-cost insurance program for lower-income families who do not qualify for Medicaid.

A daunting jobless rate continued to trouble New York City young adults in the early 1980s. Historically the YMCA had trained many resources on employment issues, and in 1981 it was still running two vocational schools: Bedford's TRY project, focusing on general office skills, and the YMCA Technical School, offering instruction in auto mechanics and commercial cooking. Occasionally other efforts were mounted to provide specific career skills, such as a program with Metropolitan Hospital to train respiratory therapy technicians.

Now, however, most jobs in New York's information- and services-based economy required at least some college, and many of the city's one million school-age youth could not qualify for them. Factory jobs, once the mainstay of the less educated, were disappearing at an alarming rate. To assist the hard-to-employ in finding work, the Association sponsored Career Opportunities for Brooklyn Youth (COBY), a program that allowed disadvantaged 17- to 25-year-olds eight weeks of exposure to a local business. In 1984, 350 youths in COBY gained full-time jobs and the program expanded rapidly. Preparatory classes were also offered for high school dropouts who wished to gain an equivalency diploma. The YMCA's Program for Assessment, Counseling and Employment (PACE) enrolled only students on public assistance, and claimed an 80-percent job placement rate. Bedford also opened a Comprehensive Employment Opportunity Support Center (CEOSC) in 1987 for women on public assistance entering the workforce. Flushing introduced Positive Approaches to Youth, a teen employment program, in 1988.

In the mid-1990s, the Association developed a Youth Skills Certification (YSC) program in each borough. YSC offered an introduction to the workplace and skills in greatest demand by teaching teens the computer software programs used most in business as well as customer service. Graduates of this popular program

Most Branches now have computer learning centers.

The COBY program offered Brooklyn youth training in job skills and exposure to local businesses.

received certificates that helped them gain part-time jobs while still in school. It also introduced the Youth Entrepreneurship Program (YEP) in 1998, which allowed participants to learn about the requirements of starting one's own venture and gain basic business skills. Teens staff stores in three Branches, learn to develop a business plan, and some launch their own enterprises. Both YSC and YEP have provided numerous participants an introduction to a career path, and are being combined in 2002 in a new program. FutureWorks will serve ninth and tenth graders at eight Branches with career awareness and educational enrichment activities.

The YMCA launched its boldest and most comprehensive initiative for teens in partnership with the public schools in 2000. *Teen Action NYC*, an in-school YMCA program modeled on the *Virtual Y*, addresses the full range of unmet needs among city teens for academic support, personal counseling, decisions about careers and/or colleges, and development of positive leadership skills. A trained social worker leads each YMCA *Teen Action* program, requiring significant outside funding. The intensive effort, with its staff/student ratio of 1:20, allows the YMCA to reach teenagers from various milieus who have not sought out Branch-based programs, and assists middle and high schools by providing extra support for students who require it.

Further underscoring the importance the YMCA places on education, in 1998 the Association began awarding college scholarships annually, named for long-time volunteer Karl M. von der Heyden, to one or more Teens of the Year.

The YMCA has continued to focus on teenagers at risk of not completing high school through its specialized YouthBuild program, funded by the U.S. Department of Housing and Urban Development (HUD). Initiated at the Flushing YMCA in 1995, the 10-month program provides training in construction trades and puts participants ages 17 to 21 to work maintaining YMCA Branch buildings. The program boasts a very high success rate in preparing participants for the high school general equivalency diploma (GED). Some go on to college and all graduate with skills that are needed in the workplace.

In 1994, the YMCA adopted as its motto, "Every Kid Deserves a Y," indicating its intention to serve every child who could benefit from a YMCA program. Financial assistance was readily available, either through reductions in program fees or subsidized, free-of-charge programs. The Association strengthened its promise to more provide young people with opportunities to learn, grow, and reach their potential, and a safe haven in an insecure world, by aiming to reach one in ten New York children by 2000. It achieved this goal without losing a focus on individual young people. "By helping just one child, we make great changes in the community," Gavin noted.

Young adults learn construction skills and prep for equivalency diplomas in the YouthBuild program.

Camping Spreads its Wings

Summer day camps draw thousands of children, like these anglers on Staten Island.

CAMPING, LONG A popular YMCA program, flourished in the 1980s and 1990s. In 1981, YMCA resident camping, under the auspices of YMCA-YWCA Camping Services, was at a record capacity of 6,500 campers with others on waiting lists. In 1983, 35 day camps enrolled a total of 15,000 campers, a reflection of increasing numbers of families with two working parents as well as single-parent families. Specialized camps such as a new computer studies camp, introduced for resident campers in 1984, focused on

education and drew enthusiastic participation. In 1990 a high ropes and climbing course was introduced at the Huguenot camps to provide an innovative and exciting way to help participants develop confidence and self-esteem. The Greenkill Sports Camp's coaching staff enjoyed an international reputation.

Camps put strong emphasis on developing international understanding, aided by scores of counselors from other countries, and on the Association's values initiative. In 1996, the Camps Values program, with a grant from the Templeton Foundation, began awarding prizes for essays by summer counselors on how they imparted the YMCA values of respect, responsibility, honesty and caring to their young charges. All YMCA camps gained accreditation through the American Camping Association (ACA). In 1998, new mandatory camping standards, more rigorous than ACA's, went into effect at each Y camp program providing for daily values-based activities and greater parental or guardian involvement. The next year resident camps introduced the Ragger program, a YMCA tradition nationwide, in which participants set personal goals on seven levels of challenge.

Year-round environmental education at Camp Greenkill was the most popular program by the early 1980s, enrolling 100 young people each week. The winter Outdoor Explore Program drew 2,000 New York City students. By 1990, the YMCA's outdoor education center was

Special resident sports camps attract volleyball enthusiasts.

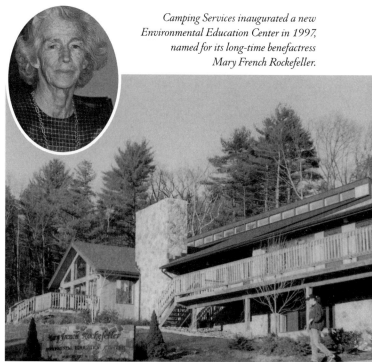

Camping Services inaugurated a new Environmental Education Center in 1997, named for its long-time benefactress Mary French Rockefeller.

deemed one of the best in the nation. In recognition of its expertise, the Environmental Protection Agency (EPA) awarded the center a grant to write an environmental education program curriculum for New York City schools. Greenkill added handicap-access housing so even more could take advantage of this program, and the two other Huguenot camps will eventually be winterized to accommodate more students year-round. Mary French Rockefeller, a major benefactor of Camping Services, donated funds to construct a new Outdoor Environmental Education Center, which opened at the Huguenot site in 1997 bearing her name.

In another important effort to enhance learning in New York City schoolchildren, Schools Chancellor Rudy Crew initiated grants for the new Break-Aways Camps in 1998 in order to keep children focused on literacy and learning year-round. In recognition of its successful *Virtual Y* program, the YMCA was awarded several Break-Aways sites where it used the *Virtual Y* curriculum to provide three hours of reading enhancement, offering traditional camp activities the rest of the day. The YMCA continues to host Break-Aways programs both at urban day camps and at its resident camps, and in 2000 added the Face-to-Face program, bringing a curriculum focused on Mexican culture to city campers.

Programs with Global Impact

IN AN ERA characterized by increasing globalization as well as conflict, and the unceasing movement of people to other countries, the YMCA drew upon its considerable strengths in international and immigrant work to add meaningful programs. In 1981, the YMCA of Greater New York was designated as the first American International YMCA Program Center, based on its commitment to internationalizing its staff, developing and expanding international programs, and supporting YMCA World Service. The New York YMCA committed to work toward "internationalization" of its Branches through each one's efforts to form partnerships with Ys in other countries and prepare cultural programs to increase understanding. Today most New York Branches have international partnerships, among them Staten Island with Mexico, McBurney with Kenya, and West Side with Myanmar, Venezuela, and the Dominican Republic. These partnerships involve visits and technical assistance as needed.

By 1983 the YMCA's International Program Services department was operating several of the largest international

The International Branch, led by Executive Director Bonnie Mairs (left), brings thousands of foreign students to work as camp counselors each summer.

programs for the YMCA of USA, which had moved its headquarters to Chicago from New York City three years earlier. As the most cosmopolitan of cities, and home to the United Nations, New York was and still is unrivaled as the perfect base for these programs. All YMCA international efforts seek to advance the ideal of worldwide understanding and peace. One program, the International Student Service, assisted more than 16,000 international arrivals in the city in 1983. The International Camp Counselor Program extended its efforts to forty nations, involving 500 youth who worked in 220 summer camps outside their home countries. International exchanges were an important facet of the program, such as one between Greenpoint Y campers and their German counterparts. (These are one-time visits as opposed to the ongoing partnerships.)

The New York YMCA, in addition to operating the state's largest English as a Second Language (ESL) program, sponsored important programs for significant immigrant populations in this period. Its Tokyo–New York Partnership provided orientation and acculturation for increasing numbers of Japanese families in the metropolitan area on company assignments. It also offered a fitness program for wives and children, weekend family camping, sports for youth and social activities. Special summer camps, staffed by counselors from the Tokyo Y, allowed Japanese children to stay current with their own language and culture. The Tokyo–New York program was transferred to the White Plains YMCA in 1988.

In 1984, in recognition of the city's growing Korean population, the YMCA of Greater New York joined in a formal partnership with the Seoul Y. A core group of ten Koreans had begun meeting at the McBurney Y in the early 1970s, primarily as a Bible study group. Members provided services to Korean permanent residents and college students, through outreach to Korean Christian clubs on local campuses. The group enjoyed weekend outings, and operated its first resident camp in 1988.

The Korean Program relocated in 1978 to the YMCA in Flushing, a community which by then had one of the largest Korean populations in the United States. Dr. William K. Lee, grandson of a Seoul Y founder, was instrumental in the Korean program's growth, and now serves on the Board of YMCA of the USA. Joe Min, a member of the core group while still a student, became the program's first executive director in 1989. It finally merged with the Flushing YMCA in 1991, where overall Branch membership is now 68 percent Korean. The Korean Program focuses on teaching basic English to help members, for example, understand swimming instruction at the YMCA. It also offers job training, computer literacy and, until 1999, offered the INS citizenship test on site. Its core program is for youth born in the United States or in Korea, offering them English classes from age 7, Korean culture and history courses to help Korean-American youngsters develop self-confidence and a strong identity, and summer camps. In addition to leadership development, immigration education, health, and recreation, the program provides counseling and translation services.

In recognition of significant new waves of immigrants, the Association introduced its ELESAIR program

Global Teens widen their worlds through experiences in countries like Venezuela (above), Estonia and Thailand.

(English Language and Employment Services for Adult Immigrants and Refugees) in 1980, initially focusing on 1,500 refugees from Southeast Asia. Soon they were joined by others from China, the Caribbean nations, the Soviet Union, Africa, Central and South America. By 1985, ELESAIR became a permanent program center of the McBurney YMCA. Students in the program have hailed from seventy-two countries, from Afghanistan to Yugoslavia. In addition to teaching English, ELESAIR offers services such as job-search skills and in 1992 conducted AIDS education in the Hispanic community. In its two decades the program has served more than 30,000 students.

The International department, chartered as a Branch in 1991, introduced an innovative new program, Global Teens, in 1996. Each summer youth are selected through their Branches to participate in a three-week stay in another country, living with families, experiencing a new culture and participating in community service with teen counterparts in the home-stay country. For many participants, this is their first experience abroad. Upon return, through year-long activities, they bring their newfound awareness to other city teens. More than 200 New York City youth have enjoyed life-changing experiences by gaining new perspectives in countries such as Mexico, Estonia, Venezuela, Korea and Thailand. Financial support comes from the DeWitt Wallace Youth Travel Enrichment Fund of the New York Community Trust.

As New York continues to be a prime portal for welcoming immigrants, the YMCA has strengthened its

ELESAIR students learn English and job skills, and travel to Albany to raise legislators' awareness of the needs of immigrants.

focus on programs for New Americans. It has naturally occurring opportunities: In the *Virtual Y* program alone, more than 60 percent of students live in homes where English is not spoken. As the world seeks to ease international conflicts and resolve the continuing crisis brought about by terrorism, the worldwide YMCA no less than the New York Association is positioned to play a major role as a conduit for understanding and resolution of conflict. Today there are YMCAs in 130 countries, serving more than 30 million people.

Welcoming All People

"The YMCA encourages the mingling of people," noted the 1981 annual report, and the word "Christian" was notably absent from the Association's mission statement. The 1983 strategic plan set forth the YMCA's new identity as values-based. In a city where every country and culture of the world was represented, the Association determined to reaffirm traditional values and be an advocate for them.

A visit to any Branch or YMCA program site in New York City today reveals a splendid diversity. Boys and girls, men and women of all ages, races, religions, income levels and nationalities come and go at Ys every day, as do people with disabilities, taking advantage of a multitude of programs. The unparalleled mix of people in the twenty-first-century YMCA extends beyond its membership to its own staff. Of the 4,300 staff members in 2001, 62 percent were women, 30 percent African

American, 18 percent Hispanic, and 9 percent Asian. Similar diversity is present in the YMCA's citywide cadre of nearly 2,900 volunteers. In its totality, the contemporary YMCA is a microcosm of New York City itself.

Family programs, which have been a YMCA focus for generations, today are broadly defined in the New York Association. Any two adults, whether related or not, qualify for family memberships, including gay and lesbian couples and parents. In this way, the YMCA reflects the changing definition in society of what constitutes family, especially in New York City, where eight percent of couples are same-sex partners and many stable heterosexual partners are unmarried.

In the latter half of the twentieth century, the YMCA's traditional middle-class Protestant purpose has gradually but firmly evolved into a mission based on positive values that *all* can live by. Without reference to a particular religious credo, the YMCA of Greater New York champions respect, responsibility, caring and honesty as principles at the core of all its programs. Marshall Klein, executive director of the Flushing/Bayside YMCA in 1988, described this broad perception by noting that "C stands for caring as well as for Christian." While non Christians had been members of the Association's Board of Directors since the 1960s, the longstanding written requirement that they be Protestant was finally removed from the by-laws in 1991. Inspirational "opening thoughts" replaced prayers at the start of meetings.

With the passage of the Americans with Disabilities Act (ADA) in 1990, a new emphasis was placed on making Branch facilities accessible to all. However, the YMCA had pioneered in this area by introducing programs in the two preceding decades for the physically and mentally challenged. By 1981, the Eastern Queens (later, Cross Island) Branch had five programs designed for the disabled, and in 1991 was designated a training center for aquatics in the Special Olympics with its swimming pool for the physically challenged. Cross Island, Flushing, and Staten Island devised "arthritic aquatics" programs to give sufferers therapeutic relief. Staten Island

The contemporary YMCA, with its unprecedented diversity, is a microcosm of the city itself.

Many YMCA Older Adults enjoy water exercise programs.

Elderhostel programs are popular at the Holiday Hills YMCA Conference Center in Pawling, NY.

provided physical fitness programs for asthmatics, autistic children and other special groups, and the West Side YMCA cultivated its Achilles Club for disabled runners. The Bronx YMCA added special computer programs for autistic and mentally handicapped individuals in 1986.

The Association introduced its Older Adults Program at most Branches in the 1990s, in recognition of special needs of New York's growing cadre of people over age 55, who are some of the YMCA's most loyal adherents. The program offers exercise tailored especially to older people's needs for balance, muscle strength, endurance and flexibility. It also provides opportunities for companionship, outings and community service. The Staten Island Branch in 1991 became coordinator of the Senior Olympics program, and popular Elderhostel programs are based at Holiday Hills and West Side Branches.

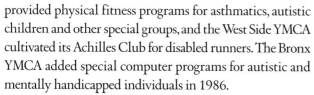

Mission Statement 1996–2002

The YMCA of Greater New York is a community service organization which promotes positive values through programs that build spirit, mind and body, welcoming all people, with a focus on youth.

A Profusion of Programs

THE YMCA'S PHYSICAL program for all ages remains firmly at the core of its "spirit, mind and body" mission. In the 1980s, the "Y's Way to a Healthy Back" and the Cardiovascular Institute were among the Association's leading fitness offerings. The cardiovascular program, which included stress tests and risk factor evaluations, served employees of major corporations as well as YMCA members. A growing population of Baby Boomers reaching middle age inspired a new focus on personal training in Branch fitness programs, a personal commitment program based on goal-setting with a counselor, and a program designed for first-time or lapsed exercisers. The overall emphasis was on cultivating habits for life-long "wellness." The Association gradually but steadily added new equipment, such as Nautilus Centers and Spinning cycles, and remodeled facilities as funds permitted. By 1988, it claimed a full array of "state-of-the-art" fitness programs and was quick to add popular new programs such as step aerobics. Continuing the YMCA tradition of inventiveness, it offered a rowing exercise called "oar-row-bics."

By 1990, special programs featured back pain, stress and weight management, as well as smoking cessation. Lending important support for community wellness, many Branches hosted meetings of Alcoholics Anonymous and other twelve-step groups. By this decade, the YMCA of Greater New York had become the city's largest and most diverse fitness provider, offering members the greatest variety in programs and equipment. The YMCA swimming certification program for all ages, the country's oldest and most comprehensive, continued to attract countless New Yorkers. Gymnastics, one of the earliest YMCA physical programs, enjoyed a resurgence even

Gymnastics enjoyed renewed popularity among the younger set.

YMCA water babies offer their parents a special bonding experience.

among young children, who were also drawn to various martial-arts programs.

Several Branches offered arts programs, in particular the West Side YMCA. One that gained national prominence is the Writer's Voice, started in 1980 by a young poet, Jason Shinder, at West Side. The program enrolls beginning and advanced writers, up to 700 per session, in courses to polish their skills and works in progress, and has given many noted writers their start. Writer's Voice took hold in other YMCAs and in 1997 became a national program through the YMCA of the USA. Several Branches also offer drama programs for youth, such as the West Side Kids Company and Harlem's Theatre Arts program, and programs in the plastic arts, such as ceramics at West Side. The Harlem YMCA Bookmarks program, introduced in 1997, brings African-American authors to the Branch to read from their works. In 2002, the West Side Y formed a partnership with the Lyric Chamber Music Society to introduce and teach musical instruments to children.

Branches continued to develop programs to serve the most pressing needs in their communities. The Bronx YMCA initiated a program for the homeless in 1987, and the Harlem YMCA Annex was renovated to serve more people in need in that community. Prospect Park joined other agencies in dedicating rooms to the homeless in 1992. Existing YMCA residences began to cater to a variety of special populations. Although the Association adopted a policy of no longer building new residences, in line with a national YMCA trend, it makes full use of existing accommodations. Several Branches, notably Flushing, Greenpoint, Vanderbilt and West Side, continue to house

international visitors and others seeking affordable accommodations on visits to New York. The New York YMCA has registered as many as 300,000 foreign and out-of-town visitors annually in recent boom years for tourism. Its Y's Way International service arranges stays for groups in New York Branches and YMCAs elsewhere.

The West Side YMCA alone, which hosts the largest Elderhostel program in New York State, receives as many as 35,000 tourists per year in its nearly 500 guest rooms. The Branch dedicates a special wing, known as Y House, for out-of-town families visiting hospitalized relatives as well as recuperating patients. In 1999, when a notorious construction accident displaced elderly residents from the Woodstock Hotel in midtown, the West Side Y provided seventy-six displaced individuals with temporary housing for several months.

Before its closing in 1991, the Sloane House Y housed hundreds of college students, a population the twenty-first- century YMCA is again focusing on to alleviate a shortage of student housing for the city's many colleges. To address the growing epidemic of HIV/AIDS in New York City, Sloane House and McBurney opened specialized residential programs for afflicted individuals in need of transitional housing in the late 1980s. The program continued in the 1990s at the McBurney YMCA, and is now located at the Jamaica (formerly Central Queens) Branch. Other supportive housing programs, at Harlem and North Brooklyn's Twelve Towns site, house populations of recovering substance abusers and homeless individuals transitioning to permanent housing. These programs are supported by grants from government agencies such as the city's Departments of AIDS Services and HPD.

New York and the Nation in Crisis

LIKE ALL NEW YORKERS and institutions based in the city, the YMCA of Greater New York was profoundly shocked by the terrorist action that destroyed the World Trade Center and claimed thousands of lives on September 11, 2001. It immediately committed people and resources to aid the rescue and recovery effort, and to comfort the many New Yorkers traumatized by the unprecedented attack on the United States and grieved by their losses. In the weeks immediately following, the YMCA developed a six-point action plan to coordinate its response to the tragedy.

The Association devised immediate actions to address community needs. Committing its residence rooms, it housed 250 passengers stranded by the disaster at airports in Queens at its nearby Flushing Branch, at nominal cost or without charge. The West Side Y served as an overnight hostel for rescue workers, providing more than 7,000 room nights, while volunteer lawyers processing death certificates were permitted to use its recreational facilities at no charge. The Association produced booklets in four languages to help parents talk to their children about tragedy.

Numerous North American YMCAs collected more than $600,000 for those in need and channeled the funds through the YMCA of Greater New York. The YMCA of the USA also sent the Association $500,000, and Cisco Systems Inc. donated another $500,000. With these generous donations, the New York City YMCA set up a fund to help families of victims and rescue workers and produced a brochure on tolerance. Free annual memberships were offered to workers who lost jobs as a result of the disaster. Children who lost a parent qualified for free day-care and after-school programs. Designated YMCA staff members received training in trauma counseling, and every Branch offered counseling services to those who requested them.

As the recovery of New York and the war on terrorism proceed in early 2002, the YMCA of Greater New York continues to provide a unique community resource to the city, its neighborhoods and its people. Branches and programs offer respite from the stresses of daily living and provide a welcoming place where all New Yorkers may come together in the most diverse of settings. YMCA International programs strive, as always, to work for peace and understanding among all people and to promote tolerance in a troubled time. Once again, in the aftermath of this unprecedented catastrophe, the New York YMCA has been able to fulfill its pledge of building strong kids, strong families and strong communities.

Timeline

1800-50	*Industrial Revolution*
1844	✤ YMCA is founded in London.
1850	✤ German Association forms in New York, but is short-lived.
1852	✤ New York Association forms.
1853	✤ Brooklyn Association forms.
1855	✤ Williamsburg (Brooklyn) Association forms; reorganized 1866 as Eastern District Association.
1857	✤ Brooklyn YMCA adds physical work; first gym classes offered by Brooklyn and New York Ys.
	✤ New York Association leads noontime prayer meetings following financial panic.
	✤ Independent Association organized on Staten Island.
1858	✤ Young Women's Christian Association (YWCA) founded in New York City.
1859	✤ Brooklyn YMCA reports adding women as members.
1860s-70s	✤ Steam railroads introduced, street railways electrified.
1861-65	*Northern and Southern states engage in Civil War.*
	✤ New York member Vincent Colyer begins work among troops.
1861	✤ Fifteen national YMCA representatives meet in New York City in November, creating U.S. Christian Commission to provide support for troops.
1862	✤ Robert Ross McBurney becomes first paid staff member of New York Association.
1865	✤ William Earl Dodge Jr. elected president of New York YMCA.
	✤ First job placements recorded.
	✤ First New York City "Colored" Association formed (closes 1872); its leader, E.V.C. Eato, is first African-American delegate to a national YMCA convention in 1867.
1866	✤ New York YMCA adds physical work to its mission.
	✤ National YMCA executive committee created, locates temporarily in New York, permanently in 1883.
1868	✤ First Harlem YMCA opens on 125th Street.
	✤ Eastern Branch opens on Grand Street, discontinued 1873.
	✤ Western Branch opens on Varick Street, discontinued 1872.
1869	✤ First "purpose-built" YMCA building opens at Twenty-Third Street and Fourth Avenue, containing a gymnasium to house "physical" work.
	✤ First YMCA evening high school offers classes in new building.
	✤ Greenpoint, Brooklyn, YMCA organized (disbands 1874).
	✤ New Utrecht YMCA opens in Brooklyn.

1871	✣ North Shore YMCA building opens on Staten Island; closes 1886.
	✣ East Eighty-Sixth Street Branch opens, becomes independent YMCA in 1880, rejoins New York Association 1884 as Yorkville Branch.
1872	✣ Bowery Branch opens, offering relief to destitute young men.
1873-77	✣ During financial panic, New York and Brooklyn YMCAs sponsor religious revivals led by Dwight Moody.
1874	✣ New York Association leaders form New York Society for the Suppression of Vice, with Anthony Comstock as salaried agent.
1875	✣ First New York Railroad YMCA opens in Grand Central Depot.
1876	*Alexander Bell invents the telephone.*
	✣ Brooklyn Association removes "evangelical" as Board member requirement.
1877	*Post-Reconstruction Period*
	✣ American Library Association holds first annual meeting at Twenty-Third Street YMCA. Association helps to compile the first Index of Periodical Literature.
1878	✣ New Lots and German YMCAs organized in Brooklyn.
1878-79	✣ Brooklyn Association holds first meetings for men in specific industries.
1879	✣ Railroad YMCA opens at Thirtieth Street depot.
1880s	*Brooklyn, now fourth largest industrial city, handles more waterfront tonnage than New York City.*
1881	✣ German Branch formed in New York City.
	✣ Brooklyn Association takes boys on first camping excursion.
1882	✣ New York Association forms Work for Boys.
1883	✣ East Shore YMCA forms on Staten Island; disbands by 1905.
	Brooklyn Bridge is completed.
1884	✣ Yorkville Branch starts up.
1885	✣ New Brooklyn Central Branch on Fulton Street features first indoor pool in a YMCA.
	✣ Young Men's Institute opens on the Bowery for working men; closes 1932.
	✣ Sumner Dudley takes boys on a first organized camping trip.
	✣ Greenpoint Association reorganized.
1885-86	✣ Leaders Corps organized at Young Men's Institute.
1886	*Statue of Liberty is dedicated.*
	✣ Railroad Branch opens at New Durham and Weehawken in New Jersey.
1887	✣ Railroad YMCA opens at Seventy-Second Street Roundhouse.
	✣ Charles Pratt founds Pratt Institute in Brooklyn.
	✣ New York YMCA adopts metropolitan form of organization; Twenty-Third Street is parent Branch.
	✣ First English classes offered to immigrants at Young Men's Institute.
	✣ Railroad Branch opens new building, 361 Madison Avenue; six years later capacity is doubled, all financed by Cornelius Vanderbilt II.
1888	✣ Eastern District Association becomes Branch of Brooklyn YMCA.
	✣ Twenty-Third Street Branch starts outreach to boys on ships.
1889	✣ Dr. Luther Gulick, YMCA Physical Director, introduces concept of unity of spirit, mind, and body.
	✣ French Branch established, New York YMCA.
	✣ Bedford Branch added, Brooklyn.
1890	✣ First Inter-Branch Athletic Contest, New York.
	✣ Twenty-Sixth Ward Branch added, Brooklyn (renamed Highland Park, 1921).
1890s	*Jim Crow laws, segregating blacks and whites, take hold in all aspects of U.S. life.*
1891	✣ Instructor James Naismith invents basketball at YMCA's Springfield College in Massachusetts.
	✣ Washington Heights Branch opens in New York.
	✣ Prospect Park Branch added in Brooklyn.
	✣ First student YMCA in Brooklyn opens at Long Island College.

	❖ Mott Haven Railroad YMCA launched in Bronx.
1894	❖ Brooklyn YMCA opens Branch for Long Island Rail Road men.
	National railroad strike is largest in history.
	❖ Brooklyn YMCA sponsors acclaimed social-economic lectures.
1895	❖ Eastern District and German Branches consolidate in Brooklyn.
	❖ First Association Business Schools and Day Business Institute for Young Men open at Twenty-Third Street.
	❖ Permanent Council on Educational Work established, New York YMCA.
1896	*Brooklyn opens Public Library.*
	Supreme Court condones "separate but equal" public accommodations.
	❖ West Side Branch opens on Fifty-Seventh Street, first in city to house dormitory.
	❖ Brooklyn YMCA adopts metropolitan structure.
1897	❖ Red triangle adopted as national YMCA symbol, representing spirit, mind, and body.
1898	*Manhattan and Brooklyn, Bronx, Queens, and Staten Island are consolidated as the City of New York.*
	Spanish-American War.
	❖ Robert Ross McBurney dies.
	❖ Overall YMCA attendance in New York City: 2 million.
1899	❖ Brooklyn YMCA opens Army Branch at Fort Hamilton; New York Association an Army Y on Governors Island (renamed Fort Jay, 1928; closes 1948).
	❖ First Navy YMCA in nation opens in Brooklyn; closes in 1964.
1900	*Brooklyn's population now 1 million.*
	❖ Railroad YMCA opens in Pennsylvania Terminal (moves to new Penn Station 1968; closes 1979).
	❖ New York Association initiates Army work at Fort Wadsworth, Staten Island (discontinued 1918).
1901	❖ "Colored Branch" forms in New York Association.
	❖ New York YMCA opens Intercollegiate Branch; disbands 1965.
	❖ Brooklyn Rapid Transit Railroad Branch organized for streetcar employees.
1902	❖ Branch for African American men and boys opens on Carlton Avenue, Brooklyn (disbands 1954).
1903	*Wright Brothers flight at Kitty Hawk; automobile replaces horse and carriage.*
	❖ West Side YMCA Trade and Technical School opens, followed by Automobile School in 1904.
1904	❖ Bronx Union, Williamsbridge Branches formed.
	❖ New Twenty-Third Street YMCA (renamed "McBurney" in 1943) opens on West 23rd Street.
	First New York City subway opens.
1904-06	❖ Brooklyn Association opens new buildings: Bedford, Eastern District and Greenpoint (a Branch since 1903).
	❖ Brooklyn YMCA forms Brooklyn Sunday School Athletic League.
1905	*Labor reform movements gather strength.*
1907	*Forty percent of New York City residents are foreign-born.*
	❖ Charles Merrill and Edmund Lynch meet at Twenty-Third Street Branch, form financial firm in 1915.
1907-17	*Junior colleges develop in California.*
1908	*Henry Ford introduces his model-T automobile.*
	❖ Bedford YMCA offers first auto mechanics course in nation.
	❖ Brooklyn Association opens building for Long Island Rail Road Branch.
1909	*Two more bridges open, linking Manhattan to Brooklyn.*
	❖ Charles and Homer Pace offer their standard accounting course in Brooklyn and New York YMCAs.
1910	❖ National YMCA leads in organization of Boy Scouts of America.
	Protestant Church in rapid decline in Brooklyn, the "City of Churches."
	❖ YMCA Aquatic Leaders Corps trains swimming instructors in lifesaving skills.
	❖ Columbia University offers courses at Brooklyn Central Branch.
	❖ YMCA opens Ellis Island Branch to reach new immigrants at port of entry.

1911	*Shirtwaist Triangle fire in Manhattan factory kills 146 workers, mainly immigrants.*
	✢ Pennsylvania Railroad, Merchant Seaman's Branches open.
	✢ Bedford opens Evening School for Employed Boys.
1912	*Supreme Court orders break-up of Standard Oil Company.*
	✢ Dale Carnegie gives his first public speaking course at Harlem YMCA (125th Street).
1913	✢ New Railroad YMCA building opens at 309 Park Avenue.
1914	✢ Brooklyn Association opens Camp Pratt on Staten Island.
1915	✢ Brooklyn YMCA opens new Central Branch, "largest YMCA in world," on Hanson Place.
	✢ Bronx Union dedicates new building.
	✢ New Bowery Branch building opens, 8 East Third Street.
1916	✢ McBurney School, a preparatory institution for boys, holds first sessions.
1918	✢ Brooklyn opens new Carlton Avenue building and Bethelship Seamen's Branch.
	✢ Brooklyn organizes Industrial Branch in Long Island City, Queens.
	✢ New York Association raises more than $1 million for YMCA buildings in military camps.
1919	✢ Bedford YMCA opens Trade School, which gains national prominence.
	✢ "Colored" Branch opens in Harlem and is soon renamed the 135th Street Y.
	✢ New York YMCA forms Wall Street Branch for working boys (disbands 1935).
1920	*Women's suffrage and Prohibition laws take effect.*
	✢ YMCA begins offering sex education for both genders.
	✢ The Vatican asks bishops to monitor the YMCA for potential corruption of Catholic youth.
	✢ Educational course enrollment at Bronx Union, East Side, Harlem, Twenty-Third Street and West Side Branches reaches 10,760 students. Ten Branch libraries contain a total of 103,100 books.
	✢ New York Law School joins Twenty-Third Street Branch educational program; departs in 1933.
	✢ Brooklyn Association's industrial program reaches 326,000 workers in 87 industries; eight Branches offer Americanization programs.
	✢ Long Island City Branch begins league play for teams in Queens.
	✢ New York Association opens Merchant Seamen's Branch.
1920-21	*American Association of Junior Colleges founded.*
1920s-40s	*Great Migration of African Americans to northern states.*
1923	✢ Brooklyn hosts first National YMCA Swimming Championships.
1924	✢ Brooklyn Association becomes Brooklyn and Queens YMCA.
	✢ Flatbush Branch organized for men and boys.
	Fulton Ferry discontinued; automobile gains favor.
1926	✢ Vast construction program begins in New York Association.
	✢ Highland Park (formerly Twenty-Sixth Ward) Branch building opens in Brooklyn.
	✢ Flushing Branch opens in Queens.
1927	✢ $4 million raised in New York building campaign.
1928	✢ Central Queens Branch opens in Jamaica, Queens.
1929	*Stock market crash*
1930-39	*Great Depression. First public housing projects.*
1930	✢ Two enormous New York Branches open within one month: William Sloane House and West Side.
	✢ All New York YMCA educational work consolidated at West Side Branch.
	✢ Bedford Trade School offers aviation course.
1930s	✢ Group work overtakes traditional YMCA program.
1931	*Floyd Bennett Field, first airport, opens.*
	✢ Seaman's House opens building in Manhattan.
	✢ Schools Branch organized at West Side.
1932	✢ Grand Central Railroad Branch opens new building (renamed Vanderbilt YMCA, 1972).

1933	✤ National YMCA allows women to be admitted as full members.
	✤ New Harlem Branch opens on West 135th Street as largest "Colored" YMCA.
	✤ Uptown Branch created on Upper West Side to work with youth gangs.
1934	✤ West Side YMCA admits its first woman member; begins work with local gangs of boys.
1936	✤ YMCA Youth and Government program created in New York State.
1939-40	✤ New York Association erects, staffs House of Friendship pavilion at World's Fair in Flushing, a YMCA first.
1940	✤ YMCA joins in formation of USO.
	✤ Bowery Branch's Penny Cafeteria serves nearly 50,000 meals in one month.
1941	*Pearl Harbor attacked, U.S. enters World War II.*
1943	✤ National Council of YMCAs rules that Associations must open membership to people of all races.
1944	✤ Vocational Service Center consolidates work of five Branches; assumes work of Bowery Branch in 1946.
	✤ Camp Custer opens as fully interracial summer camp.
1945	✤ New York educational work reorganized as YMCA Schools Branch.
	✤ Walter Hervey Junior College created (closes 1957).
1946	✤ YMCA leader John R. Mott awarded Nobel Peace Prize.
	✤ Camp and Outing Branch organized.
1946-64	*Post-War Baby Boom will produce 76 million children.*
1947	✤ Staten Island, Westchester-Bronx Branches established.
	✤ Holiday Hills acquired as "rustic resort for the relaxation of young men."
	✤ Jackie Robinson becomes first African-American major-league baseball player and signs on as coach for boys at Harlem YMCA.
1949	✤ "Evangelical" officially abandoned as membership requirement by Brooklyn and Queens YMCA.
1950	*Brooklyn population peaks at 2.7 million.*
	Beginning of substantial Puerto Rican immigration.
	Federal highway act spurs flight of residents and industries to suburbs.
	Title I programs encourage massive slum clearance programs.
1951	✤ YMCA Centennial Campaign seeks $10 million to construct seven new buildings, modernize existing New York YMCAs.
	✤ CORE pickets Bedford YMCA, claiming it practices discrimination.
1954	*Supreme Court decision effectively puts an end to segregation.*
	✤ Juvenile delinquency becomes a major concern of New York Association.
1955	✤ Camp McAlister opens as multi-racial, low-cost summer camp.
	✤ Westchester-Bronx opens Neighborhood Youth Branch, and forms earliest YMCA Golden Age Club.
1956	✤ New York YMCA opens extension projects in two public housing developments.
1957	✤ New York and Brooklyn and Queens Associations merge as the YMCA of Greater New York.
	✤ Staten Island Branch building opens.
	✤ Leaders' Clubs for boys formed at Branches.
1958	✤ YMCA of Greater New York offers its first annual Learn-to-Swim campaign.
1958-62	✤ New York Branches raise $1 million for YMCA Buildings for Brotherhood, 20 percent of total.
1959	✤ Russell Service becomes first African-American director of a Brooklyn Y.
1960	✤ West Side YMCA opens facilities to women.
	✤ Lynn Burke of Flushing Y wins Olympics Gold Medal for swimming.
1960s	*Civil rights movement peaks; women's liberation movement begins.*
	✤ YMCA adds coffeehouse programs for youth.
1961	*President John F. Kennedy revives President's Council on Physical Fitness and Sports.*
1962	✤ YMCA appoints first executive for health and fitness; begins $14 million fund drive for 28 Branches.
1963	*Demolition of Pennsylvania Station begins.*
	✤ YMCA of Greater New York affirms policy of complete racial equality.

❖ Measured Mile walking program introduced at all Branches.

1964   *Verrazano Bridge opens, connecting Brooklyn to Staten Island and New Jersey, prompting an exodus of white population.*

❖ Harlem is first YMCA residence to house women.

❖ Sloane House, Prospect Park alter structures to accommodate women and couples.

1965   *Urban renewal ends. Crime rises, race relations worsen; riots in Harlem and Bedford-Stuyvesant.*

❖ Physical fitness clinics inaugurated.

❖ YMCA closes at Brooklyn Navy Yard.

❖ Camp Greenkill becomes co-ed.

❖ Catholic Church lifts barriers to adherents joining YMCAs.

❖ West Side Branch offers nursery program, one of first YMCA child-care initiatives.

1966   *John V. Lindsay elected mayor; subway strike.*

Brooklyn Navy Yard is shut down, leaving waterfront inactive.

❖ TRY program for high-school dropouts opens at Bedford.

❖ Cardio-Vascular Program introduced for middle-age men.

1967   ❖ Eastern Queens (now Cross Island) opens first family-center YMCA in state.

❖ Jobmobiles and Youthmobiles organized for neighborhood outreach.

❖ Clinton Youth Center added as Branch; opens experimental junior high school in 1974.

❖ Mrs. Julius Leicher named a YMCA "Man of the Year."

❖ Elizabeth Noel, an African American from the Bronx, is elected first female governor, New York State Youth and Government program.

❖ Brooklyn Central YMCA sells building, reorganizes as decentralized program.

❖ Flatbush added as Branch, based in former cinema building.

❖ Holiday Hills becomes conference and continuing education center.

1968   ❖ Central Queens opens pre-school nursery in Baisley Park housing project.

❖ Association introduces Youth Fitness program, endorsed by President's Council.

❖ Wayne Anderson of Flushing Y Flyers swim team competes in Olympics.

❖ Bronx YMCA offers program for brain-damaged children.

1969   ❖ CHOICE program opens at Bedford and Harlem to train adults in job skills.

❖ YMCA Board endorses Kerner Commission Report on Civil Disorders.

❖ YMCA-YWCA Day Care Inc. formed.

1970   *Garbage collectors strike.*

NYC in largest financial crisis since Depression with mounting debt.

❖ YMCA finances imperiled.

❖ At annual all-staff meeting, YMCA employees call for greater racial inclusion, more relevant programs.

❖ First four women "unit directors" named; first women appointed to Board.

❖ New YMCA building opens in Bronx on Westchester Avenue.

❖ Association opens Independence House, short-term program for young ex-offenders.

❖ McBurney adds Chinatown youth outreach program.

❖ Holiday Hills offers environmental education; Camp Greenkill follows in 1973.

Stonewall riots over gay rights.

❖ First NYC Marathon, organized at West Side Y, is staged in Central Park.

1971   ❖ First Black Achievers Award dinner; becomes national YMCA program.

❖ Harlem YMCA launches YEP (Youth Enrichment Program) for drug prevention.

❖ Association opens facility at Fort Totten for youth-police dialogues.

1972   ❖ Former Queens courthouse on Catalpa Avenue becomes a YMCA.

1973   ❖ YMCA-YWCA Camping Services Council formed.

❖ Specialized Sports Camps offered at Huguenot site.

❖ McBurney School becomes co-ed.

1974	✣ Henry Lenoir of Harlem Branch becomes first YMCA director of urban affairs.
	✣ Association is running programs in six public housing projects.
1975	*NYC fiscal crisis starts to abate.*
1976	✣ "Y's Way to a Healthy Back" program debuts at Branches.
	✣ Eastern District sells building, moves program to two housing projects.
1977	✣ 33 percent of YMCA members are women and girls.
	✣ Bronx Union and Westchester-Bronx merge as Bronx YMCA; current site purchased on Castle Hill Road.
	✣ Staten Island opens Counseling Program, South Shore extension.
1978	*Village People release popular song "YMCA."*
	✣ Flushing adds Bayside Center.
1979	✣ New York Association designated International YMCA Program Center.
1980	*New wave of immigration; 40 percent of New Yorkers now born outside USA.*
	✣ ELESAIR program begins in New York YMCA.
	✣ Writer's Voice program begins at West Side, develops as national YMCA program.
	✣ Women comprise 40 percent of YMCA membership.
	✣ National YMCA headquarters leaves New York for Chicago.
1982	✣ New York is "largest YMCA in the world," with 21 Branches and $34 million budget.
1983	✣ Richard Traum, West Side member, co-founds Achilles Club for disabled runners.
1985	✣ Vanderbilt YMCA sells development rights, doubles program space.
1987	✣ YMCA residences, containing 4,000 rooms, attract increasing numbers of budget-minded tourists.
1989	✣ YMCA is city's largest non-governmental child care provider.
1990	✣ Paula Gavin becomes first woman president, first from outside YMCA ranks.
	✣ Women comprise half of YMCA membership.
1991	✣ Sloane House closed; sold in 1994.
	✣ Bedford revives youth program.
	✣ Junior Knicks, Junior Mets programs launched.
	✣ Cross Island named aquatics training center for Special Olympics.
	✣ Staten Island becomes coordinator for Senior Olympics.
1996	✣ Harlem renovates, reopens Jackie Robinson Youth Center.
	✣ Global Teens sends first groups of Y youth abroad.
1997	✣ YMCA launches *Virtual Y*, an innovative after-school partnership with NYC public school system.
	✣ Staten Island opens new South Shore YMCA.
	✣ Camps dedicates new Outdoor Environmental Education Center.
1998	✣ YMCA develops $150 million master plan to bring aging facilities to standard of equal excellence.
	✣ Prospect Park reopens residence as Community House.
	✣ Main Harlem YMCA building and 222 Bowery (former Young Men's Institute) accorded landmark status.
1999	✣ Staten Island dedicates new Counseling Center.
	✣ Long Island City YMCA opens its first full facility.
	✣ McBurney YMCA buildings sold, new site purchased on West Fourteenth Street to open in 2003.
	✣ Most Branches now offer Older Adult programs.
2000	✣ *Teen Action NYC*, in-school program, is launched.
2001	✣ Association announces $50 million Capital Campaign for Kids.
	✣ West Side YMCA development sale allows renovation of McBurney wing for programs and residents.
	World Trade Center attacked and destroyed in September.
	✣ YMCA offers emergency assistance, administers aid reaching $2.4 million.
2002	✣ Bronx YMCA completes major property expansion.
	✣ FutureWorks offers career awareness, educational enrichment for middle-school students.

Honor Roll

NEW YORK ASSOCIATION
CHIEF EXECUTIVES (*staff*) 1852-2002

1862-1898   Robert Ross McBurney (General Secretary)
1898-1917   Henry M. Orne (General Secretary)
1917-1942   Walter T. Diack (General Secretary)
1942-1956   R.L. Dickinson (Executive Vice President)
1956-1965   Gayle J. Lathrop (Executive Vice President)
1966-1981   William A. Howes (Executive Vice President; President, 1976-81)
1982-1990   William A. Markell (President)
1990-present   Paula L. Gavin (President)

VOLUNTEER (*lay*) LEADERS 1852-2002

Presidents

Oliver P. Woodford (1852-53)
Howard Crosby (1853-56)
S.W. Stebbins (1856-57)
Robert Bliss (1857-58)
Benjamin F. Manierre (1858-60)
S.G. Goodrich (1860-61)
P. Harwood Vernon (1861-62)
S.W. Stebbins (1862-65)
William E. Dodge Jr. (1865-72)

Morris K. Jesup (1872-75)
William E. Dodge Jr. (1875-77)
Elbert B. Monroe (1877-83)
W.W. Hoppin Jr. (1883-87)
Elbert B. Monroe (1887-90)
Cleveland H. Dodge (1890-1903)
William Fellowes Morgan (1903-19)
William M. Kingsley (1919-25)
Cleveland E. Dodge (1925-35)

Richard W. Lawrence (1935-45)
Frank Totton (1945-53)
Robert S. Curtiss (1953-63)
Alfred H. Howell (1963-66)
Reese H. Harris, Jr. (1966-68)
Herbert B. Woodman (1968-72)
Charles W. Carson Jr. (1972-73)
John S. Schumann (1973-76)

Chairmen

Quigg Newton (1976-77)
Daniel E. Emerson (1977-82)
Charles T. Stewart (1982-86)

Ralph B. Henderson (1986-88)
Barry MacTaggart (1988-90)
Donald K. Ross (1990)
Richard Boyle (1990-95)

Benjamin R. Jacobson (1995-1998)
Richard A. Grasso (1998-2000)
Robert Annunziata (2000-present)

BROOKLYN AND QUEENS ASSOCIATION (1853-1956)

Presidents (volunteer)

Andrew A. Smith (1853-56)
James McGee (1856-57)
George A. Bell (1857-58)
John M. Doubleday (1858-59)
Henry H. Lloyd (1859-60)
Robert Spier Bussing (1860-61)
James M. Ives (1861-62)
O. Vincent Coffin (1862-63)
Charles A. Righter (1863-64)

William Edsall (1864-66)
Ezra D. Barker (1866-67)
William Edsall (1867-68)
William W. Wickes (1868-69)
Joseph T. Duryea (1869-70)
Darwin G. Eaton (1870-72)
David H. Cochran (1872-74)
Tasker H. Marvin (1874-76)
John P. Adams (1876-77)
Charles H. Dillingham (1877-79)

Daniel W. McWilliams (1879-80)
Andrew L. Taylor (1880)
Robert Fulton Cutting (1880-83)
Edwin Packard (1883-90)
Frederick B. Schenck (1890-98)
Edward P. Lyon (1898-1920)
Frank C. Munson (1920-36)
Roy M. Hart (1937-47)
Rodney C. Ward (1947-56)

General Secretaries (staff)

Thomas J. Wilkie (1880-86)
Edwin F. See (1886-1906)
Harvey L. Simmons (acting) (1906-10)

John W. Cook (1910-24)
James C. Armstrong (1924-31)
Arthur H. Greeley (acting) (1931-32)

Arthur H. Greeley (1932-37)
Eugene Field Scott (1937-56)

ORDER OF THE RED TRIANGLE

This highest YMCA award is designated for lay leaders who have given unstintingly of their abilities and resources to advance the work of the YMCA among youth in New York City. Names are listed in chronological order of award.

Cleveland E. Dodge
Frank M. Totton
William H. Pouch
Winston Paul
Maurice T. Moore
Herbert H. Schwamb
James M. Trenary
Robert S. Curtiss

Alfred H. Howell
Reese H. Harris Jr.
Herbert B. Woodman
John S. Schumann
Rev. Mannie Wilson
Alger B. Chapman
Henry J. Mali
John W. Raber
Charles F. Dalton

Daniel E. Emerson
John H. Schwieger
Jack Kleinoder
Charles T. Steward
William W. McCormick
Myrtle G. Whitmore
Peter Howard Munch
Donald K. Ross
Barry MacTaggart

Richard L. Brecker
Carrie Terrell
Norman and Esther Lau Kee
Roscoe C. Brown, Jr.
Richard J. Boyle
Harold Smith
Arthur Taylor
William K. Lee, M.D.

THE DODGE AWARD

Given annually by the YMCA of Greater New York, the Dodge Award is a living memorial to the New York City family that founded and continuously supports and guides numerous institutions, including the YMCA. It is awarded to individuals who have acted unselfishly for others, in the spirit of the Dodge family.

Mr. and Mrs. Laurance S. Rockefeller (1974))
J. Henry Smith (1975)
William M. Ellinghaus (1976)
William M. Batten (1977)
Gabriel Hauge; Robert M. Gutkowski (1978)
R. Manning Brown, Jr. (1979)
Dr. William J. McGill (1980)
J. Peter Grace (1981)
William I. Spencer (1982)

Delbert C. Staley (1983)
Donald V. Siebert (1985)
Harold W. McGraw Jr. (1986)
Thomas M. Macioce (1987)
John B. Cater (1988)
Donald K. Ross (1989)
Edmund T. Pratt, Jr. (1990)
Elizabeth and Zachary Fisher (1991)
Eugene M. Lang (1992)
Jack Kemp (1993)

Richard Jalkut; Sally Jesse Raphael (1994)
Henry R. Kravis; Anthony L. Watson (1995)
The Dodge Family (1996)
Karl M. von der Heyden (1997)
Deryck C. Maughan (1998)
Karen Katen (1999)
Gary Wininick (2000)
David H. Komansky (2001)
Jeffrey S. Maurer (2002)

Branches of the YMCA of Greater New York, 2002

Bedford
1121 Bedford Avenue
Brooklyn, NY 11216

> Bedford Youth Center
> 139 Monroe Street
> Brooklyn, NY 11216

Bronx/Howard & Minerva Munch
2 Castle Hill Avenue
Bronx, NY 10473

> Glebe Senior Center
> 2125 Glebe Avenue
> Bronx, NY 10462

Brooklyn Central
153 Remsen Street
Brooklyn, NY 11201

Camping Services
Big Pond Road
Huguenot, NY 12746
> Camps: Greenkill, McAlister, Talcott

Chinatown
100 Hester Street
New York, NY 10002

Cross Island
238-10 Hillside Avenue
Bellerose, NY 11426

Flatbush
1401 Flatbush Avenue
Brooklyn, NY 11210

Flushing/Korean Center
138-46 Northern Boulevard
Flushing, NY 11354

> Bayside Program Center
> 214-13 35th Avenue
> Bayside, NY 11361

> Flushing Beacon/Junior High School 189
> 144-80 Barclay Avenue
> Flushing, NY 11355

> Flushing Beacon/Junior High School 194
> 154-60 17th Avenue
> Whitestone, NY 11357

Greenpoint
99 Meserole Avenue
Brooklyn, NY 11222

> Kids in Control (KIC)
> 224 Berry Street
> Brooklyn, NY 11211

Harlem
180 West 135th Street
New York, NY 10030

> Jackie Robinson Youth Center
> 181 West 135th Street
> New York, NY 10030

Holiday Hills
2 Lakeside Drive
Pawling, NY 12564

International
5 West 63rd Street
New York, NY 10023

Jamaica
89-25 Parsons Boulevard
Jamaica, NY 11432

Long Island City
32-23 Queens Boulevard
Long Island City, NY 11101

McBurney
215 West 23rd Street
New York, NY 10011

> Chelsea Center/ELESAIR
> 122 West 17th Street
> New York, NY 10011

North Brooklyn/Twelve Towns
570 Jamaica Avenue
Brooklyn, NY 11208

> Eastern District
> 125 Humboldt Street
> Brooklyn, NY 11206

> Beacon Center
> 35 Starr Street
> Brooklyn, NY 11221

Prospect Park
357 Ninth Street
Brooklyn, NY 11215

Staten Island/South Shore
3939 Richmond Avenue
Staten Island, NY 10312

> Broadway Center
> 651 Broadway
> Staten Island, NY 10310

> Brooklyn Expansion
> 3939 Richmond Avenue
> Staten Island, NY 10312

> Counseling Center
> 3911 Richmond Avenue
> Staten Island, NY 10312

Vanderbilt
224 East 47th Street
New York, NY 10017

West Side
5 West 63rd Street
New York, NY 10023

PROGRAM CENTERS
Catalpa Center
69-02 64th Street
Ridgewood, NY 11385

CORPORATE OFFICE
333 Seventh Avenue, 15th floor
New York, NY 10011

Organization of the YMCA

The YMCA of Greater New York is an independent, charitable, non-profit organization qualifying under Section 501 (c) (3) of the United States Tax Code. It pays annual dues to the YMCA of the USA, refrains from discrimination and supports the national YMCA mission. Its programs, staffing and mode of operation are determined locally by a Board of Directors.

About the Author and Editor

PAMELA BAYLESS, author, served the YMCA of Greater New York as vice president, communications, from 1997 to 2001. Ms. Bayless, now a principal in Coronado Consultants, strategy/communications advisors, has been a journalist and writer based in New York City for 25 years. She holds a masters degree from the Columbia University Graduate School of Journalism.

MINDA NOVEK, picture editor and researcher, specializes in New York City cultural history, including multi-media exhibits, books, and documentariesx. For PBS she worked on the School series, Voices & Visions, and the Academy Award-winning documentary Ten-Year Lunch: The Wit and Legend of the Algonquin Round Table. Ms. Novek is curator of the YMCA's 150th anniversary exhibit at the Municipal Art Society.

ACKNOWLEDGEMENTS

Many people have contributed to the publication of this 150th anniversary history. The author especially thanks Paula L. Gavin and J. Frederick Rogers for their unwavering support on a challenging project. Herman Eberhardt and Ellen Snyder-Grenier also provided helpful guidance in this effort.

The Kautz Family YMCA Archives at the University of Minnesota and archivists Andrea Hinding, Dagmar Getz, Todd Mahon and Susan Larson-Fleming provided extensive support and guidance into the massive array of documents, articles and images in the collections of the YMCA of Greater New York and YMCA of the USA. Minda Novek, in addition to her role as picture editor, supplied extensive and invaluable research. Members of the YMCA Communications Leadership Team and Executive Leadership Team cooperated generously with efforts to unearth important pieces of Association history at their Branches. Thanks also to the staff of the YMCA of USA and *Discovery* magazine.

Great appreciation goes as well to Carolyn Benbow-Ross and James A. Rubins, who read the manuscript and provided valuable insights and editorial comments. Jessie Santiago brought order and dedication to the movement and cataloging of image materials. Susan Vitucci gave generously of her time and resources. Communications Department staffers Laura Fowler and Amy DeLorenzo provided much-needed support. Thanks to the staff of Neuwirth & Associates, especially to Pauline Neuwirth, whose design sense added immeasurably to this book.

SOURCES

Many sources were used in the compilation of this history. The Kautz Family YMCA Archives at the University of Minnesota and its archivists were essential to this project in supplying annual reports for the Brooklyn & Queens and New York Associations and YMCA periodicals such as *Brooklyn Central, Men of New York, Outlook, West Side Lights* and *YMCA Armed Services News*. Local archival sources were especially helpful in providing YMCA-related materials, especially the Brooklyn Collection of the Brooklyn Public Library, the Brooklyn Historical Society, the New-York Historical Society, and the Queens Borough Public Library, Long Island Division.

The following publications were especially useful:

Brainerd, Ira H. and E.W. "Cephas Brainerd Biography." (Manuscript, 1947, Kautz Family YMCA Archives).

Burns, Ric, James Sanders, and Lisa Ades. *New York: An Illustrated History* (New York: Alfred A. Knopf, 1999).

Burrows, Edwin G., and Mike Wallace, Gotham: *A History of New York City to 1898* (New York: Oxford University Press, 1999).

Colwin, Cecil M. "The 50 Year Saga Of The Breaststroke Rules," *Swimnews,* April 1997.

Dodge, Phyllis B. *Tales of the Phelps-Dodge Family: A Chronicle of Five Generations* (New-York Historical Society, 1987).

Doggett, L.L. *History of the YMCA, Part I,* 1922.

Doggett, L.L. *Life of Robert R. McBurney* (New York: Association Press, 1925).

Donoghue, Terry. *An Event on Mercer Street: A Brief History of the YMCA of the City of New York* (privately printed, undated).

Falkner, David. *Great Time Coming: The Life of Jackie Robinson, from Baseball to Birmingham,* 1995.

Gustav-Wrathall, John Donald. *Take the Young Stranger by the Hand* (University of Chicago Press, 1998).

Hall, Dr. Robert King. *A Strategy for the Inner City, A Report of the Program Evaluation and Priority Study,* YMCA of Greater New York, 1963.

Hopkins, Howard. *The American YMCA Movement* (New York, Association Press, 1951).

Kenneth Jackson, editor. *Encyclopedia of New York* (Yale University Press, 1995).

Johnson, Elmer L. *The History of YMCA Physical Education* (Chicago: Follett, 1979).

Johnson, James Weldon. *Black Manhattan* (New York, Alfred A. Knopf, 1930).

Lancaster, Richard C.. *Serving the U.S. Armed Forces: 1861-1986* (Armed Services YMCA of the USA, 1987).

McAfee, Joseph Ernest. "Self-Imposed Handicaps," *The New Republic,* Dec. 21, 1918.

McCleod, David I. *Building Character in the American Boy: The Boy Scouts, YMCA and Their Forerunners, 1870-1920* (Madison: University of Wisconsin Press, 1983).

Mjagkij, Nina, and Margaret Spratt. *Men and Women Adrift: The YMCA and the YWCA in the City* (New York University Press, 1997).

Mjakij, Nina. *Light in the Darkness: African Americans and the YMCA, 1852-1946* (The University Press of Kentucky, 1994).

Moore, John F. *The Story of the Railroad "Y"* (New York: Association Press, 1930).

Morse, Richard C. *My Life With Young Men* (New York: Association Press, 1918).

Nesbett, Peter T., and Michelle DuBois. *The Complete Jacob Lawrence* (University of Washington Press © 2000)

O'Neill, Thomas, with William Novak. *Man of the House: the life and political memoirs of Speaker Tip O'Neill* (Random House, 1987).

Pence, Owen E. *The YMCA and Social Need: A Study of Institutional Adaptation* (New York: Association Press, 1939).

Rampersad, Arnold. *Jackie Robinson, a Biography* (Alfred A. Knopf, 1997).

Rampersad, Arnold. *The Life of Langston Hughes, Vol 1* (New York: Oxford University Press, 1986).

See, Edwin F. *Fifty Years in Brooklyn, 1853-1903.*

The Survey of the Young Men's Christian Association of the City of New York, June, 1925-July, 1926 (New York: Association Press, 1926).

The Survey of the Young Men's Christian Association, Brooklyn and Queens, May 1927-June 1928. (New York: Association Press, 1928).

Vandenberg-Daves, Jodi. "The Manly Pursuit of a Partnership between the Sexes: The Debate over YMCA Programs for Women and Girls, 1914-1933," *The Journal of American History,* March 1992.

Ware, Louise. *George Foster Peabody: Banker, Philanthropist, Publicist* (University of Georgia Press, 1951).

Weld, Ralph Foster. *Brooklyn Is America* (New York: AMS Press, NY 1967).

Worman, E. Clark. *History of the Brooklyn and Queens Young Men's Christian Association 1853-1949* (New York: Association Press, 1952).

Photo Credits

Unless otherwise noted, images are from *The YMCA of Greater New York Collection*, Kautz Family YMCA Archives, University of Minnesota

Archives of The J. Pierpont Morgan Library: 23 (top, right)

Brooklyn Collection, The Brooklyn Public Library: 76 (top), 77 (top), 84 (bottom), 86 (bottom, left)

Brown Brothers, Sterling, PA: 62, 69 (left), 82 (top), 98 (left inset), 109 (bottom)

Courtesy of Rockefeller Archive Center: 122 (bottom, right)

Courtesy of The Brooklyn Historical Society: 99 (bottom), 146 (right), 164 (bottom)

Library of Congress: 7 (top right), 15 (top, left), 16, 17, 54

New York Public Library, Picture Collection: 11 (top, left), 71 (bottom inset)

Queens Borough Public Library, Picture Collection: 78 (top), 79 (bottom), 110 (bottom, right), 143 (bottom)

Robert Levine Collection: 44 (bottom), 69 (background), 115 (bottom, left), 119, 129 (bottom, right), 189 (bottom, right)

Smithsonian American Art Museum, Peter Juley & Son Collection: 132 (left inset)

Special Collections, University of Virginia: 7 (top)

Stevenson-Ives Library, McLean County Historical Society: 14 (top)

The Colgate Story, Shields T. Hardin, Vantage Press, NY © 1959: 36 (all images, except fourth, down)

Watertown Free Library: 100 (top)

YMCA of Greater New York Corporate and Branch Collections:
Camping Services: 210 (bottom, right)

Corporate Communications: 3 (right, top and bottom), 4 (top, right; bottom, both), 5 (top), 6, 7 (bottom, background), 8, 12, 13, 21 (background), 26 (top, right), 27 (bottom), 28 (top, left), 29 (bottom, left), 30 (top), 31, 32, 34 (top, right), 35, 36 (fourth down), 43 (top, center), 46 (entire spread), 50, 63 (top), 74 (top), 85 (top), 88 (bottom), 102 (top, left), 110 (bottom, left), 116 (top), 117 (top, left), 121 (bottom), 122 (top, left), 127 (bottom), 157, 158, 165 (background), 166 (bottom), 167 (bottom), 168 (both, top), 169 (top), 170 (both), 172, 173, 174 (right and bottom left), 176 (top), 182, 183 (top left; bottom right), 185, 187, 196-199, 201 (bottom, both), 202 (top), 203-206, 207 (both, right), 208, 209, 210 (all), 211, 212 (both), 214 (both)

Bedford-Stuyvesant Branch: 61 (bottom), 73 (entire spread), 86 (top, right), 87 (top), 93 (middle; bottom, both), 94 (top), 96 (bottom, left and right), 98 (top), 99 (top), 104 (bottom, right)

Bronx Branch: 75 (top)

Harlem Branch: 132 (background), 133 (bottom, right), 162 (all), 163, 167 (top), 207 (left)

Long Island City Branch: 107 (middle, right), 184 (all)

McBurney Branch: Title page, 4 (top, left), 21 (inset right), 27 (top), 42 (both), 53 (all), 65 (bottom), 67 (all), 70 (both), 71 (top and middle), 85 (bottom), 89 (bottom), 90 (bottom, left), 91 (top and middle), 97 (bottom, right), 104 (background), 107 (top and middle, left), 110 (top), 122 (middle, left), 123 (all), 138 (bottom), 140 (top, left), 147 (background), 156, 172 (top), 176 (bottom), 178 (right), 181 (bottom), 202 (bottom), 215 (right)

Prospect Park Branch: 52 (bottom), 200, 201 (top), 213

Vanderbilt Branch: 56, 57 (all), 58, 60, 76 (bottom), 111 (top, both), 118, 183 (top)

West Side Branch: 75 (bottom), 128 (bottom, left), (top and bottom, right), 139 (right inset), 148 (top, right)

Index